Power and Resistan

MW00584192

Power and Resistance:

Foucault, Deleuze, Derrida, Althusser

Yoshiyuki Sato

VERSO

London • New York

This English-language edition published by Verso 2022
First published in French as *Pouvoir et résistance: Foucault, Deleuze, Derrida, Althusser*, Éditions L'Harmattan, Paris, 2007
© Yoshiyuki Sato 2007, 2022
Preface © Étienne Balibar 2007, 2022

1 3 5 7 9 10 8 6 4 2

Verso
UK: 6 Meard Street, London W1F 0EG
US: 388 Atlantic Avenue, Brooklyn, NY 11217
versobooks.com

Verso is the imprint of New Left Books

ISBN-13: 978-1-83976-351-9
ISBN-13: 978-1-83976-358-8 (US EBK)
ISBN-13: 978-1-83976-357-1 (UK EBK)

British Library Cataloguing in Publication Data
A catalogue record for this book is available from the British Library

Library of Congress Cataloging-in-Publication Data
A catalog record for this book is available from the Library of Congress

Typeset in Minion by Hewer Text UK Ltd, Edinburgh
Printed and bound by CPI Group (UK) Ltd, Croydon, CR0 4YY

Contents

Part II:
Becoming of the Structure: Althusser and Derrida 117

Contents

Preface

Étienne Balibar

This book, which Yoshiyuki Sato publishes under the title of *Power and Resistance*, is the result of a brilliant PhD thesis on 'Structuralism and the problem of resistance', defended at the University of Paris X Nanterre before a jury composed, besides myself, of Judith Butler, Pierre Macherey, Catherine Malabou and Bertrand Ogilvie. It brilliantly testifies to the acuteness, depth and originality of the readings of twentieth-century French philosophy that *young* foreign, especially Japanese, philosophers are producing today. Their readings bring a freshness, a re-perspective and a re-questioning — and such conditions are ripe to relaunch previously passionate debates at this opportune moment. As a participant in these debates, which I — quite wrongly — believed to have travelled all avenues, it is with great pleasure that I welcome this critical return and relaunch.

Yoshiyuki Sato's book is characterized both by its fascinating content and by its qualities of form. The author's extreme condensation here is a sign of mastery, along with the clarity and rigour of the argumentation and the strength of the architectonics. In this essay, not an ounce is too much. Is it all said there? All it takes, for sure, is to investigate what is perhaps *the* fundamental question raised by structuralism (in the broad sense, including post-structuralism) which has persisted throughout its existence. Sato's knowledge of the texts and their philosophical background is perfect. From the outset, he establishes the idea of the double comparison — Foucault with Deleuze, Althusser with Derrida — which forms the guiding thread of his work, but this idea revolves and is renewed around two paradoxical questions that arise herein: that of 'the immanence of resistance to domination' and that of the contradiction of the Freudian concept of 'death drive', key to the relationship of all structuralisms to psychoanalysis. We thus escape any banality, and above all we ensure that the fundamental notion — that of resistance — is effectively problematized.

Sato has constructed a schema with remarkable structural properties: it *raises questions* rather than just summarizing and classifying answers. Among the formally identifiable questions, some concern the grouping of discourses. Sato is aware of the insistence in contemporary critical discourse of a Derrida–Deleuze (philosophies of difference) grouping against Foucault–Althusser (philosophers of power and conflict). But he prefers a transversal coupling: Foucault with Deleuze (and Guattari), Althusser with Derrida. It is in this way, in particular, that he brings out the singular place of Lacan's discourse: *the other* of structuralism, unless it is, rather, its most typical representative, in the sense of a discourse that seems to cancel any possibility of thinking resistance. Sato takes into account the fact that this thesis can be articulated at two levels: on the one hand, the historical and psychological level of political pessimism ('as revolutionaries, you seek a master: well, you will have one!'); on the other, the transcendental level of a 'philosophy of destiny', as Althusser would say, where 'the excentration of the centre' (about which Lacan forges the neologism 'extimacy', which makes one necessarily think of Saint Augustine) marks forever the impossibility of freeing the subject from the hold of the Other. This demonstration opens up an extraordinary reading of the antithetical relationships of Derrida and Lacan to the texts of Freud, which, in turn, contains the key to the relationship between subjection to structure and subjection to power, or even their identification, in particular, with Foucault, from whom Sato borrows his initial formulations. Finally, the same formal schema, by its inducement of the parallelism between Deleuze–Foucault and Althusser–Derrida, leads us to wonder whether, in this second case too, we are dealing with a sort of 'second position' mediated by the confrontation between the discourses, both close and irreducible, of the two philosophers. It is not impossible that the key to this great analogy is to be sought in particular in the philosophy of Judith Butler, used at length here. This explains the interest that Butler, during Yoshiyuki Sato's viva, showed in his analysis, particularly on the relationship between the problematic of the death drive and the question of the contingency of structures, understood as the uncontrollable rupture of their effects of subjection. A dialogue took shape there, and it is expected to continue.

Among the many questions of interpretation and doctrine discussed in Sato's essay that I, for my part, would like to continue to reflect on while widening the circle of debate to new participants, I will mention two in particular. They communicate with each other precisely through the intermediary of the profound idea of the 'new antinomy', specifically linked to the death drive in both its necessity and its indeterminacy, destruction and conservation of life, and which appears here in the strong sense of 'lifting [relever]' the classical (Kantian) antinomy of causality and freedom.

The first concerns the relativization of the opposition between 'exteriority' and 'interiority', and the central importance of the problematic of activity and passivity in the development of structuralism and its critical elaborations. The paradoxical possibility of an 'active passivity' or, better, of a *beyond of passivity* by means of passivity itself, intended to dismiss the perspective of a purely *reactive* 'resistance', draws a new figure of the transcendental, distinct from what, according to Foucauldian critique of Kant, Sato called the 'transcendental gaze'. It is regarding Derrida (and therefore, virtually, Althusser) that Sato examines its significance. What about Foucault, Deleuze and Guattari? We are tempted to find here the relevance of the idea of 'philosophies of difference' because it is in Deleuze, as well as in Derrida, that the idea of a beyond of passivity — where it becomes resistance (to cruelty, to mastery or to domination) or the idea of a 'becoming-other' — is the most explicit. This is where the question arises as to whether the idea of 'resistance' is really univocal.

The same remark applies to the most difficult question posed by Derrida's discourse — at least, in any case, by its presentation here: does the eventual rupture of the time of reproduction necessarily open up to a liberation, to an emergence of justice, or does it still contain the possibility of another outcome, an oppressive and a 'demoniac' one, which would mean that it is always necessary to intervene, in the abyss, in a decision or a practical freedom choosing between antinomic possibilities? It is perhaps to avoid this 'flight forwards [fuite en avant]' or this reiteration of the political difficulty, ad infinitum, that Althusser maintained, in the face of his other idea of 'overdetermination', the idea of 'determination in the last instance' in his presentations on the schema of the 'absent cause'. For, in accordance with Marxist tradition, this last

instance 'guaranteed' him the correct orientation of history, especially
since in fact 'the hour of last instance never struck'.

We do not labour under the illusion of believing that these speculative questions (but which are also directly linked to ethics and politics)
can be definitively 'settled'. However, the presentation, both clear and
subtle, that Yoshiyuki Sato has given them should not remain without
effects. I say thank you to him for coming from so far (and yet so close)
to bring them to us.

Introduction

1 The subject and internalized power

This book offers a critical reinterpretation of 'structuralist' theories of power. But before embarking on this attempt, it is necessary to define 'structuralist' thought. In the lecture entitled 'What Is an Author?' delivered by Michel Foucault in 1969 — where he advocates a 'return to the text itself' (reexamining Freud's texts modifies, he says, psychoanalysis itself, just as a reexamination of Marx's would modify Marxism[1]) — Jacques Lacan, then present in the room, intervenes as follows:

> I would like to point out that, structuralism or not, it seems to me that there is no question anywhere, in the field vaguely determined by this label, of the negation of the subject. It's about the subject's dependence, which is extremely different; and especially, regarding the return to Freud, about the subject's dependence on something really elementary, and which we tried to isolate under the term 'signifier'.[2]

Lacan's remarks provide us with two important perspectives. First, structuralist thought is not a 'negation of the subject': it is, rather, that of

---

1 Michel Foucault, « Qu'est-ce qu'un auteur ? », in *Dits et écrits*, T. I, Gallimard, 1994, 809; 'What Is an Author?', in *Essential Works*, Vol. 2, New Press, 1998, 219. This is an allusion to the works of Lacan and Althusser.

2 Intervention by Jacques Lacan in the lecture of Michel Foucault : « Qu'est-ce qu'un auteur ? », in *Dits et écrits*, T. I, 820.

'the subject's dependence on something really elementary'. By affirming that the subject is formed by the elements that are external to it, this theory privileges the problematic of subject formation. In this sense, it is not a theory of negation of the subject but a 'theory of the subject'.[3] In other words, as Étienne Balibar points out, it is not a simple disqualification of the subject but, a movement of 'reversal of the constituent subject into constituted subjectivity', comprised of 'a simultaneous operation of deconstruction and reconstruction of the subject, or of deconstruction of the subject as *arche* (cause, principle, origin) and of reconstruction of the subjectivity as effect'.[4] It thus appears as a theory of constituted subjectivity.

The second point is about 'something really elementary'. In Lacanian theory, the subject depends on the 'signifier' or the 'signifier of lack'. Influenced by this 'structuralist' reading of Freud by Lacan, certain structuralist theories of power substitute 'internalized power' for 'signifier'. In such theories, the subjected subject depends on internalized power.

However, we must immediately note that this substitution never means that internalized power is identical to the signifier. The borrowings of these theories of power from psychoanalytic theory rather concern the mechanism of 'internalization [*Verinnerlichung*]' or 'introjection [*Introjektion*] of the object' (Freud) and the 'excentric position of the subject' (Lacan) which follows from this: the subject is determined by 'something' it internalizes but which is not under its own control; it is in this sense that the subject is 'excentric' in relation to this 'something'. In the same way that the internalized signifier determines the subject, the internalized power determines the subject, from within the subject itself, through the effect of its internalization. Since the subject itself is constituted by this internalization, it is then 'excentric' in relation to the internalized power. This conception is at the heart of the theories of power developed by Althusser, Deleuze/Guattari and Foucault. By way of critical approaches, but undeniably influenced by Lacan's 'structuralist' theory, Althusser theorized the mechanisms of interpellation and ideological recognition/denial [*reconnaissance/méconnaissance*]; Deleuze/Guattari,

---

3 See Alain Badiou, *Théorie du sujet*, Seuil, 1982; *Theory of the Subject*, Continuum, 2009.

4 Étienne Balibar, « Le structuralisme : une destitution du sujet ? », *Revue de métaphysique et de morale* 1, 2005, 15.

those of Oedipal subjection [*assujettissement*] by the capitalist family system; and Foucault, those of investment and internalization of power achieved by the disciplinary dispositives (*dispositifs*: the set of power tactics).[5] These three apparently different theorizations share the same theory of subjection effected by the internalization of power, as well as that of the subject's 'excentric' position. It is in this sense that we denote by 'structuralist' theories of power those three theorizations, which all base their approaches on the 'structuralist' psychoanalytic theory of Lacan.

If this 'something really elementary' (Lacan) corresponds, in these theorizations, to the power that the subject internalizes, is there then a possibility for it to resist this subjection effected by power? This is precisely the question we would like to address in this essay. We can identify the 'structuralist' theory of power by the theorization in which the formation of the subject depends on 'internalized' power, and the theory seeking resistance to this power will therefore necessarily include the internal critique of this 'structuralist' theory as well as its self-transformation. Insofar as the problem of resistance to power implicitly includes the internal overcoming of structuralist thought itself, we will deal with the philosophers who are situated beyond the very domain determined by 'structuralism' (notably Deleuze/Guattari and Derrida). We can call this movement of going beyond a 'post-structuralism', which can be provisionally defined as a theory of *power* [*pouvoir/puissance*] *capable of transforming the structure*,[6] but it will suffice here to note that it shares certain problematics (for example, subjectivity constituted as effect, the negation of the *arche*) with the structuralist movement and that it tries to surpass its limits internally.

5 See Louis Althusser, « Idéologie et appareils idéologiques d'État » (1970), in *Sur la reproduction*, PUF, 1995; 'Ideology and Ideological State Apparatuses', in *On the Reproduction of Capitalism*, Verso, 2014; Gilles Deleuze/Félix Guattari, *L'Anti-Œdipe : Capitalisme et schizophrenie*, Minuit, 1972/73; *Anti-Oedipus: Capitalism and Schizophrenia*, University of Minnesota Press, 1983; Michel Foucault, *Surveiller et punir : Naissance de la prison*, Gallimard, 1975; *Discipline and Punish: The Birth of the Prison*, Vintage Books, 1977. We discuss the Foucauldian notion of dispositives [*dispositifs*] in Appendix 2. On the translation of '*dispositif*' as 'dispositive', see Jeffrey Bussolini, 'What is a Dispositive?', *Foucault Studies* 10, 2010. According to Bussolini, the term 'dispositive' is the best choice to translate '*dispositif*' in differentiating it from '*appareil* [apparatus]'.

6 See the definition of post-structuralism as a 'thought of power' by Akira Asada: *Kôzô to chikara* [*Structure and Power*], Keisô-shobô, 1983. Judith Butler, for her part, uses the term 'agency' to designate this transformative power paradoxically produced by the normalizing power. See Judith Butler, *The Psychic Life of Power: Theories in Subjection*, Stanford University Press, 1997, 'Introduction'.

Our intention is, it must be repeated, a reinterpretation of 'structural-ist' thought and an *internal* overcoming of the problem it postulates. We do not therefore criticize it externally — for example, on the basis of the modern concept of constituent subject (structuralist thought is a 'regres-sion' towards the premodern idea, etc.), and therefore do not deduce too easily from it a 'return to the subject'.[7] If the question is a 'return', it must be, as Foucault pointed out in 'What Is an Author?', *a return to the text itself*: 'an effective and necessary task of transforming the discursivity itself',[8] to which the structuralist thought belongs.

If the thesis of 'dependence of the subject on power' results from the way in which psychoanalytic theory — notably Lacanian theory — affects philosophy, then the theory of resistance to power also implies a 'resistance' to psychoanalytic theory which postulates the 'subject's dependence on something' and the subject's 'excentricity'. The 'structuralist' philosophies, affected by psychoanalysis, and this 'other' of philosophy were transformed by trying to overcome the problem that the latter raised. In fact, this process constitutes a kind of self-transformation of structuralist thought to include both philosophy and psychoanalysis. In the course of this research, we will often approach psychoanalytic theory critically; however, our intention is never to deny its revolutionary contribution to the renewal of human sciences. The question for us is, rather, to analyse the self-transformation of structuralist thought in relation to psycho-analytic theory.

2 What is internalization?

Before starting to reinterpret 'structuralist' theories of power, we must ask a fundamental question: what is the internalization or introjection that produces and reproduces the subject? Freud's texts provide us here with a framework for reflection. In *Group Psychology and the Analysis of*

---

7 See the banal neo-Kantian criticism of '(post-)structuralist' thought: Luc Ferry/ Alain Renaut, *La Pensée 68 : Essai sur l'anti-humanisme contemporain*, Gallimard, 1985. For a more systematic criticism of '(post-)structuralist' thought through communicational reason, see Jürgen Habermas, *Der Philosophische Diskurs der Moderne*, Suhrkamp, 1985; *The Philosophical Discourse of Modernity*, MIT Press, 1990.

8 « Qu'est-ce qu'un auteur ? », in *Dits et écrits*, T. I, 808; 'What Is an Author?', in *Essential Works*, Vol. 2, 219. Translation modified.

the Ego (1921), Freud analyses the mechanism of the formation of masses by constructing a psychoanalytic theory of the mechanism of power. Considering identification as a mechanism of mass formation, he uses the notion of 'introjection': the subject identifies with a certain object by introjecting it into the ego. This process is especially revealed in melancholia:

> Another such instance of introjection of the object has been provided by the analysis of melancholia, an affection which counts among the most notable of its exciting causes the real or emotional loss of a loved object. A leading characteristic of these cases is a cruel self-depreciation of the ego combined with relentless self-criticism and bitter self-reproaches.[9]

In short, in melancholia, the subject identifies with the lost object of affection by introjecting it into the ego; by this introjection, the structure of the ego is strangely modified: 'A leading characteristic of these cases is a cruel self-depreciation of the ego combined with relentless self-criticism and bitter self-reproaches'. In this cruel self-depreciation, 'the shadow of the object has fallen upon the ego'. But what exactly is going on in the ego by introjecting this lost object? Freud explains:

> They [the melancholias] show us the ego divided, fallen apart into two pieces, one of which rages against the second. This second piece is the one which has been altered by introjection and which contains the lost object. But the piece which behaves so cruelly is not unknown to us either. It comprises the conscience, a critical instance within the ego, which even in normal times takes up a critical attitude towards the ego, though never so relentlessly and so unjustifiably. On previous occasions [note: In my paper on narcissism and in 'Mourning and Melancholia'] we have been driven to the hypothesis that some such instance develops in our ego which may cut itself off from the rest of the ego and come into conflict with it. We have called it the 'ego ideal [*Ichideal*]', and by way of functions we have ascribed to it

---

9 Sigmund Freud, 'Massenpsychologie und Ich-Analyse', in *Gesammelte Werke*, Bd. XIII, Fischer, 1999, 120; 'Group Psychology and the Analysis of the Ego', in *Standard Edition*, Vol. XVIII, Hogarth Press, 1961, 109.

self-observation, the moral conscience, the censorship of dreams, and the chief influence in repression.[10]

Melancholias show 'the ego divided, fallen apart into two pieces, one of which rages against the second', writes Freud. The introjection of the lost object thus creates the division of the ego [*Ichspaltung*], which is observed reflectively and inflicts violence on itself. This analysis allows us to identify two essential points. First, what he calls here the 'ego ideal [*Ichideal*]' is the higher instance of the ego, which regards the lower instance of the ego as the object of 'self-criticism' and 'self-reproach'. It denotes the formation of the reflective subject, whose higher instance watches and controls the lower instance. He will later name the first one 'superego', established by the introjection of paternal or parental authority.[11] Second, if this system of self-reflectivity arises from the introjection of the *lost* object, it functions, through this introjection, both independently of the *real* object and dependently on the internalized object. We can notice here a kind of autonomization of the subject, which depends on the *internalized object*.

From this principle of introjection, Freud analyses the mechanism of the formation of 'masses' such as the army and the Church. He defines the mechanism of introjection as the 'installation of the object in the place of the ego ideal [*Einsetzung des Objekts an die Stelle des Ichideals*]'.[12] In this case, the object is introjected and placed at the higher level of the ego, which watches and controls the lower instance in a reflective manner. This analysis leads us directly to that of Althusser's ideological state apparatuses. According to Althusser, the introjection of the object

10 'Massenpsychologie und Ich-Analyse', in *Gesammelte Werke*, Bd. XIII, 120–1; 'Group Psychology and the Analysis of the Ego', in *Standard Edition*, Vol. XVIII, 109–10. Translation modified.

11 Freud introduced the term 'superego [*Über-ich*]' in *The Ego and the Id* (1923). On the relationship between the superego and the introjection of parental authority, see, for example, Sigmund Freud, 'Der Untergang des Ödipuskomplexes', in *Gesammelte Werke*, Bd. XIII, 399; 'The Dissolution of the Oedipus Complex', in *Standard Edition*, Vol. XIX, 176–7: 'The object-investment are given up and replaced by identifications. The authority of the father or the parents is introjected into the ego, and there it forms the nucleus of the super-ego, which takes over the severity of the father and perpetuates his prohibition against incest, and so secures the ego from the return of the libidinal object-investment'. Translation modified.

12 'Massenpsychologie und Ich-Analyse', in *Gesammelte Werke*, Bd. XIII, 145; 'Group Psychology and the Analysis of the Ego', in *Standard Edition*, Vol. XVIII, 130. Translation modified.

corresponds to the internalization of the ideological interpellation. By internalizing the ideological interpellation of the ideological state apparatuses, subjects identify with the dominant ideology; by this identification, they 'work by themselves' as subjected subjects.[13] Later in our analysis, we find the same problematic of internalized power in Foucault (*Discipline and Punish*) and Deleuze/Guattari (*Anti-Oedipus*). Such 'structuralist' theories of power thus construed the introjection of the object in the Freudian sense as the internalization of power.

3 Trajectory of the text

At this point in our reflection, we can thus formulate our fundamental question to reinterpret 'structuralist' theories of power: how can the subject resist the power internalized or introjected by 'itself'?

In Part I of our work, we will consider the theories of Foucault and Deleuze/Guattari as theories of subject formation in their relation to power dispositives. It is within these theories that we will identify the possibility of resistance to these dispositives.

In the first chapter, 'Topic', we start from the 'empirico-transcendental doublet' (the reflective system of the subject), defined by Foucault as the structure of the modern subject. We follow the deconstruction of this 'doublet' (which we will name 'topical subject') through the Nietzschean 'thought of the outside'. It is during this process that an aporia of the Foucauldian theory of power emerges, namely the impossibility of resistance to power.

In the second chapter, entitled 'Economics', Deleuze and Guattari's *Anti-Oedipus* allows us to shed light on this Foucauldian aporia from another angle. Their struggle both against and for psychoanalysis indeed offers the possibility of resistance to power. It is in their internal critique of psychoanalytic theory that another concept of subject is to be found: the economic subject that is constantly becoming through its impersonal power [*puissance impersonnelle*]. This notion of an economic subject suggests a possibility of thinking about the resistance to power that is lacking in *Discipline and Punish*. This possibility is inscribed in

---

13 See Louis Althusser, « Idéologie et appareils idéologiques d'État », in *Sur la reproduction*, 310–11; 'Ideology and Ideological State Apparatuses', in *On the Reproduction of Capitalism*, 269.

their articulation of libidinal economy to capitalist economy and in their strategy to transform the 'subjected group [*groupe assujetti*]' to a 'subject-group [*groupe-sujet*]'.

In the third chapter, we return to Foucault in order to find a strategy of resistance to power in his *Kehre* [turn] located between the first volume (*The Will to Know*, 1976) and the second and third volumes (*The Use of Pleasure* and *The Care of the Self*, 1984) of *The History of Sexuality*. For this, we will start — by referring to *Bodies That Matter* by Judith Butler — from the relationship between the body and the formation of the ego, and we will show that the point of resistance to the 'reactive ego' (Deleuze/Nietzsche) formed by disciplinary power resides, in the last Foucault, in the body, the self and the singularity. The issue will therefore be to transform the regulatory structure of the 'empirico-transcendental doublet' into a heterogeneity in which domination and resistance intersect. We find here a consequence of his internal critique of the Kantian concept of subject.

In Appendix 1, we focus on the Foucauldian analysis of neoliberalism in *The Birth of Biopolitics* (1978–79) in order to define neoliberal governmentality as the production of competition and the modality of the neoliberal subject as a competitive subjectivity. Then, in the conclusion to Part I, we seek a strategy of resistance in the era of neoliberalism.

Our objective in Part I consists in looking for a modality of resistance to the power dispositives that produce and reproduce the subjected subject. However, these dispositives produce and reproduce not only the subjected subject, but also the structure or social formation. Around this point, we must therefore reflect on the thought of the 'rupture' — what we call the theory of structural change — which resists the reproduction of the structure itself. This theory of structural change must be posed with the 'theory of the subject', since the subject is included, as a minimal structured element, in the structure of the social formation itself. In Part II, we will thus analyse, in the thoughts of Derrida and Althusser, this other modality of resistance that can achieve structural change.

In the fourth chapter, we consider the problem of contingency and resistance in Derrida by referring to his analysis of the drive, particularly the death drive in the Freudian sense. Our reflection then takes two directions. First, by referring to the Derridian theory, we show that the Lacanian theory cannot conceive the problem of structural change and of contingency, and it is indeed by altering this theory that Derrida himself endeavours to conceive it. Second, Derrida analyses power from the question of 'drive' ('drive for domination: *Bemächtigungstrieb*'), and considers the problem of resistance and structural change in relation to the notion of 'death drive'. We therefore elucidate, by referring to Freud's texts, the two antinomic modalities of the death drive (that which threatens human life and that which resists this very cruelty of the drive), and then we will show how resistance in the Derridian sense (gift, forgiveness, hospitality) is linked to these two modalities. This reflection ultimately convenes the analysis of *Specters of Marx* around the thematic of event and rupture.

Returning to our analysis of the contingency and alteration of Lacanian theory in Derrida, we address, in the fifth and sixth chapters, the issue of the causality of structural change and contingency in Althusser. The fifth chapter is devoted to the theory of ideological interpellation, which produces and reproduces the subjected subject and social formation. We show here how the contingent factor intervenes, as a 'deviation' of the interpellation, in the process of the ideological interpellation/introjection. The aim of this argument is to shed light on the way in which Althusser intervenes in Lacanian psychoanalytic theory and modifies, even *materializes*, its theoretical dispositives.

This analysis of the contingent 'deviation' of the ideological interpellation is linked, in the sixth chapter, to the problem of the causality of structural change. We argue that the theory of causality of structural change is conceptualized and developed, as a consequence of a singular reading of Marx's texts by Althusser, in relation to contingency (perturbation and deviation from the law). Our intention is to show how social formation — namely, structure — constantly reproduced by the power dispositives in a repetitive manner, can be altered by the eruption of an 'other' in relation to the law of reproduction.

In Appendix 2, we return to Foucault in order to analyse *Penal Theories and Institutions* (1972–73) and *The Punitive Society* (1973–74), two lecture courses influenced by and confronting Althusser. In this analysis, we see that Foucault created the notion of 'disciplinary power' and 'power dispositives' as his response to Althusserian theory of state apparatuses and reproduction. Through such reflection, we examine the relation of disciplinary power to the state apparatus.

Finally, in the conclusion to Part II and the general conclusion, we define the post-structuralist strategies of resistance in Foucault, Deleuze/Guattari, Derrida and Althusser to de-subject the subjected subject and transform the capitalist structure — in other words, to realize the 'anti-pastoral revolution'.

*　*　*

This essay was originally written as a doctoral thesis submitted at the University of Paris X Nanterre in 2004. The English edition is the revised and enlarged version (with two appendixes) written in 2020–21. I sincerely thank Étienne Balibar, director of my thesis; without his support and our many discussions, this work would not exist. I also thank Akira Asada, Judith Butler, Yves Duroux, Yoshihiko Ichida, Pierre Macherey, Catherine Malabou and Bertrand Ogilvie, who read my work and gave me detailed and precise advice. This work has also been realized with the support of my friends, to whom I address my gratitude for their reactions, their suggestions and their advice — among others, Livio Boni, Mathias Lavin, Izumi Sekizawa, Masaaki Takeda and Jun Fujita Hirose.

This publication was supported by Grants-in-Aid for Scientific Research of JSPS (Japan Society for the Promotion of Science).

Topic and Economics: Foucault and Deleuze/Guattari

1

Topic I (Foucault)

Introduction to Part I

During the 1960s and 1970s, structuralist thought radically changed the dominant perspective on the theory of power, notably in the apprehension of its relation to the subject. Until that time, in fact, most of these theories were based on the 'repressive hypothesis',[1] where power is identified with the *repressive* state apparatus that alienates and oppresses the original nature of the subject, while 'structuralist' theories, for their part, would focus on the *productivity* of power, which is supported by the 'dispositives [*dispositifs*]'[2] within the social field: it is the power dispositives which produce and reproduce the docile subject. These dispositives correspond, in Althusser, to 'ideological state apparatuses'; in Foucault, to 'disciplinary power'; and in Deleuze/Guattari, to the 'Oedipal family'. 'Structuralist' analysis thus revealed the productivity of power that was lacking in the 'repressive hypothesis'. In this sense, they constructed more detailed theories to analyse the mechanism of power.

---

1 See Michel Foucault, *La volonté de savoir : Histoire de la sexualité 1*, Gallimard, 1976, Ch. II « L'hypothèse répressive »; *The History of Sexuality*, Vol. 1, Pantheon Books, 1978, Part Two, 'The Repressive Hypothesis'. By this expression, we refer to a series of theories of power from Marx (notably his political writings) to the Frankfurt School (notably Herbert Marcuse, who emphasized the importance of the young Marx's theory of alienation).

2 About the notion of 'dispositive [*dispositif*]', see Gilles Deleuze, « Qu'est-ce qu'un dispositif ? », in *Deux régimes de fous : textes et entretiens 1975–1995*, Minuit, 2003; 'What Is a *Dispositif* ?', in *Two Regimes of Madness: Texts and Interviews 1975–1995*, Semiotext(e), 2007. We will discuss this notion in Appendix 2.

There seems to be, however, an aporia in these 'structuralist' theories of power. If the subject is effectively 'produced' by the power dispositives, then it is passively determined by power. This is how Althusser defines structuralism as a variant of formalism; its particularity is the suppression of the subject and the virtual existence of the truth in the object (namely, the formal structure), which can be formulated as a variation of the invariant (Subject = Object) = Truth:

(= Object) = Truth (formalist-structuralist variant)[3]

If we apply this schematization to 'structuralist' theories of power, the subject is in fact removed from the relation to power and all productivity is then found in the 'object', namely the power:

(= Object) = Power ('structuralist' variant of power)

The suppression of the subject therefore means that of its productivity in relation to power, or even the 'subject's dependence' (Lacan) with regard to power. The subject then becomes, as an object produced by the power dispositives, incapable of resisting the productive mechanism of power. Thus *the impossibility of thinking about the subject's resistance to power*: how can 'structuralist' theories of power overcome this aporia?

In Part I, we analyse this impossibility and we will seek, within the very thought of Foucault and Deleuze/Guattari, the possibility of overcoming this aporia. These 'dramas' of thought will lead us into the difficult endeavour of constructing a new concept of subject which will replace the existing modern concept. We first consider Foucault's attempt to construct this new concept against that of the Kantian subject, then that of Deleuze/Guattari against the Oedipal subject.

1.1 Double empirico-transcendental operation

Foucault deconstructs the Kantian subject through Nietzschean thought, and it is in this *Nietzscheanization of Kant* that the possibility and the impossibility of the Foucauldian theory of power intersect.

---

3 Louis Althusser, « Du côté de la philosophie (cinquième Cours de philosophie pour scientifiques) », in *Écrits philosophiques et politiques*, T. II, Stock/IMEC, 1995, 278–80.

In *The Order of Things* (1966), Foucault situates the Kantian subject
— the one he intends to deconstruct — at the starting point of modernity, defining it as follows:

> Man, in the analytic of finitude, is a strange empirico-transcendental
> doublet, since he is a being such that knowledge [*connaissance*] will
> be attained in him of what renders all knowledge possible.[4]

For Foucault, the Kantian subject is an 'empirico-transcendental doublet'
defined as 'a being such that knowledge will be attained in him of what
renders all knowledge possible': this subject 'appears in his ambiguous
position as an object of knowledge and as a subject that knows'.[5] How
should we understand this ambiguity? Let us refer to Kant's *Anthropology*,
a work translated into French by Foucault himself in the early 1960s.
Kant clearly demonstrates the ambiguous position of the subject
between spontaneity and receptivity:

> If we consciously represent two acts: inner activity (spontaneity), by
> means of which a *concept* (a thought) is possible, or *reflection*, and
> receptiveness (receptivity) by means of which a *perception* (*perceptio*),
> i.e., empirical *intuition*, becomes possible, or *apprehension*, then
> consciousness of oneself (*apperceptio*) can be divided into that of
> reflection and that of apprehension. The first is a consciousness of
> understanding, *pure* apperception; the second a consciousness of
> inner sense, *empirical* apperception [. . .]. Now here the 'I' appears to
> us to be double (which would be contradictory): 1) The 'I' as subject
> of thought (in logic), which means pure apperception (the purely
> reflecting 'I'), and of which there is nothing more to say except that it
> is an very simple idea. 2) The 'I' as *object* of perception, therefore of
> inner sense, which contains a manifold of determinations that make
> an inner experience possible.[6]

---

4 Michel Foucault, *Les mots et les choses*, Gallimard, 1966, 329; *The Order of Things*,
Routledge, 2002, 347.

5 Ibid., 323; 340.

6 Immanuel Kant, *Anthropologie in pragmatischer Hinsicht*, in *Werkausgabe*, Bd. XI,
1977, Suhrkamp, 416–17, Anmerkung; *Anthropologie d'un point de vue pragmatique :
précédé de Michel Foucault, Introduction à l'*Anthropologie, tr. Michel Foucault, Vrin,
2008, 95, note 1; *Anthropology from a Pragmatic Point of View*, Cambridge University
Press, 2006, 23, note b. Translation modified.

'The "I" appears to us to be double', writes Kant. This reduplication designates the structure in which the ego assumes both 'reflection' and 'apprehension', 'spontaneity' and 'receptivity'. They correspond respectively to "'I" as subject of thought' and to "'I" as object of perception'. According to the *Critique of Pure Reason*, the ego first receives things as intuition (receptivity) and then transforms them into concepts using its understanding (spontaneity): 'Our knowledge [*Erkenntnis*] arises from two fundamental sources in the mind, the first of which is the reception of representations (receptivity of impressions), and the second the faculty for cognizing an object by means of these representations (spontaneity of concepts); through the former an object is *given* to us, through the latter it is *thought* in relation to that representation (as a mere determination of the mind). Intuition and concepts therefore constitute the elements of all our knowledge.'[7]

The 'spontaneity' of the ego is defined as 'pure apperception', which is opposed to the 'receptivity' of the ego. According to Kant, any representation of intuition accompanies the representation of 'I think [*Ich denke*]'. The 'I think' corresponds to the self-consciousness and to the act of spontaneity: it is in this very representation that the multiplicity of representations achieves its unity. Kant calls it 'pure apperception' and defines it as 'transcendental unity of self-consciousness.'[8] The multiplicity of representations in intuition (the empirical) is thus based on the representation of 'I think' (the transcendental). It is the ego carrying out this double operation that Foucault calls 'an empirico-transcendental doublet'.

Regarding the term 'transcendental', let us refer to the well-known definition in the *Critique of Pure Reason*: transcendental knowledge designates 'all knowledge [. . .] that is occupied not so much with objects but rather with our mode of knowledge of objects insofar as this is to be possible *a priori*.'[9] Transcendental knowledge is not that of the external object, but that of 'our mode of knowledge', namely the reflective recognition of the self. In this operation, the transcendental ego is found superior to the empirical ego and produces knowledge through the gaze brought onto this empirical ego. Let us call this reflective gaze the *transcendental gaze*.

The ego establishes, by this double operation, a demarcation between

7 Immanuel Kant, *Kritik der reinen Vernunft*, in *Werkausgabe*, Bd. III, Suhrkamp, 1974, 97; *Critique of Pure Reason*, Cambridge University Press, 1998, 193. Translation modified.

8 Ibid., 136; 247.

9 Ibid., 63; 149. Translation modified.

the ego and things in themselves, and it grasps them as representations. By way of this operation, the ego recognizes them while remaining within the ego. Hence things in themselves remain, as the 'impossible' of knowledge, outside the ego. In this sense, Kant effectively finds the *outside* of knowledge. However, he establishes a demarcation between ego and things in themselves and creates a structure in which the ego produces concepts, as an internalized object, through intuition. By this process, Kant detaches the ego from its exterior. It is this structure of the ego that Foucault calls 'an empirico-transcendental doublet': 'a being such that knowledge will be attained in him of what renders all knowledge possible'. The Kantian subject thus internalizes his exterior through the double empirico-transcendental operation (the correlation between intuition and concept) and establishes the foundation of all knowledge within himself. We can then define the Kantian subject as the one who internalizes his exterior by virtue of the transcendental gaze.

Given that the Kantian subject is thus determined by the very particular double operation of the transcendental gaze, what then is Foucault's position with regard to this Kantian theory of the doublet? In *The Order of Things*, he deals with the Kantian problem of the 'finitude of man' and the 'limits' it imposes:

> Finitude of man is heralded — and imperiously so — in the positivity of knowledge; we know that man is finite, as we know the anatomy of the brain, the mechanics of production costs, or the system of Indo-European conjugation; or rather, like a watermark running through all these solid, positive, and full forms, we perceive the finitude and limits they impose, we sense, as though on their blank sides, all that they make impossible.[10]

The Kantian subject is marked by 'finitude' and 'limits' that allow objects to be recognized by establishing a 'positivity': the field of knowledge. But they also make the 'impossible' of knowledge appear 'on their blank sides'. The thesis of the 'finitude of man' is borrowed from Heidegger,[11] but we must immediately point out that by relying on Heidegger, Foucault ultimately ruins this Heideggero-Kantian strategy.

---

10 *Les mots et les choses*, 324–5; *The Order of Things*, 342. Translation modified.

11 On the correlation between *The Order of Things* and Heideggerian thought, see Hubert L. Dreyfus/Paul Rabinow, *Michel Foucault: Beyond Structuralism and Hermeneutics*, University of Chicago Press, 1983, 37–43.

In *Kant and the Problem of Metaphysics*, Heidegger writes: 'we must maintain that intuition constitutes the authentic essence of knowledge and that, despite the reciprocity of the relationship between intuiting and thinking, [intuition] does possess authentic importance. [. . .] only with this interpretation of knowledge is it also possible to grasp what is essential in this definition, namely, the finitude of knowledge. That first sentence of the *Critique of Pure Reason* is already no longer a definition of knowing in general, but rather is already the determination of the essence of human knowledge.'[12] According to Heidegger, intuition constitutes the essence of 'the finitude of knowledge': it is 'the determination of the essence of human knowledge'. Man as finitude cannot grasp things in themselves: he can only recognize objects through intuition. This finitude commands the need for double empirico-transcendental operation: 'The finitude of knowledge directly demonstrates a peculiar inner dependency of thinking upon intuition, or conversely: a need for the determination of the latter by the former.'[13] The finitude of knowledge therefore necessarily summons empirico-transcendental reduplication ('*Zwiefalt*' [twofoldness], writes Heidegger[14]), that is to say, man marked by finitude must confine himself, by this very finitude, in the empirico-transcendental doublet.

In *Anthropology*, Kant asks three questions: '*Was kann ich wissen?*' [What can I know?], '*Was soll ich tun?*' [What should I do?], and '*Was darf ich hoffen?*' [What may I hope?], which correspond respectively to the *Critique of Pure Reason*, the *Critique of Practical Reason* and the *Critique of Judgment*. However, Kant refers these three questions to the fourth anthropological question: '*Was ist der Mensch?*' [What is man?].[15] This is, according to Heidegger, a necessary consequence of the 'finitude' of reason: 'human reason is not finite just because it poses the three

---

12 Martin Heidegger, *Kant und das Problem der Metaphysik*, in *Gesamtausgabe*, Bd. 3, Vittorio Klostermann, 1991, 23–4; *Kant and the Problem of Metaphysics*, Indiana University Press, 1997, 16–17.

13 Ibid., 58; 41.

14 See, for example, Martin Heidegger, *Was heißt Denken?*, Max Niemeyer, 1984, 134; *What is Called Thinking?*, Harper & Row, 1968, 221. By 'twofoldness', Heidegger designates the duality of *Sein* [Being] and *Seiendes* [being], namely the transcendental and the empirical: 'In keeping of that dual nature, a being has its being in Being, and Being persists as Being of being. There does not exist another kind of twofoldness that can compare with this'.

15 Foucault evokes this problem without citing Heidegger's name: see *Les mots et les choses*, 352; *The Order of Things*, 371.

questions cited above, but the reverse: it poses these questions because it is finite, indeed it is so finite that in its Being-rational this finitude itself is at issue. Because these three questions ask about this one [problem], finitude, "they let themselves be related" to the fourth: What is man?'.[16] Since man is a being who is finite and lacking, he must question his *Bedürftigkeit* [need/lack]. From there are justified the questions about his *Können*, *Sollen* and *Dürfen* — the infinite being would not even need to ask these questions. From this, Heidegger deduces the following proposition:

> [H]uman reason does not just disclose finitude in these [three] questions; rather, its innermost interest is with finitude itself. For this reason, it is not a matter of doing away with the ability [*Können*], duty [*Sollen*], and allowing [to hope] [*Dürfen*], in this way to extinguish finitude, but rather the reverse. It is precisely a question of becoming certain of this finitude in order to hold oneself in it.[17]

According to Heidegger, the interest of human reason is 'becoming certain of this finitude in order to hold oneself in it'. It is on this point that Foucault will move away from Heidegger while referring to him. Heidegger affirms that the finitude of man, of *Dasein*, gives access to the understanding of *Sein*, always already forgotten in the history of philosophy: 'The finitude of *Dasein* — the understanding of Being [*Sein*] — lies in forgetfulness. This [forgetfulness] is nothing accidental and temporary, but on the contrary is necessarily and constantly formed'.[18] It is from there that he considers Kantian 'finitude' as a possibe way for rediscovering the forgotten *Sein*. It is exactly this Kantian 'finitude' that Foucault criticizes, drawing on the Heideggerian reading of Kant.

Let us refer to Foucault's complementary PhD thesis entitled *Introduction to Kant's* Anthropology (1961). He attaches there great importance to Kant's *Opus Postumum*, because *Anthropology* offers no answer to the fourth question: '*Was ist der Mensch?*'. It is in the *Opus Postumum* that we must look for it. To announce the programme of his

---

16 *Kant und das Problem der Metaphysik*, in *Gesamtausgabe* Bd. 3, 217; *Kant and the Problem of Metaphysics*, 152. Translation modified.

17 Ibid., 216–17; 152.

18 Ibid., 233; 163–4. This structure of Being [*Sein*] — which has fallen into forgetfulness, but which is always found closest [*Dasein* = Being there] — Foucault will call 'the retreat and the return of the origin'. See *Les mots et les choses*, 345; *The Order of Things*, 365.

transcendental philosophy, Kant reiterates the definition of the relationship between God, the world and man. Man finds himself there in the role of 'medius terminus', founding the unity between the world and God. But why does man, the finite being, assume this role?

> If man gives unity to the world and to God, it is to the extent that he exercises his sovereignty as a thinking subject — thinking the world and thinking God: 'Der medius terminus . . . ist hier das urteilende Subjekt (das denkende Weltwesen, der Mensch . . .)'.[19]

Kant's answer is quite clear: as a thinking subject, man thinks of God and the world. In other words, it is from thought that the unity emerges. The question 'What is man?' opens up to the problem of the finitude of human reason. This finitude refers the three 'critical' questions to that of an 'anthropological' order, where they are repeated. It is human finitude that ensures the 'positivity' of the knowledge of the world: the world represented in human thought is the basis of the unity of the world. It is in this regard that Foucault writes: 'it [the world] is not given in the opening of the All; it is present in the flection of the Ganz on itself'.[20] The world is thus folded down in human thought and represented in the 'flection' of the transcendental ego on the empirical ego. If Kant's 'anthropological' question rests on this structure of 'flection' or pli, then we can formulate the structure of Kantian anthropology as representing the exteriority of the world in the interiority of human thought (positivity) and confining it within this positivity.

In addition, the 'anthropological' question is called up by and given as a repetition of the Critique. If the anthropology that is closed within the finitude of the subject is so called into question by Foucault, it is because it repeats the Kantian Critique, even the double empirico-transcendental operation that it presupposes ('anthropologico-critical repetition'[21]). Foucault will call this closure that of menschliches Wesen [human essence]:

---

19 Michel Foucault, Introduction à l'Anthropologie de Kant, in Immanuel Kant, Anthropologie d'un point de vue pragmatique : précédé de Michel Foucault, Introduction à l'Anthropologie, Vrin, 2008, 48; Introduction to Kant's Anthropology, Semiotext(e), 2008, 77. Translation modified.

20 Ibid., 50; 80. Translation modified.

21 Ibid., 52; 83.

And the paradox is this: freeing itself from a preliminary critique of knowledge and an initial interrogation of the relationship to the object, philosophy did not manage to free itself from subjectivity as the fundamental thesis and starting point of its reflection. On the contrary, it confined itself into subjectivity by conceiving of it as thickened, hypostasised and enclosed in the impassable structure of '*menschliches Wesen*', in which the extenuated truth that is the truth of truth silently keeps vigil and gathers itself.[22]

The *menschliches Wesen* signifies the mark of finitude worn by man. With this mark, the subject establishes a demarcation between the inside and the outside and represents the exteriority within itself, closing itself off within its 'limit'. It is this process that the expression 'to hold oneself in the finitude' (Heidegger) designates, this very closure of the subject that Foucault, for his part, calls 'anthropology'. The 'anthropological' thought thus encloses, in the finitude of man (representation), the exteriority of thought that the Critique brought to light. And *it is this thought that represses exteriority for the subject*: 'What possibilities generated this thought from which everything, up until our time, has seemingly diverted us, but as if to lead us to the point of its returning? From what impossibilities does it derive its hold on us? Undoubtedly, it can be said that it comes to us through that opening made by Kant in Western philosophy when he articulated, in a manner that is still enigmatic, metaphysical discourse and reflection on the limits of our reason. However, Kant ended by closing this opening when he ultimately relegated all critical investigations to an anthropological question.'[23] Anthropology thus *sutures* the opening of knowledge that the Critique practised. By this suture, the empirical ego is doubled by the transcendental ego, and the Other of knowledge is repressed. This structure of the empirico-transcendental doublet produces the 'positivity' of the field of knowledge and necessarily denies any power relation that lies outside this doublet:

[I]n fact, it concerns [. . .] an empirico-critical reduplication by means of which an attempt is made to make the man of nature, of exchange, or of discourse, serve as the foundation of his own finitude. In this

---

22 Ibid., 78; 123. Translation modified.
23 Michel Foucault, « Préface à la transgression », in *Dits et écrits*, T. I, Gallimard, 1994, 239; 'A Preface to Transgression', in *Essential Works*, Vol. 2, New Press, 1998, 75–6.

Fold, the transcendental function is doubled over so that it covers with its dominating network the inert, grey space of empiricity; inversely, empirical contents are given life, gradually pull themselves upright, and are immediately subsumed in a discourse which carries their transcendental presumption into the distance. And so we find philosophy falling asleep once more in the hollow of this Fold; this time not the sleep of Dogmatism, but that of Anthropology.[24]

Through the effect of the transcendental gaze focused on the empirical, the subject represses the Other of thought ('the inert, grey space of empiricity'), in a movement of reduction of the Other to the Same — 'for modern thought is one that moves no longer towards the never-completed formation of Difference, but towards the ever-to-be-accomplished unveiling of the Same'.[25] To repress the exteriority of thought and reduce it to the Same, to remain within the 'limit' and to deny the external relations of forces constitutes 'anthropological sleep', a consequence of the empirico-transcendental operation. If Heideggero-Kantian thought poses this double operation as the programme of modern philosophy, and if it signifies the internalization of exteriority, namely the *denial* of the power relations that exist in the empirical and social field, then Foucault's strategy will be constituted as the *deconstruction of interiority through exteriority* — in other words, the *Nietzscheanization of Kant*.

1.2 Nietzsche and the thought of the outside

Foucault, in qualifying the structure of the Kantian subject as 'anthropological', radically criticized the confinement of thought within the subject. But what, then, is the other thought capable of breaking this deadlock of 'anthropological thought'? Foucault calls it 'the thought of the outside':

A thought that stands outside subjectivity, setting its limits as though from without, articulating its end, making its dispersion shine forth, taking in only its invincible absence; and that, at the same time, stands at the threshold of all positivity, not in order to grasp its foundation or justification but in order to regain the space of its unfolding, the void

24 *Les mots et les choses*, 352; *The Order of Things*, 371–2.
25 Ibid., 351; 370.

serving as its site, the distance in which it is constituted and into which its immediate certainties slip the moment they are glimpsed — a thought that, in relation to the interiority of our philosophical reflection and the positivity of our knowledge, constitutes what in a phrase we might call 'the thought of the outside'.[26]

The 'thought of the outside' remains outside the subject, reveals the 'limit' of subjectivity, and by this very fact makes it empty. It tacitly designates the Nietzschean thought of exteriority that allows Foucault to deconstruct the Kantian subject. Let us refer to Foucault's lecture entitled 'Truth and Juridical Forms' (1974), where he deals in detail with the possibility of Nietzschean 'thought of the outside'. To put it briefly, this possibility resides in considering the problem of knowledge through practice and history: 'The subject of knowledge itself has a history; the relation of the subject to the object; or, more clearly, truth itself has a history'.[27] The 'thought of the outside' is therefore nothing other than what questions the foundation of knowledge through exteriority understood as historicity.

Foucault initially focuses his attention on the meaning of the word 'invention [*Erfindung*]' in Nietzsche, who always uses it in the opposite sense to the word 'origin [*Ursprung*]'.[28] For example, in *The Gay Science*, he deals with the problem of the *Ursprung* of religion, concluding that it does not belong to the *Ursprung* but only to the *Erfindung*.[29] According to *On the Genealogy of Morals*, 'ideals are fabricated [*fabriziert*]' by a series of mechanisms.[30] This is what allows Foucault to assert that knowledge was 'invented' and has no metaphysical origin. If we apply this principle to the knowledge of things, it follows that there is no identity, no similarity between knowledge and a thing; there is only heterogeneity between them, because the knowledge that man 'fabricated' is determined by 'a small beginning, one that is low, mean, unavowable'.[31]

---

26 Michel Foucault, « La pensée du dehors », in *Dits et écrits*, T. I, 521; 'The Thought of the Outside', in *Essential Works*, Vol. 2, 50.

27 Michel Foucault, « La vérité et les formes juridiques », in *Dits et écrits*, T. II, 539; 'Truth and Juridical Forms', in *Essential Works*, Vol. 3, New Press, 2001, 2.

28 Ibid., 543; 6.

29 Friedrich Nietzsche, *Die fröhliche Wissenschaft*, in *Kritische Studienausgabe*, Bd. 3, Walter de Gruyter, 1999, 589; *The Gay Science*, Vintage Books, 1974, 296.

30 Friedrich Nietzsche, *Zur Genealogie der Moral*, in *Kritische Studienausgabe*, Bd. 5, 281; *On the Genealogy of Morals*, Vintage Books, 1967, 46. Translation modified.

31 Michel Foucault, « La vérité et les formes juridiques », in *Dits et écrits*, T. II, 544; 'Truth and Juridical Forms', in *Essential Works*, Vol. 3, 7.

Knowledge is 'a violation of the things to be known'.[32] In other words, it does not rely on any identity with the object of knowledge: it is always 'fabricated' by way of violence carried out against the things to be known.

If knowledge is not determined by the object of knowledge, by what mechanism is it so? In *The Gay Science*, Nietzsche writes:

> The meaning of knowing. — *Non ridere, non lugere, neque detestari, sed intelligere!* says Spinoza as simply and sublimely as is his wont. Yet in the last analysis, what else is this *intelligere* than the form in which we come to feel the other three at once? One result of the different and mutually opposed desires to laugh, lament, and curse? Before knowledge is possible, each of these drives must first have presented its onesided view of the thing or event; after this comes the fight of these onesided views, and occasionally this results in a mean, one grows calm, one finds all three sides right, and there is a kind of justice and a contract; for by virtue of justice and a contract all these drives can maintain their existence and assert their rights against each other. Since only the last scenes of reconciliation and the final accounting at the end of this long process rise to our consciousness, we suppose that *intelligere* must be something conciliatory, just, and good — something that stands essentially opposed to the drives, while it is actually nothing but *a certain restraint of the drives toward one another*.[33]

For Nietzsche, knowledge is equivalent to a 'certain restraint of the drives toward one another': the struggle of the drives to conquer one another achieves 'a kind of justice and contract'. In Nietzsche, this scene of 'reconciliation' means 'knowledge'. Foucault, for his part, radically interprets this Nietzschean theory. According to traditional philosophy, knowledge is first revealed in the act of approaching and identifying with the object. But the drives such as '*ridere, lugere, et detestari* [to laugh, to lament, and to detest]' make it possible to 'keep the object at a distance, to differentiate oneself from it or to mark one's separation from it'. Knowledge, therefore, does not signify identification with the object, but its domination and destruction: 'Behind knowledge there is a will,

---

32 Ibid., 546; 9.
33 *Die fröhliche Wissenschaft*, in *Kritische Studienausgabe*, Bd. 3, 558–9; *The Gay Science*, 261. Translation modified.

no doubt obscure, not to bring the object near to oneself or identify with it but, on the contrary, to get away from it and destroy it'. Knowledge is the product of the 'radical malice' that dominates the object, and it is permeated by power relations such as the domination of the object by the subject of knowledge.[34]

Second, if knowledge for Nietzsche is a struggle between drives, Foucault then interprets this interior struggle of the subject as that of powers in the social field. In other words, knowledge is not 'the possibility of a knowledge of the in-itself' that Kant imagined, but an *effect* of the struggle of powers in the social field:

> What the Kantian critique questioned was the possibility of a knowledge of the in-itself, a knowledge of a truth or a reality in itself. In *On the Genealogy of Morals*, Nietzsche says: 'Henceforth, dear philosophers, let us be on guard against . . . the snares of such contradictory concepts as "pure reason", "absolute spirit", "knowledge in itself"'. Or again, in *The Will to Power*, Nietzsche states that there is no being in itself, just as there cannot be any knowledge in itself. And when he says this, he has in mind something completely different from what Kant understood by knowledge in itself. Nietzsche means that there is not a nature of knowledge, an essence of knowledge, of the universal conditions of knowledge; rather, that knowledge is always the historical and circumstantial result of conditions outside the domain of knowledge. In reality, knowledge is an event that falls under the category of activity.[35]

Foucault's interpretation makes it possible to grasp knowledge in its relation to external powers or, more exactly, to power relations. 'Anthropological' thought — criticized in *The Order of Things* — internalizes the exteriority of the subject through the double empirico-transcendental operation and excludes external power relations. But the confinement of this thought is destructed by the Nietzschean 'thought of the outside'. For Foucault, knowledge is a 'historical result' and an 'event' produced in social relations. He puts it this way: 'knowledge is always a certain strategic relation in which man is placed. This strategic

---

34 « La vérité et les formes juridiques », in *Dits et écrits*, T. II, 548; 'Truth and Juridical Forms', in *Essential Works*, Vol. 3, 11.
35 Ibid., 550–1; 13.

relation is what will define the effect of knowledge; that's why it would be completely contradictory to imagine a knowledge that was not by nature partial, oblique, and perspectival.'[36] Knowledge is, therefore, the product of 'a certain strategic relation'; the subject of knowledge is thus determined by power relations. It is exactly in this sense that Foucault *transgresses* the 'limit' of the Kantian subject by Nietzschean thought. It is this transgression that leads him to the deconstruction of the subject:

> When we retrace the philosophical tradition starting from Descartes, to go no further back than that, we see that the unity of the subject was ensured by the unbroken continuity running from desire to knowledge, from the instincts to knowledge, from the body to truth. All of that ensured the subject's existence. If, on the one hand, it is true that there are mechanisms of instinct, the play of desire, the affront-ment between the mechanisms of the body and the will, and on the other hand, at a completely different level of nature, there is knowl-edge, then we don't need the postulate of the unity of the human subject. We can grant the existence of subjects, or we can grant that the subject doesn't exist.[37]

If there exist, in the subject's empirical instance, 'mechanisms of instinct, the play of desire, the affrontment between the mechanisms of the body and the will', then the empirical instance is *multiple*. Based on the discrepancy [*décalage*] between the multiplicity of the empirical instance and unicity of the transcendental instance, Foucault announces the destruction of the subject's unity. He interprets the struggle of forces in the empirical instance as that of powers in social relations. So, this strug-gle in the social field produces the transcendental instance of the subject, and the 'subject' appears as an 'empty form'[38] revealed by the exteriority of power relations. Foucault thus deconstructs the Kantian subject by the Nietzschean thesis of the 'will to know', where knowledge is the product of a struggle between different forces: 'This does not mean, in

---

36   Ibid., 551; 14.

37   Ibid., 547; 10.

38   « Préface à la transgression », in *Dits et écrits*, T. I, 234; 'A Preface to Transgression', in *Essential Works*, Vol. 2, 70: 'In that zone which our culture affords for our gestures and speech, transgression prescribes not only the sole manner of discovering the sacred in its unmediated substance, but also a way of recomposing its empty form, its absence, through which it becomes all the more scintillating'.

terms of a critical procedure, that the will to truth is limited by the intrinsic finitude of knowledge, but that it loses all sense of limitations and all claim to truth in its unavoidable sacrifice of the subject of knowledge.[39] This is the moment when the Nietzschean 'thought of the outside' deconstructs the Kantian empirico-transcendental doublet and transgresses its 'limit'. But, it is also the very moment when the possibility and the impossibility of Foucauldian thought intersects.

1.3 Aporia of the Foucauldian theory of power

Based on the Nietzschean 'thought of the outside', Foucault deconstructs the Kantian empirico-transcendental doublet. But this very strategy implies a sort of aporia. In what does this aporia consist in the Foucauldian theory of power? To analyse it, let us first examine Foucault's concept of power. In the first volume of *The History of Sexuality* (1976), he defines it as 'the multiplicity of force relations':

> It seems to me that power must be understood in the first instance as the multiplicity of force relations immanent in the sphere in which they operate and which constitute their own organization; as the process which, through ceaseless struggles and confrontations, transforms, strengthens, or reverses them [. . .].[40]

For him, power relations are based on a principle of 'multiplicity' that includes ceaseless struggles and confrontations between different forces. Such a definition of power was already set out in *Discipline and Punish* (1975): power relations 'are not univocal; they define innumerable points of confrontation, focuses of instability, each of which has its own risks of conflict, of struggles, and of an at least temporary inversion of the power relations.'[41] This definition bears a resonance of Nietzschean thought as derived from *The Genealogy of Morals*: 'The 'evolution' of a thing, a custom, an organ is thus by no means its *progressus* toward a goal, even less a logical *progressus* by the shortest route and with the

---

39 Michel Foucault, « Nietzsche, la généalogie, l'histoire », in *Dits et écrits*, T. II, 156; 'Nietzsche, Genealogy, History' in *Essential Works*, Vol. 2, 388.

40 *La volonté de savoir*, 121–2; *The History of Sexuality*, Vol. 1, 92.

41 Michel Foucault, *Surveiller et punir : Naissance de la prison*, Gallimard, 1975, 32; *Discipline and Punish: The Birth of the Prison*, Vintage Books, 1977, 27.

smallest expenditure of force — but a succession of more or less profound, more or less mutually independent processes of subduing, plus the resistances they encounter, the attempts at transformation for the purpose of defence and reaction, and the results of successful coun-teractions'.[42] Struggles and confrontations constitute, writes Nietzsche, an antagonistic process of 'subduing' and 'resistance'. In this sense, the Foucauldian concept of power is manifestly Nietzschean. Power can never be reduced to a single entity: it is the totality of shifting strategic relations that always constitute the risk of inversion of the force relations ('focuses of instability', 'moving substrate of force relations'[43]). This will make him affirm: 'politics is war pursued by other means',[44] and it is precisely in this sense that the Foucauldian notion of power signifies a 'multiplicity' of power relations. We define here the 'multiplicity' of power relations as *the diagrammatic heterogeneity of domination and resistance*.

Following the Nietzschean definition of power, Foucault raises, in the first volume of *The History of Sexuality*, the problem of resistance:

> Where there is power, there is resistance, and yet, or rather conse-quently, this resistance is never in a position of exteriority in relation to power. Should it be said that one is always 'inside' power, there is no 'escaping' it, there is no absolute outside where it is concerned, because one is subject to the law in any case? Or that, history being the ruse of reason, power is the ruse of history, always emerging the winner? This would be to misunderstand the strictly relational character of power relations. Their existence depends on a multiplicity of points of resist-ance: these play the role of adversary, target, support, or handle in power relations. These points of resistance are present everywhere in the power network. Hence there is no single locus of great Refusal, no soul of revolt, source of all rebellions, or pure law of the revolutionary. Instead there is a plurality of resistances, each of them a special case

---

42 *Zur Genealogie der Moral*, in *Kritische Studienausgabe*, Bd. 5, 314–15; *On the Genealogy of Morals*, 77–8.

43 *Surveiller et punir*, 32; *Discipline and Punish*, 27. *La volonté de savoir*, 122; *The History of Sexuality*, Vol. 1, 93.

44 *La volonté de savoir*, 123; *The History of Sexuality*, Vol. 1, 93. See also Michel Foucault, « *Il faut défendre la société* », *Cours au Collège de France, 1975–1976*, Gallimard/ Seuil, 1997, 16; '*Society Must Be Defended*', *Lectures at the Collège de France, 1975–1976*, Picador, 2003, 15.

[. . .]; by definition, they can only exist in the strategic field of power relations. [. . .] They are the odd term in relations of power; they are inscribed in the latter as an irreducible opposite.[45]

According to Foucault, 'where there is power, there is resistance', and 'resistance' is inscribed in power relations as 'the odd term', as 'an irreducible opposite'. This obviously does not mean, adds Foucault, that one is necessarily 'inside' power and that one does not 'escape' it. But it is in this point, it seems to us, that the aporia of the Foucauldian theory of power resides. The power mechanism he describes *always works perfectly* and leaves the subject no possibility to resist. It is then difficult to identify in Foucauldian theory the possibility of resistance to power.[46] To explore this problem, let us turn to the analysis of Bentham's Panopticon in *Discipline and Punish*.

The Panopticon designates the architectural style invented to make the prison more efficient: a tower is located in the centre of a ring building divided into cells. Each cell is constantly visible from the inspection tower, but in return the supervisor in the tower cannot be seen by the condemned. Whoever is confined in the cell is therefore constantly aware of being watched and, therefore, is forced to control himself. Seeing without being seen enables the production of an unparalleled disciplinary mechanism. The Panopticon 'automatizes and disindividualizes power', writes Foucault: 'He who is subjected to a field of visibility, and who knows it, assumes responsibility for the constraints of power; he makes them play spontaneously upon himself; he inscribes in himself the power relation in which he simultaneously plays both roles; he becomes the principle of his own subjection'.[47]

In this case, the subject is divided into two instances: the higher ego that 'assumes responsibility for the constraints of power' and the lower ego that is subjected to it. The subject 'internalizes' the power relation:[48]

---

45 *La volonté de savoir*, 125–7; *The History of Sexuality*, Vol. 1, 95–6. Translation modified.

46 On this point, see in particular Edward W. Said, 'Foucault and the Imagination of Power', in David Couzens Hoy, ed., *Foucault: A Critical Reader*, Basil Blackwell, 1986.

47 *Surveiller et punir*, 204; *Discipline and Punish*, 202–3.

48 See Michel Foucault, « L'œil du pouvoir », in *Dits et écrits*, T. III, 198; 'The Eye of Power', in *Power/Knowledge: Selected Interviews and Other Writings 1972–1977*, Pantheon Books, 1980, 155: 'Just a gaze. An inspecting gaze, a gaze which each individual under its weight will end by internalizing [*intérioriser*] to the point that he is his own overseer, each individual thus exercising this surveillance over, and against, himself'

the higher ego, as the agent of power, disciplines the lower ego. Foucault uses the same structure here as the Kantian empirico-transcendental doublet,[49] but, at the same time, he disqualifies the Kantian limit because the empirico-transcendental doublet is constructed, for Foucault, by power relations in the social field. In other words, it is external forces that allow this reflective structure to operate. Let us refer to Kantian philosophy again. In the *Critique of Practical Reason*, Kant uses the term 'discipline': 'We stand under a discipline of reason [*Disziplin der Vernunft*], and in all our maxims must not forget our subjection to it or withdraw anything from it'.[50] For Kant, discipline is that of reason as a transcendental instance of the ego. In Foucault's case, discipline refers to the power dispositives. In other words, what ensures discipline is not reason, but power relations as external forces. Foucault thus deconstructs the Kantian empirico-transcendental doublet by the forces of the outside.

For him, power relations correspond to an interweaving of domination and resistance where there is always the risk of an inversion of power relations. They therefore signify a 'multiplicity' of power relations. In this sense, the empirical field as a field of power relations is multiple.

However, Foucault does not define the transcendental instance as multiple. As quoted above, he affirms in *Discipline and Punish* : 'He who is subjected to a field of visibility, and who knows it, assumes responsibility for the constraints of power; he makes them play spontaneously upon himself; he inscribes in himself the power relation in which he simultaneously plays both roles; he becomes the principle of his own

---

(translation modified). Foucault borrows the concept of 'internalization' from the second Freudian topic (*Verinnerlichung, Introjektion*). According to this, the 'ego' is watched and controlled by the 'superego' (higher ego), which is formed by the 'internalization' or introjection of parental authority. This structure is very similar to that of the Kantian 'empirico-transcendental doublet'. However, unlike Kant, the higher instance is, in Freud, established by an external force relation: the Oedipal relation.

49 The theory of empirico-transcendental reduplication is not manifestly formulated in Bentham's text, except in the following sentence: the Panopticon is 'a new mode of obtaining power of mind over mind' (Jeremy Bentham, *Panopticon*, in *Works*, Vol. IV, Russel & Russel, 1962, 39; quoted by Foucault in *Surveiller et punir*, 208; *Discipline and Punish*, 206). The theory of reduplication and self-surveillance is therefore based on the properly Foucauldian (Kantian) interpretation of Bentham's text.

50 Immanuel Kant, *Kritik der praktischen Vernunft*, in *Werkausgabe*, Bd. VII, 204; *Critique of Practical Reason*, Cambridge University Press, 2015, 52.

subjection.'[51] The subject inscribing 'in himself the power relation' allows the system of self-surveillance to function within the subject itself: the transcendental ego watches and disciplines, as the agent of power, the empirical ego. In this sense, as Foucault notes, the 'power relation' is internalized in the subject. But this 'power relation' established between the transcendental ego (agent of power) and the empirical ego (dominated instance) is completely fixed and does not face the possibility of being overthrown: it only functions as a system of domination. Hence, the Panopticon is, according to Foucault, 'the diagram of a mechanism of power reduced to its ideal form; its functioning [is] *abstracted from any obstacle, resistance or friction*.'[52] The subject is nothing other than the object of the investment of power and its resistance is neutralized by the effects of disciplinary power.[53]

According to Foucault in the first volume of *The History of Sexuality*, such power relations constitute a diagrammatic interweaving of domination and resistance. In this sense, the possibility of resistance is immanently inscribed in the empirical field. However, in *Discipline and Punish*, the transcendental instance produced by disciplinary power is only an agent of power that operates the system of self-surveillance in the subject. It is a field of unique force insofar as it is reduced to a system of domination, while the empirical field appears in the multiplicity of relationships between domination and resistance. It is this *discrepancy* between the multiplicity of the empirical field and the unicity of the transcendental instance that makes the intervention of resistance difficult in the first Foucauldian theory of power (up to the first volume of *The History of Sexuality*). In other words, this discrepancy is revealed as a theoretical discrepancy between *Discipline and Punish* and the first volume of *The History of Sexuality*. And it is precisely this discrepancy concerning resistance that will lead the last Foucault to turn his thought.

---

51 *Surveiller et punir*, 204; *Discipline and Punish*, 202–3.
52 Ibid., 207; 205. Our emphasis.
53 Ibid., 221; 219: 'It [discipline] must also master all the forces that are formed from the very constitution of an organized multiplicity; it must neutralize the effects of counter-power that spring from them and which form a resistance to the power that wishes to dominate it'.

2

Economics (Deleuze/Guattari)

2.1 Body without organs and death instinct

Reflecting on the formation of the subject by disciplinary power, Foucault defined the subject by its radical passivity. In contrast, Deleuze and Guattari start from absolute activity. *Anti-Oedipus* (1972) was written three years before Foucault's *Discipline and Punish*. But, in a sense, their theory provides a solution to the aporia of the Foucauldian theory of power: they formulate it outside of Foucault's problematic of the deconstruction of the Kantian subject. By following the course of this theoretical struggle, we can clarify the predicament in which Foucauldian theory has become stuck, presenting instead a strategy of resistance to power. In order to consider this problem, we will move away, in this second chapter, from the analysis of Foucauldian theory to examine the strategy of resistance in Deleuze and Guattari.

In *Anti-Oedipus*, the authors presuppose that subjection is produced and reproduced, in capitalist society, by the Oedipal family, an omnipresent 'dispositive' in the social field, which makes the subject internalize power, and they criticize its main support, psychoanalysis. They therefore advance literally 'anti-Oedipus' as a strategy of resistance: their aim is the *internal* critique of the Oedipal nucleus of Freudo-Lacanian psychoanalysis by the anti-Oedipal theory virtually present in Freud and Lacan. In this sense, *Anti-Oedipus* resists psychoanalysis *while relying on psychoanalytic theory*, and it is from there that the authors develop their own theory of 'schizoanalysis'. To analyse this theoretical course, it is essential to refer carefully to Freudo-Lacanian psychoanalytic theory.

Anti-Oedipus presents a seemingly strange concept, the 'body without organs':

> The full body without organs is the unproductive, the sterile, the unengendered, the unconsumable. Antonin Artaud discovered this one day, finding himself with no shape or form whatsoever, right there where he was at that moment. The death instinct: that is its name, and death is not without a model. For desire desires death also, because the full body of death is its immobile motor, just as it desires life, because the organs of life are the *working machine*.[1]

In this passage that introduces the 'body without organs', Deleuze and Guattari refer to Antonin Artaud, but we will interpret this concept beyond him. When they refer to the 'body without organs' as the 'death instinct',[2] in what sense are they using it?

Freud's *Beyond the Pleasure Principle* (1920) provides an important key to interpreting *Anti-Oedipus*. Let us first examine the relationship that this text has with the Oedipus complex. In a letter to Fliess dated 15 October 1897, Freud gave for the first time a sketch of the Oedipus complex. But 'he doesn't give a generalized theoretical form to it until 1923, in *The Ego and the Id*; and that, between these two formulations, Oedipus leads a rather marginal existence'.[3] When the death drive is introduced in *Beyond the Pleasure Principle*, it is therefore not 'contaminated' by the Oedipal notion. However, when it is reused in *The Ego and the Id*, it is then joined to the 'superego' and used in the proper Oedipal

---

1 Gilles Deleuze/Félix Guattari, *L'Anti-Œdipe : Capitalisme et schizophrenie*, Minuit, 1972/73, 14; *Anti-Oedipus: Capitalism and Schizophrenia*, University of Minnesota Press, 1983, 8. Translation modified.

2 *Todestrieb* is currently translated as 'death drive'. However, in this chapter, we use 'death instinct' to quote the Deleuzian notion. Let us remember that since *Presentation of Sacher-Masoch* (1967) and *Difference and Repetition* (1968), Deleuze has consistently used 'death instinct' not simply as a translation of *Todestrieb*, but as his own concept. We see this later in this chapter.

3 *L'Anti-Œdipe*, 62; *Anti-Oedipus*, 53. Translation modified. See also Jean Laplanche/ J.-B. Pontalis, *Fantasme originaire, fantasme des origines, origine du fantasme*, Hachette, coll. « Pluriel », 1985, 63; 'Fantasy and the Origins of Sexuality', in Dana Birksted-Breen *et al.* eds., *Reading French Psychoanalysis*, Routledge, 2010, 324–5, note 21.

sense. This tells us that the death drive is free from Oedipal interpretation only in *Beyond the Pleasure Principle*.

Second, what is the relationship with the economic point of view? In Freudian theory, the mechanism of thinking is based on the investment of psychic energy in goal representation [*Zielvorstellung*]. Freud borrows the notions of 'free energy' and 'bound energy' from Breuer and assigns them a new meaning. In the primary process (the unconscious system), energy is completely free and mobile; therefore energy investment 'can easily be completely transferred, displaced and condensed [*leicht vollständig übertragen, verschoben, verdichtet werden könnte*]'.[4] For example, the manifest content of the dream is constituted in the displacement from one representation to another and in the condensation of several representations. On the other hand, in the secondary process (the preconscious-conscious system), it is the 'contact-barriers [*Kontaktschranken*]' between the neurons that bind the energy investment and limit the passage of energy from one neuron to the other. Freud calls 'free energy' this energy of the primary process, and 'bound energy' that of the secondary process. He sought thus to explain the mechanism of the psychic apparatus through neurological models. This neurological theory appears initially in *Project for a Scientific Psychology* (1895), then in *The Interpretation of Dreams* (1900), and reappears in *Beyond the Pleasure Principle* (1920).[5] These texts are therefore distinguishable from other Freudian texts by the importance given to the energy model.

Based on these premises, let us examine *Beyond the Pleasure Principle*. Freud considers the problem of the compulsion to repeat: it designates the process by which the subject places itself in painful situations, thus repeating traumatic experiences.[6] In the compulsion to repeat, the patient is 'obliged to *repeat* [wiederholen] the repressed material as a contemporary experience instead of [. . .] *remembering* [erinnern] it as

---

4 Sigmund Freud, *Jenseits des Lustprinzips*, in *Gesammelte Werke*, Bd. XIII, 35; *Beyond the Pleasure Principle*, in *Standard Edition*, Vol. XVIII, 34.

5 Jean Laplanche/J.-B. Pontalis, *Vocabulaire de la psychanalyse*, PUF, 1967; coll. « Quadrige », 1997, 133–6. But in *Project for a Scientific Psychology*, the primary process and the secondary process both belong to the memory system (ψ system), which corresponds to 'impermeable neurons' having contact grids. We must therefore remain attentive to the fact that, even if, through the Freudian theory from *Project for a Scientific Psychology* to *Beyond the Pleasure Principle*, the terms 'primary process' and 'secondary process' are retained, their definition is constantly modified.

6 *Vocabulaire de la psychanalyse*, 86.

something belonging to the past'.[7] For example, the war neurotic repeats his painful experiences in his dreams. In other words, 'the compulsion to repeat also recalls from the past experiences which include no possibility of pleasure, and which can never, even long ago, have brought satisfaction'.[8] This observation being manifestly contradictory with the pleasure principle, Freud is forced to seek another principle 'beyond the pleasure principle', namely the 'death drive [*Todestrieb*]'.

According to Freud, all drives [*Triebe*] have a 'regressive character', which is based on 'observed material', namely on the compulsion to repeat.[9] If this compulsion repeats the traumatic experiences of the past, the drives are strictly regressive. From this reasoning, Freud develops a 'speculation': if the origin of all living being as an organism is the inorganic, all drives 'tend towards the restoration of an earlier state of things'[10] and this regressive character therefore brings them back to the inorganic. Then he affirms:

If we are to take it as a truth that knows no exception that everything living dies for *internal* reasons, returns to the inorganic [*ins Anorganische zurückkehrt*], then we shall be compelled to say that *the aim of all life is death* and, looking backwards, that *inanimate things existed before living ones.*[11]

Death is the 'return to the inorganic' and the 'aim of all life'. The death drive signifies, therefore, the drive to 'return to the inorganic'. Freud opposes the death drive to the life drive: the first attempts a return to the inorganic; while the second tries to conserve the organic life. Life is therefore based on this opposition between the two drives, and this tension of drives constitutes the subject.

Let us now come back to *Anti-Oedipus*. The 'body without organs' was named, in this text, the 'death instinct'. If the organism means a unified set of organs, the 'body without organs' is to be understood here as an anti-organism. To refuse to be the unified organic and to remain inorganic — this is the state that Deleuze and Guattari call the 'body

---

7 *Jenseits des Lustprinzips*, in *Gesammelte Werke* Bd. XIII, 16; *Beyond the Pleasure Principle*, in *Standard Edition*, Vol. XVIII, 18.
8 Ibid., 18; 20.
9 Ibid., 64; 59.
10 Ibid., 38; 37.
11 Ibid., 40; 38. Translation modified.

without organs'. But they do not use this notion in the metaphysico-
biological sense that Freud gave to the death drive.[12] They use it in the
properly structural sense,[13] where the 'body without organs' cannot be
reduced to any representation: 'The body without organs is not the proof
of an original nothingness, nor is it what remains of a lost totality. Above
all, it is not a projection; *it has nothing whatsoever to do with the body
itself, or with an image of the body*. It is the body without an image'.[14] It is
therefore defined as an unrepresentable body, as a counter-representa-
tion. In this sense, the body without organs is not 'actual' but 'virtual'. It
exists only as a *structural* function.

It is in this structural sense that *Anti-Oedipus* chooses the 'death
instinct' rather than the 'death drive'. Differentiating these two notions,
Deleuze writes in *Presentation of Sacher-Masoch* (1967):

> In *Beyond the Pleasure Principle*, Freud distinguished between the life
> instincts and the death instincts, Eros and Thanatos. But in order to
> understand this distinction we must make a further and more
> profound distinction between the death or destructive drives [*les
> pulsions de mort ou de destruction*] and the death *instinct* [*l'instinct de
> mort*]. The former are actually given or exhibited in the unconscious,
> but always in combination with the life drives; this combination of the
> death drives with Eros is as it were the precondition of the 'presenta-
> tion' of Thanatos. So that destruction, and the negative at work in
> destruction, always manifests itself as the other face of construction
> and unification as governed by the pleasure principle. It is in this
> sense that Freud can state that we do not find a No (pure negation) in
> the unconscious, since all opposites coincide there. By contrast when
> we speak of the death instinct, we refer to Thanatos in the pure state.
> Thanatos as such cannot be *given* in psychic life, even in the uncon-
> scious: it is, as Freud pointed out in his admirable text, essentially

---

12 See *Beyond the Pleasure Principle*, Ch. VI.

13 Noticing the Freudian definition 'death is the return to the inorganic', Deleuze
interprets, in *Difference and Repetition*, the death instinct as a 'pure form': 'Death does
not appear in the objective model of an indifferent inanimate matter to which the living
would 'return'; it is present in the living in the form of a subjective and differentiated
experience endowed with its prototype. It is not a material state; on the contrary, having
renounced all matter, it corresponds to a pure form — the empty form of time' (Gilles
Deleuze, *Différence et répétition*, PUF, 1968, 148; *Difference and Repetition*, Columbia
University Press, 1994, 112).

14 *L'Anti-Œdipe*, 14; *Anti-Oedipus*, 8. Our emphasis.

silent. And yet we must speak of it for it is a determinable principle, the foundation and even more of psychic life. Everything depends on it, though as Freud points out, we can only speak of it in speculative or mythical terms. To designate it, we must, in French, keep the name instinct, the only one capable of suggesting such a transcendence or of designating such a 'transcendental' principle.[15]

The life and death drives, always 'mixed' in the unconscious (coincidence of opposites: construction and destruction), exist there as psychic givens. In this sense, the life and the death drives are 'the *representatives* in the given of Eros and Thanatos':[16] they are essentially empirical in psychic life. On the other hand, the death instinct denotes 'Thanatos in the pure state' and constitutes a *transcendental principle* of psychic life, which Deleuze defines as 'ground' or, more precisely, as 'absence of ground':[17] 'beyond the ground which resists all forms and cannot be represented'.[18] This is why the death instinct is discussed only in a speculative and *transcendental* manner.

When the body without organs is called the 'death instinct', we should not understand the word 'death' in the biological sense. The 'death' in Deleuze and Guattari is a structural and transcendental principle. It should be understood as a 'second death' in the Lacanian sense. In the seminar on 'The Ethics of Psychoanalysis' (1959–60), Lacan evokes the 'second death' as radically different from biological death. According to him, the second death is 'the one that you can still set your sights on once death has occurred'. It appears in Sade's text as 'suffering beyond death', within the perpetual suffering inflicted on the victim. This 'second death', which designates the 'death instinct', is beyond biological death. Moreover, it is this 'second death' that gives desire *its dynamism*: 'It is this trespassing of death on life that gives its dynamism to any question that attempts to find a formulation for the subject of the realization of

---

15 Gilles Deleuze, *Présentation de Sacher-Masoch*, Minuit, 1967, 27–8; 'Coldness and Cruelty', in *Masochism*, Zone Books, 1991, 30. Translation modified. The last sentence is not translated in the English edition.

16 *Présentation de Sacher-Masoch*, 100. This sentence is not translated in the English edition.

17 *Différence et répétition*, 151; *Difference and Repetition*, 114: 'The third synthesis, however, refers to the absence of ground into which we are precipitated by the ground itself: Thanatos appears in third place as this groundlessness, beyond the ground of Eros and the foundation of Habitus'.

18 Ibid., 352; 275.

desire'.[19] In this sense, the second death is not 'the one that life brings', but 'the one that brings life'.[20]

'The full body of death is the immobile motor of desire', wrote Deleuze and Guattari. This means that 'death', the immobile motor, gives desire its dynamism and makes desiring-machines work. Therefore '[d]eath is not desired, there is only death that desires, by virtue of the body without organs or the immobile motor'.[21] The death instinct, which exists only as a structural concept, gives desire its dynamics in the Lacanian sense. The authors call this 'death' 'the model of death': 'The body without organs is the model of death'.[22] What does this affirmation mean?

Let us refer to Freud's 'Inhibitions, Symptoms and Anxiety'. In this text, which speculates on the relationship between the anxiety and the forma-tion of symptoms, Freud writes: 'nothing resembling death can ever have been experienced [*etwas dem Tod Ahnliches ist (. . .) nie erlebt worden*] [. . .]. I am therefore inclined to adhere to the view that the fear of death should be regarded as analogous to the fear of castration'.[23] In his course on *Anti-Oedipus* dated 14 December 1971, Deleuze interprets Freud's passage in an anti-Oedipal or schizoanalytic manner: 'why does Freud cling so strongly to the notion of a death instinct? He tells his secret in "Inhibition, Symptom and Anxiety". It seems that if there is a death instinct, it's because there is neither a model nor an experience of death. When pressed, he admits that there is a model of birth but not of death, thus, all the more reason to make of it a transcendent instinct. [. . .] Perhaps the model of death could be something like the body without organs'.[24] Man cannot experience death in his life. Why then does the death instinct exist while the death experience does not? This is because it signifies the transcendental principle opposed to the empirical — in other

---

19 Jacques Lacan, *Le séminaire*, Livre VII, « L'éthique de la psychanalyse », Seuil, 1986, 341; *The Seminar of Jacques Lacan*, Book VII, 'The Ethics of Psychoanalysis', Norton, 1992, 294–5.

20 Jacques Lacan, « Subversion du sujet et dialectique du désir dans l'inconscient freudien », in *Écrits*, Seuil, 1966, 810; 'The Subversion of the Subject and the Dialectic of Desire in the Freudian Unconscious', in *Écrits: The Complete Edition*, Norton, 2006, 686.

21 *L'Anti-Œdipe*, 393; *Anti-Oedipus*, 329.

22 Ibid.

23 Sigmund Freud, 'Hemmung, Symptom und Angst', in *Gesallemte Werke*, Bd. XIV, 160; 'Inhibitions, Symptoms and Anxiety', in *Standard Edition*, Vol. XX, 130.

24 Gilles Deleuze, « Nature des flux », Cours du 14 décembre 1971, webdeleuze.com; 'The Nature of Flows', Lecture on 14 December 1971, webdeleuze.com.

words, the plane of immanence (the recording surface) that records the empirical flows in order to give them dynamism. Let us remember, for example, the Marxian transcendental principle such as capital: it is the plane of immanence that records monetary or material flows and gives them dynamism.[25] It is in this way that the model of death or the death instinct only exists as a transcendental principle.

In Freud, the death drive opposing the life drive provides the subject with the dynamism of desire. In Deleuze and Guattari, the 'body without organs' is opposed to 'desiring-machines'. The first is the 'second death', the 'model of death' which, as the plane of immanence (the recording surface), records the seconds and gives desire its dynamism and, at the same time, 'anti-production', which refuses organization.[26] On the other hand, the seconds correspond to the 'production of production'; by this functioning, desiring-machines 'make us an organism'.[27] Ultimately, the body without organs, which corresponds to anti-organization, and desiring-machines, which correspond to organization, are in a relationship of 'repulsion'.[28]

As we can understand from their comparison with Freudian theory, Deleuze and Guattari choose Freudian economics as a model for their theorization. However, they reject the Freudian topic, in particular the second Oedipal topic of the ego and the superego. In other words, they reject the 'empirical-transcendental doublet' where the higher instance controls the lower instance. This means that they choose a different path than Foucault's, which is limited to the deconstruction of the Kantian subject. We find in Foucault's thought a topical problematic and in that of Deleuze/Guattari an *economic* problematic.[29] Foucault limits himself to the relativization of the empirico-transcendental doublet, while Deleuze and Guattari situate themselves in the anti-Oedipal economy. This difference in problematic between Foucault and Deleuze/Guattari will constitute a radical difference for theorizing resistance to power.

---

25 *L'Anti-Œdipe*, 16–17; *Anti-Oedipus*, 10–11.
26 Ibid., 21; 15.
27 Ibid., 14; 8.
28 Ibid., 15; 9.
29 In Freud, the economic point of view refers to a hypothesis 'according to which psychic processes consist of the circulation and distribution of quantifiable energy (drive energy)' (*Vocabulaire de la psychanalyse*, 125). We are not using the terms 'economics' and 'topic' only in the context of psychoanalytic theory. For example, the triad 'id – ego – superego' (second Freudian topic) will correspond, in its functioning, to the Kantian triad 'thing in itself – empirical ego – transcendental ego'.

2.2 Machinic assemblage and becoming-other

In *Anti-Oedipus*, Deleuze and Guattari start from Freudian economics. But why do they choose this problematic? We can answer briefly: to affirm the flows of desire, namely to 'introduce desire into the mechanism' and to 'introduce production into desire'.[30] Let us consider this point in the psychoanalytic context. According to Guattari's *Schizoanalytic Cartographies*, the aim of the Freudian energetic is to 'give a scientific foundation to psychology by introducing into it abstract quantities'.[31] Freud's treatment of energy flows distinguished two processes of the psychic apparatus: the primary process (unconscious system), in which the energetic movement is completely free, and the secondary process (preconscious-conscious system), in which it is bound. In the unconscious system, the energy flows are therefore mobile and variable. They are completely free — in other words, 'multiple'. On the other hand, Lacan considers these flows of the primary process as a signifying chain:[32]

[T]he mechanisms described by Freud as those of the primary process, by which the unconscious is governed, correspond exactly to the functions this school of [structuralist] linguistics believes determine the most radical axes of the effects of language, namely metaphor and metonymy — in other words, the effects of the substitution and combination of signifiers in the synchronic and

---

30 *L'Anti-Œdipe*, 29; *Anti-Oedipus*, 22. Translation modified. On the philosophy of desire in Deleuze and Guattari, see, for example, Philip Goodchild, *Deleuze & Guattari: An Introduction to the Politics of Desire*, SAGE Publications, 1996. This work underlines the correlation between *Anti-Oedipus* and *Beyond the Pleasure Principle* (122–3), but it takes the 'body without organs' for representation and overlooks its essential relation with the 'death instinct'.

31 Félix Guattari, *Cartographies schizoanalytiques*, Galilée, 1989, 42; *Schizoanalytic Cartographies*, Bloomsbury, 2013, 29.

32 Ibid., 36; 24: 'In this respect, one could easily demonstrate that Lacan progressively substituted his concept of the signifier for that of the libido'. It is not therefore by chance that Lacan gave importance to *Project for Scientific Psychology* and *Beyond the Pleasure Principle* in 'Seminar on "The Purloined Letter"'. In the Introduction for this seminar, he tries to find, by reorganising the Freudian energetic, the system of the signifying chain in which the phallus ('the letter' as a 'fundamentally lost object') is the transcendent instance. See Jacques Lacan, « Le séminaire sur 'La Lettre volée' », in *Écrits*, 44–6; 'Seminar on "The Purloined Letter"', in *Écrits: The Complete Edition*, 33–4. We will return to this point in Chapter 4.

diachronic dimensions, respectively, in which they appear in discourse.[33]

Lacan identifies investments of the primary process in 'the effects of the substitution and combination of signifiers', which, for example, designate respectively the condensation and the displacement of signifiers in the dream.[34] According to Freud, the investments of the primary process 'can easily be completely transferred, displaced and condensed'. However, Lacan orients the signifying chain towards a signifier (the 'phallus') and tries to establish the system of absolute domination in a single transcendent signifier. By this operation, the multiplicity of signifiers is reduced to *an* absolute signifier, and the signifying chain is subsumed only to the Oedipal code. Lacan defines the system of signifiers as follows:

> For our part, we will begin with what the abbreviation S($Ⱥ$) articulates, being first of all a signifier. Our definition of the signifier (there is no other) is as follows: a signifier is what represents the subject to another signifier. This latter signifier is therefore the signifier to which all the other signifiers represent the subject — which means that if this signifier is missing, all the other signifiers represent nothing. For something is only represented to.[35]

Since the sign S($Ⱥ$) designates the 'signifier of a lack in the Other',[36] 'a signifier' means here nothing other than the phallus. 'All the other signifiers' are oriented towards 'a signifier', the phallus, and arranged by it. In this sense, Lacan calls the phallus 'the privileged signifier'.[37] It is precisely

---

33 « Subversion du sujet et dialectique du désir dans l'inconscient freudien », in *Écrits*, 799–800; 'The Subversion of the Subject and the Dialectic of Desire in the Freudian Unconscious', in *Écrits: The Complete Edition*, 676–7.

34 Jacques Lacan, « L'instance de la lettre dans l'inconscient ou la raison depuis Freud », in *Écrits*, 511; 'The Instance of the Letter in the Unconscious or Reason since Freud', in *Écrits: The Complete Edition*, 425. Lacan defines condensation [*Verdichtung*] as 'the superimposed structure of signifiers in which metaphor finds its field' and displacement [*Verschiebung*] as the 'transfer of signification that metonymy displays'.

35 « Subversion du sujet et dialectique du désir dans l'inconscient freudien », in *Écrits*, 819; 'The Subversion of the Subject and the Dialectic of Desire in the Freudian Unconscious', in *Écrits: The Complete Edition*, 693–4. Translation modified.

36 Ibid., 818

37 Jacques Lacan, « La signification du phallus », in *Écrits*, 692; 'The Signification of Phallus', in *Écrits: The Complete Edition*, 581: 'The phallus is the privileged signifier of this mark in which the role of Logos is wedded to the advent of desire'.

this transcendence of the phallus that Deleuze and Guattari reject by
refusing the domination system of free flows by the phallus: 'We owe to
Jacques Lacan the discovery of this fertile domain of a code of the
unconscious, incorporating the entire chain — or several chains — of
meaning: a discovery thus totally transforming analysis. [. . .] But how
very strange this domain seems, simply because of its multiplicity — a
multiplicity so complex that we can scarcely speak of *one* chain or even
of *one* code of desire'.[38]

The phallus is a transcendent signifier insofar as it gives an Oedipal
meaning to all the other signifiers and controls them. At the same time,
it is the signifier of a 'lack'. The subject assumes, writes Lacan, the renunciation of the satisfaction of desire by the effect of castration. In other
words, through castration, the subject assumes the lack and at the same
time *represses* the phallus that is the symbol of desire (the original
repression). Therefore, the phallus is always already 'veiled'[39] for the
subject, and, in this sense, always already the 'lost signifier'.[40] This repression of the phallus, which signifies the 'lack' of the subject, controls all
the other signifiers — in other words, all the flows of desire. Lacan
defines the 'phallus' as the 'signifier of the lack of zero symbol':

> Let us observe carefully, therefore, what it is that objects to conferring on
> our signifier S($\cancel{A}$) the meaning of *Mana* or of any such term. [. . .] Claude
> Lévi-Strauss, commenting on Mauss' work, no doubt wished to see in
> *Mana* the effect of a zero symbol. But it seems that what we are dealing
> with in our case is rather the signifier of the lack of this zero symbol.[41]

The phallus is not only a zero symbol as a 'a symbol in its pure state,
therefore liable to take on any symbolic content whatever',[42] namely the

---

38 *L'Anti-Œdipe*, 46; *Anti-Oedipus*, 38.

39 « La signification du phallus », in *Écrits*, 693; 'The Signification of the Phallus', in
Écrits: The Complete Edition, 582. Note the Heideggerian meaning of the word 'veiled
[*verborgen*]'. The phallus is always already 'veiled' for the subject, just as the *Sein* is
always already 'forgotten'. In the 'phallus' and the '*Sein*', Lacan and Heidegger share a
core association with negativity.

40 Jacques Lacan, « Remarque sur le rapport de Daniel Lagache », in *Écrits*, 683;
'Remarks on Daniel Lagache's Presentation', *Écrits: The Complete Edition*, 572.

41 « Subversion du sujet et dialectique du désir dans l'inconscient freudien », in
Écrits, 821; 'The Subversion of the Subject and the Dialectic of Desire in the Freudian
Unconscious', in *Écrits: The Complete Edition*, 695. Translation modified.

42 Claude Lévi-Strauss, « Introduction à l'œuvre de Marcel Mauss », in Marcel

symbol that represents all the other signifiers; it also establishes, as symbol zero, the system of the signifying chain and, at the same time, orders and dominates, as 'signifier of lack' (i.e., *repressed* signifier), the flows of desire. It is through this system of lack that the phallus can be the 'insignia of omnipotence'.[43] Lacan thus hypostases the *effect* of repression and calls it 'lack'. In his doing so, the phallus becomes 'the One in negative theology'[44] which dominates all other signifiers by its 'lack'. The Lacanian concept of the signifying chain arranged by the phallus introduces the lack in the free flows of desire and oppresses the production of desire. Deleuze and Guattari refuse this repression of desire realized by 'lack'. They consider desire as production, pure flow and multiplicity, which leads them, on the one hand, to criticize the Lacanian concept of the signifier and, on the other hand, to deploy unconscious desire in its multiplicity. This strategy grasps desire as radical productivity and activity.

Freud limited energetic flows to within the psychic apparatus, namely within the subject. In contrast, Deleuze and Guattari extend these flows outside the subject. The flows refer to those of libido in the Freudian sense and, simultaneously, to those of capital in the Marxian sense. For Deleuze and Guattari, 'flows' refer to 'abstract quantities' in the empirical field. This multiplicity of flows is essential for desiring production.

In his lecture dated 14 December 1971, Deleuze asserts that the notion of flow derives from the Keynesian economic notion of flow and stock:

As a point of departure in our quest for a nominal definition of flows, I'll take a recent study by a specialist in the flows of political economy: *Flows and Stocks*, by Daniel Antier. Stocks and flows are two primary notions in modern political economy remarked by Keynes to the extent that we find the first great theory in his *General Theory of Employment, Interest and Money*. Antier tells us that, 'from the economic point of view, we can call flows the values of the quantities of service goods or of money that are transmitted from one pole to

---

Mauss, *Sociologie et Anthropologie*, PUF, 1950, L; *Introduction to the Work of Marcel Mauss*, Routledge & Kegan Paul, 1987, 64.

43 « Subversion du sujet et dialectique du désir dans l'inconscient freudien », in *Écrits*, 808; 'The Subversion of the Subject and the Dialectic of Desire in the Freudian Unconscious', in *Écrits: The Complete Edition*, 684.

44 *L'Anti-Œdipe*, 70; *Anti-Oedipus*, 60.

another'; the first concept to be placed in relation with that of flows is that of pole: a flow, inasmuch as it flows on the socius, enters by one pole and exits by another.[45]

Referring to *The Study of Flows and Stocks* by Daniel Antier, Deleuze explains that flows refer to 'the values of the quantities of service goods or of money that are transmitted from one pole to another'.[46] In this sense, the notion of flow is essentially economico-political. Deleuze mentions Keynes here, but we can also evoke Marxian theory. In Marx, when the flows of labour power meet the flows of capital, exploitation of labour power is produced. In this sense, monetary or material flows imply power relations: let us recall the fact that the power relation is asymmetrical between capital and labour power. If we want to transform the power relations, we must transform the flow relations: as we will see later, this transformation will be conceptualized, in Deleuzo-Guattarian theory, as that of the subjected group into subject-group.

In *Anti-Oedipus*, the multiple flows produce a kind of 'subject'. But what kind of subject is it? The relationship between desiring-machines and body without organs constitutes the foundation of all productions. Desiring-machines are at the root of everything:

> The rule of continually producing production, of grafting producing onto the product, is a characteristic of desiring-machines or of primary production: the production of production.[47]

Desiring-machines are always 'binary machines, obeying a binary law or set of rules governing associations: one machine is always coupled with another':[48] a desiring-machine produces 'production' and connects it to another machine; the latter cuts the flows, takes them and produces the other flows (for example, connection of breast–mouth). There are only produced and withdrawn partial objects and flows. Following the

---

45 Gilles Deleuze, « Nature des flux », Cours du 14 décembre 1971, webdeleuze. com; 'The Nature of Flows', Lecture on 14 December 1971, webdeleuze.com. Translation modified. On the notion of flow and stock in Deleuze, see also Daniel W. Smith, 'Flow, Code and Stock: A Note on Deleuze's Political Philosophy', *Deleuze Studies* 5, supplement, 2011.

46 Daniel Antier, *L'étude des flux et des stocks*, Sedes, 1957, 10.

47 *L'Anti-Œdipe*, 13; *Anti-Oedipus*, 7.

48 Ibid., 11; 5.

concept of 'production of production' by desiring-machines, Deleuze and Guattari thus define desire as radical productivity. There are only desiring-machines (partial objects) and the multiple flows of desire. This connection between machines achieves the 'machinic assemblage [*agencement machinique*]' between the subjects. For Deleuze and Guattari, the subject designates thus, in principle, the *collective subject* or the *machinic assemblage*.

Desiring-machines as production are opposed to the body without organs as anti-production. The former are productive and form the organism; in contrast, the latter is anti-productive and anti-organic. The body without organs is therefore in a relationship of 'repulsion' towards desiring-machines and is opposed to their organization.

Furthermore, the body without organs serves as 'a surface for the recording of the entire process of production of desire'.[49] Desiring-machines are connected to the surface of the body without organs and produce production by reciprocally connecting with each other. They are never controlled by a privileged element such as the transcendent signifier (which differs from the Lacanian signifying chain): 'Machines attach themselves to the body without organs as so many points of disjunction, between which an entire network of new syntheses is now woven, marking the surface off into co-ordinates, like a grid'.[50] Deleuze and Guattari call this 'the disjunctive synthesis', in which several desiring-machines coexist while preserving their differences.

This disjunctive recording produces a sort of 'subject'. The 'subject' is an 'organism' with a unified body that the body without organs represses; it is produced, on the surface of the body without organs, as a 'residue [*résidu/ reste*] alongside the desiring-machines' ('return of the repressed').[51] The authors call this process the 'production of production':

[T]he production of consumption is produced in and through the production of recording. This is because something on the order of a *subject* can be discerned on the recording surface. It is a strange

---

49 Ibid., 17; 11.
50 Ibid., 18; 12.
51 Ibid., 23–4, 27; 17, 20. The 'return of the repressed', the 'residue' are key concepts of Lacanian theory ('the symptom is the return of the repressed', 'symbolization leaves an irreducible residue' etc.). However, Deleuze and Guattari constantly use in the productive sense these Lacanian terms that mean for them the repression of production. They use the most Lacanian terms in the most anti-Lacanian sense possible.

subject, however, with no fixed identity, wandering about over the body without organs, but always remaining peripheral to the desiring-machines, being defined by the share of the product it takes for itself, garnering here, there, and everywhere a reward in the form of a becoming or an avatar, being born of the states that it consumes and being reborn with each new state. 'It's me, and so it's mine . . .'[52]

A desiring-machine consumes the product produced by another desiring-machine. In this process of consumption, the 'subject' is produced as a 'residue'. The products to be consumed are different at every moment; so, the 'subject' transforms itself, too, since it is produced by this consumption. In other words, it must be a multiple being who never ceases to become and who does not have a 'fixed identity'.

The 'subject' is thus produced 'alongside desiring-machines', constantly 'decentred': 'This subject itself is not at the centre, which is occupied by the machine, but on the periphery, with no fixed identity, forever decentred, defined by the states through which it passes'.[53] Therefore, it is desiring-machines, namely the unconscious desires, that occupy the centre.[54] Let us compare with Lacan. In 'Seminar on "The Purloined Letter"' (1957), he uses the term 'ex-sistence'. This term, which comes from Heideggerian philosophy, signifies 'the excentric place'. The subject of the Lacanian unconscious is therefore placed in 'the excentric place'. It is apparently identical to the 'decentred subject' of Deleuze and Guattari (Lacan uses the word 'excentric [*excentrique*]' almost in the same sense as 'decentred [*décentré*]'[55]). However, in Lacan, unconscious desire does not occupy the centre:

---

52 Ibid., 22–3; 16.

53 Ibid., 27; 20.

54 Unconscious desires are not then disordered: in the 'transcendental unconscious', they are ordered by 'the immanence of its criteria'. See ibid., 89; 75.

55 See Jacques Lacan, *Le séminaire*, Livre II, « Le moi dans la théorie de Freud et dans la technique de la psychanalyse », Seuil, 1978, 17; *The Seminar*, Book II, 'The Ego in the Freud's Theory and in the Technique of Psychoanalysis', Norton, 1988, 9: 'Freud tells us — intelligence has nothing to do with the subject, the subject is not on the same axis, it is excentric [*excentrique*]. The subject as such, functioning as subject, is something other than an organism which adapts itself. It is something else, and for those who are capable of understanding, its entire behaviour speaks of something other than the axis we can grasp when we consider it as a function of an individual, that is to say, with a specific number of interests conceived of in relation to the individual *arétè*. / We will confine ourselves to this topological metaphor for the moment — the subject is decentred [*décentré*] in relation to the individual. That is what *I is an other* [Je est un autre] means'. Translation modified.

Our research has led us to the realization that repetition automatism (*Wiederholungszwang*) has its basis in what we have called the insistence of the signifying chain. We have isolated this notion as a correlate of the *ex-sistence* (that is, of the excentric place) in which we must necessarily locate the subject of the unconscious, if we are to take Freud's discovery seriously.[56]

In Lacan, it is a 'signifier', the phallus as a 'signifier of lack', which determines the subject. Therefore, if it is the 'lack' that occupies the centre, then the centre is nothing other than a void (a 'hole'[57]). The subject defined as the one determined by the signifier of lack turns out to be decentred *by absolute passivity*. In Deleuze and Guattari, it is *productive desires* that occupy the centre. The 'subject' is therefore always penetrated by the desiring production. For them, the 'decentred subject' is never reduced to unproductive passivity: it is produced by multiple desires and their consumption. This fact constitutes a point of fundamental difference with Lacanian theory.

The multiplicity of the 'subject' is a consequence of the multiplicity of desiring-production. Desiring-production refers to the flows that are communicated between machines. The flows, as an abstract quantity, are 'material and signaletic';[58] they correspond to the energy exchanged in the empirical field. If the 'subject' continues to transform by consuming flows in the empirical field, this subject can therefore be qualified as multiple. In other words, as a result of multiple production, the 'subject' (the transcendental field) becomes multiple. The 'subject' is then in an incessant becoming. The multiplicity of the transcendental field therefore signifies, for them, 'becoming-other'.[59]

The productivity of desiring-machines corresponds to that of the decentred impersonal subject, who transforms and connects to other subjects transversally. It derives exactly from the principle of transformation and machinic assemblage. It is precisely this subject of transformation, capable of realizing the transversal machinic assemblage, that

---

56 « Le séminaire sur 'La Lettre volée' », in *Écrits*, 11; 'Seminar on "The Purloined Letter"', in *Écrits: The Complete Edition*, 6. Translation modified.

57 See, for example, ibid., 50; 38.

58 *Cartographies schizoanalytiques*, 44; *Schizoanalytic Cartographies*, 30.

59 Gilles Deleuze/Félix Guattari, *Qu'est-ce que la philosophie ?*, Minuit, 1991, 107, 168; *What is Philosophy?*, Columbia University Press, 1994, 112, 177.

can produce social transformation.

Deleuze and Guattari call this transversal machinic assemblage 'schizophrenia as a process'.[60] But why is this process referred to as 'schizophrenia as a process'? According to Lacan's definition given in his seminar on 'The Psychoses', schizophrenia is defined as the structure in which the foreclosure or disqualification of the Other destroys the symbolic by infinitely multiplying the others. Likewise, *the process of desiring production lacks the transcendent instance (the Other) and multiplies the desiring production transversally on the plane of immanence: it is this process that realizes the transversal machinic assemblage between the subjects.*[61] What Deleuze and Guattari called 'schizoanalysis' designates exactly this theoretical position, which highlights the process of desiring production that multiplies in a transversal manner in order to realize the transversal machinic assemblage.

2.3 Subject-group and impersonal desiring power

It is through the economic problematic that Deleuze and Guattari make capable the multiple transcendental field and the transversal machinic assemblage. However, their theoretical revolution is not limited to this achievement — it also opens up the way to the problem of resistance to power. But what makes resistance to power possible in their theory?

Their starting point is the absolute productivity of desires. Unconscious desires are always productive and never stop producing. In this sense, 'desire is part of the infrastructure'.[62] But at the same time, the desiring production is always 'repressed', since the total liberation of desires means the total destruction of the social order: 'If desire is repressed, it is because every position of desire, no matter how small, is capable of calling into question the established order of a society: not that desire is asocial, on the contrary. But it is explosive; there is no

---

60 *L'Anti-Œdipe*, 155; *Anti-Oedipus*, 130.

61 On the Lacanian definition of schizophrenia, see Jacques Lacan, *Le séminaire*, Livre III, « Les psychoses », Seuil, 1981; *The Seminar*, Book III, 'The Psychoses', Norton, 1993. Regarding the formation of the notion of 'schizoanalysis', the contribution of Guattari, who was the auditor of this seminar, was important. See Félix Guattari, *Écrits pour l'Anti-Œdipe*, Lignes & Manifeste, 2004, 42–3; *The Anti-Œdipus Papers*, Semiotext(e), 2006, 30–1.

62 *L'Anti-Œdipe*, 124; *Anti-Oedipus*, 104.

desiring-machine capable of being assembled without demolishing entire social sectors. Despite what some revolutionaries think about this, desire is revolutionary in its essence [. . .] and no society can tolerate a position of real desire without its structures of exploitation, servitude, and hierarchy being compromised'.[63] How then does the mechanism of repression of desire work?

To reflect on this mechanism, Deleuze and Guattari distinguish 'social repression [*répression*]' from 'psychic repression [*refoulement*]'. 'Social repression' (*répression*: social concept) forms docile subjects and reproduces social formation, while 'psychic repression' (*refoulement*: psychoanalytic concept) dams up the flows of desire in the psychic apparatus and subordinates them to a certain representation. But this distinction is not unique to their theorization; the originality of this theoretical definition resides rather in the idea that 'psychic repression' is inextricably linked to 'social repression': 'social repression needs psychic repression precisely in order to form docile subjects and to ensure the reproduction of the social formation, including its repressive structures. But social repression should not be understood by using, as a starting point, a familial repression coextensive with civilization — far from it; it is civilization that must be understood in terms of a social repression inherent to a given form of social production'.[64] 'Family repression' therefore functions as an agent of social repression which reproduces social formation. This repression is nothing other than family oedipalization, the Oedipal family being an agent of social reproduction. This theory of social reproduction guaranteed by power dispositives is shared by Foucault to the extent that these dispositives encourage the subject to internalize power. As Foucault claims, 'Oedipus is an instrument of power'.[65]

How, in fact, does the Oedipal family become an agent of social reproduction? In primitive or despotic societies, social reproduction is not independent of family reproduction. On the contrary, it depends on family elements such as 'the relations of filiation and alliance'; it is therefore 'coextensive with the social field'.[66] In contrast, in the capitalist system, the social field becomes purely economic, since an 'abstract

63 Ibid., 138; 116.
64 Ibid., 140–1; 118.
65 « La vérité et les formes juridiques », in *Dits et écrits*, T. II, 554; 'Truth and Juridical Forms', in *Essential Works*, Vol. 3, 16.
66 *L'Anti-Œdipe*, 313; *Anti-Oedipus*, 262–3.

quantity' — like money, capital and labour — is inscribed on the social field. The family is detached from it, as placed out of the social field ('privatization of the family'). However, the family does not lose its reproductive role in society. For this removal of the family from the social field is 'the condition under which the entire social field can be *applied* to the family'.[67] The social field is thus *folded back* onto the Oedipal family theatre (the Oedipal folding, which oppresses the unconscious desire of each person). Through this operation, the Oedipal family becomes an agent of social reproduction. But what becomes of the desiring-production following this Oedipal folding? In other words, how does the multiple 'subject' change following this family repression?

> The social field, where everyone acts and is acted upon as a collective agent of enunciation, an agent of production and antiproduction, is reduced to Oedipus, where everyone now finds himself cornered and cut along the line that divides him into an individual subject of statement [*sujet d'énoncé*] and an individual subject of enunciation [*sujet d'énonciation*]. The subject of the statement is the social person, and the subject of enunciation, the private person.[68]

By oedipalization, the subject is divided into 'subject of statement' and 'subject of enunciation'. To understand these two notions, it is necessary to refer again to Lacanian theory. According to Jakobson's linguistics, from which Lacan was inspired, the subject of statement designates the 'I' in the statement, but the referent of the 'I' changes according to who utters the sentence, namely to the subject of enunciation (shifter).[69] The subject of statement is therefore determined by the subject of enunciation. On the basis of this linguistic definition, Lacan reflects on the statement in the analytical session. The 'I' designates, writes Lacan, the subject of enunciation, but 'it does not signify him'; 'There are signifiers that differ from the I'.[70] He cites an example of a dream interpreted by Freud. A man who had once nursed his father through a long and

---

67 Ibid., 314; 264.

68 Ibid., 316; 265.

69 See Roman Jakobson, *Essais de linguistique générale*, T. 1, Minuit, 1963, 178–80.

70 « Subversion du sujet et dialectique du désir dans l'inconscient freudien », in *Écrits*, 800; 'The Subversion of the Subject and the Dialectic of Desire in the Freudian Unconscious', in *Écrits: The Complete Edition*, 677. Translation modified.

painful mortal illness dreams of his father repeatedly. In this dream, 'his father was alive once more and that he was talking to him in his usual way. But he felt it exceedingly painful that his father had really died, only without knowing it'. Freud then interprets this statement at the level of unconscious desire: his father had, however, already died 'as the dreamer wished', he simply did not know 'that he wished it'. This statement is therefore interpreted as a self-reproach: that of having been obliged to wish the death of the father as a deliverance.[71] We must note here a discordance between the statement and the unconscious desire, or 'an intentional ambiguity' of the statement.[72] The analysand's statement should not be interpreted in the sense that the *I* (the conscious subject) says, but in its relation to the 'subject of the unconscious', namely the Other ('the unconscious, it is the discourse of the Other'). It is thus the enunciation of the Other (unconscious enunciation) that determines the statement of the subject. It follows that, in Lacan, the subject of state-ment corresponds to the conscious instance and the subject of enuncia-tion to the unconscious instance. The subject of unconscious enuncia-tion is then superior to the subject of statement and dominates it. We find ourselves, once again, at the centre of the *topical problematic*.

Deleuze and Guattari call the subject of statement 'the social person' and the subject of enunciation 'the private person'. In the capitalist system, individual persons are first of all social persons ('images produced by the points-signs, the breaks-flows, the pure "figures" of capitalism'), then private persons ('images of images — that is, *simula-cra* that are thus endowed with an aptitude for representing the first-order images of social persons').[73] Family oedipalization designates this folding of the social person onto the private person. Desiring-production then is changed into a fixed representation (images of images, *simula-cra*) by family oedipalization: 'The reign of images is the new way in which capitalism utilizes the schizzes and diverts the flows: composite images, images folded onto other images, so that when this operation

---

71 Sigmund Freud, 'Formulierungen über die zwei Prinzipien des psychischen Geschehens', in *Gesammelte Werke*, Bd. VIII, 237–8; 'Formulation on the Two Principles of Mental Functioning', in *Standard Edition*, Vol. XII, 225–6.

72 Jacques Lacan, « La direction de la cure et les principes de son pouvoir », in *Écrits*, 592–3; 'The Direction of the Treatment and the Principle of Its Power', in *Écrits: The Complete Edition*, 495. Translation modified. See also Roland Chemama *et al.*, dirs., *Dictionnaire de la psychanalyse*, Larousse, 1998, 120–1.

73 *L'Anti-Œdipe*, 314–15; *Anti-Oedipus*, 264.

reaches its outcome the little ego of each person, related to its father-mother, is truly the centre of the world'.[74] The multiple 'subject' decentred by the desiring-production changes into a unitary subject whose centre is the 'little ego' 'related to its father-mother'. Oedipalization thus represses the multiplicity of the 'subject' and reduces it to the fixed couple of the empirical ego and the transcendental ego: the topical oedipalized subject. In other words, because it is defined on the side of the Other, by absolute passivity, the Lacanian subject decentred by lack always remains the topical subject, namely the unitary and fixed subject.

Through oedipalization, the subject of statement (empirical ego) is subjected to the subject of enunciation (transcendental ego, or Oedipal representation). This Oedipal subjection is introduced by the capitalist system: capitalism reterritorializes the flows of desire that it has itself liberated and shifts the schizophrenic 'absolute limit' towards the internalized 'relative limit'. The first signifies the absolute liberation of desire; the second, the restriction of its liberation. Capitalism pushes back the liberated flows and oppresses their movements. And it is this internalized limit that designates family oedipalization: 'Oedipus is this displaced or internalized limit where desire lets itself be caught. The Oedipal triangle is the personal and private territoriality that corresponds to all of capitalism's efforts at social reterritorialization'.[75] This is how the multiple subject is reduced to the unitary 'little ego' by oedipalization in the capitalist system. Hence, it is the capitalist system that represses the multiple economic subject and reduces it to the topical unitary subject.

At the same time, oedipalization forms the 'subjected group' by making subjects identify with the same 'group' (such as race, nation, religion) integrated under a transcendent signifier. The 'subjected group [groupe assujetti]' and the 'subject-group [groupe-sujet]' are concepts introduced by Guattari in several articles in Psychoanalysis and Transversality.[76] In the preface of this work, Deleuze offers the following definition of these concepts:

Subjected groups [Groupes assujettis] are subjected no less by the

---

74 Ibid., 316–17; 265. Translation modified.

75 Ibid., 317; 266.

76 See Félix Guattari, « Le groupe et la personne (bilan décousu) » (1966), « Introduction à la psychothérapie institutionnelle » (1962–63), in Psychanalyse et transversalité, Maspero, 1972; 'The Group and the Person', 'Introduction to Institutional Psychotherapy', in Psychoanalysis and Transversality, Semiotext(e), 2015.

leaders they assign themselves, or accept, than by the masses. The hierarchy, the vertical or pyramidal organization, which characterizes subjected groups is meant to ward off any possible inscription of nonsense, death or dispersal, to discourage the development of creative ruptures, and to ensure the self-preservation mechanisms rooted in the exclusion of other groups. Their centralization works through structure, totalization, unification, replacing the conditions of a genuine collective 'enunciation' with an assemblage of stereotypical utterances cut off both from the real and from subjectivity (this is when imaginary phenomena such as oedipalization, superegofication, and group-castration take place). Subject-groups [*Groupes-sujets*], on the other hand, are defined by coefficients of *transversality* that ward off totalities and hierarchies. They are agents of enunciation, environments of desire, elements of institutional creation. Through their very practice, they ceaselessly conform to the limit of their own nonsense, their own death or rupture.[77]

The 'subjected group' is a notion strongly influenced by Freud's *Group Psychology and the Analysis of the Ego* (1921). It designates the totality integrated *in a hierarchical, vertical and centralized manner* through the effect of identification with the transcendent centre. It thus subjects the desiring singularities to the centred group in order to crush them. In contrast, the 'subject-group', characterized by molecular multiplicity, horizontality, and transversality, reverses this relationship to subjugate the group to desiring singularities in order to deliver them. 'The two poles are defined, *the one* [the subjected group] by the enslavement of production and the desiring-machines to the gregarious aggregates that they constitute on a large scale under a given form of power or selective sovereignty; *the other* [the subject-group] by the inverse subordination and the overthrow of power. *The one* [the subjected group] by these molar structured aggregates that crush singularities, select them, and regularize those that they retain in codes or axiomatics; *the other* [the subject-group] by the molecular multiplicities of singularities that on

---

77 Gilles Deleuze, « Préface », in Félix Guattari, *Psychanalyse et transversalité*, VI (« Trois problèmes de groupe », in *L'île déserte : textes et entretiens 1953–1974*, Minuit, 2002, 276–7); 'Preface: Three Group-Related Problems', in *Psychoanalysis and Transversality*, 13–14 ('Three Group-Related Problems', in *Desert Islands and Other Texts: Texts and Interviews 1953–1974*, Semiotext(e), 2004, 197–8). Translation modified.

the contrary treat the large aggregates as so many useful materials for their own elaborations'.[78]

What seems important here is that Deleuze and Guattari define these two notions in relation to the collective fantasy:

> The development of distinctions between group and individual fantasy shows sufficiently well, at last, that there is no individual fantasy. Instead there are two types of groups, subject-groups and subjected groups, with Oedipus and castration forming the imaginary structure under which members of the subjugated groups are induced to live or fantasize individually their membership in the group. [...] It is therefore all the more disturbing to see to what extent Freudian analysis retains from the fantasy only its lines of exclusive disjunction, and flattens it *into its individual or pseudoindividual dimensions, which by their very nature refer the fantasy to subjected groups*, rather than carrying out the opposite operation and disengaging in the fantasy the underlying element of a revolutionary group potential.[79]

According to Deleuze and Guattari, what psychoanalysis calls the 'individual fantasy' is, in reality, the collective fantasy, which organizes both the subjected group and the subject-group. Note that the family fantasy, or Oedipus, plays an essential role in the formation of the subjected group. Oedipalization as individualization produces the so-called 'individual' family fantasy, which subordinates individuals to the transcendent signifier ('phallus' or 'name of the father'). By the displacement of this transcendent signifier to the social transcendent signifier (such as state, race, and God), individuals are integrated into the totality of the subjected group and that of collective fantasy.

The formation of psychic repression by oedipalization thus coincides exactly with the subjection of the subjects to the subjected group, which takes place through individualization in the Oedipal family so that the formation of the subjugated group integrates the individual subjects with the transcendent signifier. On this point, the authors stress that the family and individual fantasy is nothing other than the collective fantasy. Oedipalization thus constitutes a means of integrating subjects into the subjected group.

---

78 *L'Anti-Œdipe*, 439–40; *Anti-Oedipus*, 366–7.
79 Ibid., 75–6; 64. Our emphasis.

However, in Deleuze and Guattari, the means of resisting the Oedipal power are always already given in capitalism itself. How do Deleuze and Guattari define capitalism? According to them, capitalism was born from the encounter [*rencontre*] between decoded flows of production (in the form of money-capital) and decoded flows of labour (in the form of the 'free worker').[80] This definition borrows from the Marxist theory of the emergence of capitalism, developed by Étienne Balibar in *Reading Capital* (1965), where he quotes the following passage of Marx's *Grundrisse*:

> But the mere presence of monetary wealth, and even the achievement of a kind of supremacy on its part, is in no way sufficient for this dissolution into capital to happen. Or else ancient Rome, Byzantium etc. would have ended their history with free labour and capital, or rather begun a new history. There, too, the dissolution of the old property relations was bound up with development of monetary wealth – of trade, etc. But instead of leading to industry, this dissolution led in fact to the supremacy of the countryside over the city. [. . .] [Capital's] original formation is that, through the historic process of the dissolution of the old mode of production, value existing as money-wealth is enabled, on one side, to buy the objective conditions of labour; on the other side, to exchange money for the living labour of the workers who have been set free. *All these moments are present; their divorce is itself a historic process, a process of dissolution, and it is the latter which enables money to transform itself into capital.*[81]

Commenting on this passage by Marx, Balibar points out that the emergence of capitalism is achieved through the combination [*Verbindung*] or the encounter [*rencontre*] between the accumulation of money-capital and the 'free worker' detached from the land.[82] Based on this

---

80 Ibid., 41; 33.

81 Karl Marx, *Grundrisse der Kritik der politischen Ökonomie*, Marx-Engels Werke, Bd. 42, Dietz, 1983, 413–14; *Grundrisse*, Penguin, 1993, 506–7. This passage is translated, quoted and emphasized by Étienne Balibar in *Lire le Capital* (nouvelle édition revue, PUF, 1996, 530–1).

82 Étienne Balibar, « Sur les concepts fondamentaux du matérialisme historique », in Louis Althusser et coll., *Lire le Capital*, nouvelle édition revue, coll. « Quadrige », PUF, 1996, 529–33; 'On the Basic Concepts of Historical Materialism', in *Reading Capital: The Complete Edition*, Verso, 2015, 448–51. This reference is explicitly indicated in the second volume of *Capitalism and Schizophrenia*. See Gilles Deleuze/Félix Guattari, *Mille*

formulation, Deleuze and Guattari define capitalism as a movement of decoding flows (flows of capital-money and of labour power), given that it introduces the abstract quantity of money in place of the precapitalist code. The axiomatics of the abstract quantity of money pushes the movement of decoding to the limit and deterritorializes the flows of desire.[83]

Capitalism is defined as the decoding and deterritorialization of flows — in other words, as a schizophrenic movement towards its absolute limit. Meanwhile, capitalism simultaneously represses these deterritorialized flows in order to confine them to its internal and relative limit: it constantly reproduces this internal limit by widening it so that deterritorialized flows never reach the absolute limit: 'one can say that schizophrenia is the *exterior* limit of capitalism itself or the conclusion of its deepest tendency, but that capitalism only functions on condition that it inhibit this tendency, or that it pushes back or displaces this limit, by substituting for it its own immanent relative limits, which it continually reproduces on a widened scale. It axiomatizes with one hand what it decodes with the other'.[84]

This Deleuzo-Guattarian theorization of capitalism is based on Marx's *Capital*, where capitalism is defined, on the one hand, as a movement towards the absolute limit: 'the circulation of money as capital is an end in itself, for the valorisation of value takes place only within this constantly renewed movement. The movement of capital is therefore limitless'.[85] However, this movement towards the absolute limit is controlled, on the other hand, by the internal limit, which is necessary to contain this movement within the framework of capitalism: 'Capitalist production constantly strives to overcome these immanent barriers [*immanenten Schranken*], but it overcomes them only by means that set up the barriers afresh and on a more powerful scale. / The true barrier [*die wahre Shranke*] to capitalist production is capital itself'.[86] Quoting

plateaux: Capitalisme et schizophrenie, Minuit, 1980, 565, note 43; *A Thousand Plateaus: Capitalism and Schizophrenia*, University of Minnesota Press, 1987, 569, note 48. We will discuss the Althusserian notion of *Verbindung* and *rencontre* in section 6.3.

83 *L'Anti-Œdipe*, 41; *Anti-Oedipus*, 33.

84 Ibid., 292; 246.

85 Karl Marx, *Das Kapital*, Bd. 1, *Marx-Engels Werke*, Bd. 23, Dietz, 1962, 167; *Capital*, Vol. 1, Penguin, 1990, 253. Quoted in *L'Anti-Œdipe*, 296; *Anti-Oedipus*, 248.

86 Karl Marx, *Das Kapital*, Bd. 3, *Marx-Engels Werke*, Bd. 25, Dietz, 1964, 260. *Capital*, Vol. 3, Penguin, 1991, 358. Quoted in *L'Anti-Œdipe*, 274, note 82; *Anti-Oedipus*, 231, note. The translation of this passage quoted in *L'Anti-Œdipe* is that of Étienne

this passage from Marx, Balibar deals with, in *Reading Capital*, the notion of 'immanent limit': 'The "limits" towards which the movement of the mode of production tends (its dynamics) are not therefore a question of a ladder, of a *threshold* to attain. If the tendency cannot pass these limits, it is because they are inside it, and as such *never reached*: in its movement it carries them with it, they coincide with the causes which make it a "mere" tendency, i.e., they are simultaneously its actual conditions of possibility. To say that the capitalist mode of production has internal limits is quite simply to say that the mode of production is not a "mode of production in general", but a *delimited, determinate* mode of production.'[87] Balibar maintains that the 'immanent limit' of the capitalist mode of production prevents the passage to another mode of production, namely the passage to communism. In this sense, it corresponds exactly to the 'internal limit' (that which prevents movement towards the absolute limit) in the Deleuzo-Guattarian sense of the term. Therefore, the Deleuzo-Guattarian theorization of capitalism is owed entirely to Balibar's reading of *Capital*.

The capitalist state is the regulator of decoded flows. It controls, at the request of the axiomatics of capital, the decoded flows: this control is done both to widen the relative limit of capitalism (namely, to achieve capitalist development and the deterritorialization of capital) and to confine the capitalist movement within the internal limit (namely, to prevent social revolution).[88] The welfare state, the neoliberal state, and even the socialist state can be interpreted within this framework of the axiomatic of capital: the welfare state and the socialist state take the initiative in economic development and redistribute income to the workers; the neoliberal state does not intervene directly in the movement of capital, but controls it by creating a state of competition in the entire society.[89]

How then can we overthrow capitalism endlessly reproduced at the

---

Balibar in *Lire le Capital*. See « Sur les concepts fondamentaux du matérialisme historique », in *Lire le Capital*, 545.

87 « Sur les concepts fondamentaux du matérialisme historique », in *Lire le Capital*, 545; 'On the Basic Concepts of Historical Materialism', in *Reading Capital: The Complete Edition*, 461.

88 *L'Anti-Œdipe*, 299–300; *Anti-Oedipus*, 251–2.

89 On the role of the state in neoliberal government, see Michel Foucault, *Naissance de la biopolitique, Cours au Collège de France, 1978–1979*, Gallimard/Seuil, 2004; *The Birth of Biopolitics, Lectures at the Collège de France, 1978–79*, Palgrave Macmillan, 2008. We discuss this point in Appendix 1.

level of desire? According to Deleuze and Guattari's strategy, capitalism will be undermined through the transformation of the oedipalized subjected subject and of the hierarchical subjected group into a molecular multiplicity of desire and into a transversal subject-group:

> The paranoiac and the schizoid investments are like two opposite poles of unconscious libidinal investment, one of which subordinates desiring-production to the formation of sovereignty and to the gregarious aggregate that results from it, while the other brings about the inverse subordination, reverses the power, and subjects the gregarious aggregate to the molecular multiplicities of the productions of desire. [. . .] it is not enough to construct a new socius as full body; one must also pass to the other side of this social full body, where the molecular formations of desire that must master the new molar aggregate operate and are inscribed. Only by making this passage do we reach the revolutionary inconscient break and investment of the libido. This cannot be achieved except at the cost of, and by means of a rupture in causality.[90]

Reversing the subordination of the molecular multiplicity of desire to the socius (subordination achieved by the oedipalization of desire) with the aim of subordinating the socius to the molecular multiplicity of desire — it is this very reversal of the power of desire that will achieve 'the revolutionary inconscient break and investment of the libido' and the transformation of the subjected group into a subject-group. And this transformation will be possible only by 'a rupture in causality' of the reproduction of capitalist society, namely by the revolution at the level of interest. We must emphasize that the 'unconscious revolution' — the deterritorialization of the molecular multiplicity of desire ('break of break') — becomes possible within the 'preconscious revolution' itself, that is to say, within the revolution at the level of interest ('Leninist break'):

> In fact, the unconscious revolutionary break implies for its part the body without organs as the limit of the socius that desiring-production subordinates in its turn, under the condition of a reversed power, a reversed subordination. The preconscious revolution refers to a new

---

90 L'Anti-Œdipe, 451–2; Anti-Oedipus, 376–7. Translation modified.

regime of social production that creates, distributes, and satisfies new aims and interests. But the unconscious revolution does not merely refer to the socius that conditions this change as a form of power; it refers within this socius to the regime of desiring-production as a reversed power on the body without organs. It is not the same state of flows and schizzes: in one case the break is between two forms of socius, the second of which is measured according to its capacity to introduce the flows of desire into a new code or a new axiomatic of interest; in the other case the break is within the socius itself, in that it has the capacity for causing the flows of desire to circulate following their positive lines of escape, and for breaking them again following *productive breaks of breaks.*[91]

In *Anti-Oedipus*, which recognizes the revolutionary potentiality of the proletarians, the transformation of the subjected group into a subject-group is possible only through the pursuit of proletarian class interests. It is through this pursuit of class interests that the proletarians (a group subjected to their interests) find the productive power of desire, a power that remained subjected to the socius. But at the same time, if the proletarians are content to pursue class interests, they will never be able to detach themselves from the group subjected to capitalist interests. The proletarians must therefore form the subject-group of the schizos, detaching their desiring production from the pursuit of interests. It is this deterritorialization of the molecular multiplicity of desire operated at the level of the unconscious that transforms the subjected group — which is integrated in a hierarchical, vertical, and centralized manner — into a horizontal, transversal, and de-subjected group-subject; this deterritorialization reverses desire subjected to the capitalist principle (Oedipus), produces the 'break of break' submitting the socius to the molecular multiplicity of desire and, finally, undermines capitalism. The 'revolutionary inconscient break and investment of the libido' then refers to the abolition of capitalism through the transformation of the subjected group into a subject-group.[92]

---

91 Ibid., 416; 347–8. Translation modified and our emphasis.

92 We discussed this point in our following work: Yoshiyuki Sato/Jun Fujita Hirose, *Mittsu no kakumei: Duruzu-Gatari no seiji tetsugaku* [*Three Revolutions: Political Philosophy of Deleuze and Guattari*], Kôdan-sha, 2017; *Comment imposer une limite absolue au capitalisme ? : Phiolsophie politique de Deleuze et Guattari*, Hermann, forthcoming.

Deleuze and Guattari started with productivity or the absolute activity of desire to develop a strategy of resistance. This movement is in fact capable of transforming the topical unitary subject into an economic and collective multiple subject. The activity of desire is not then identical to that of the subject, since, for these authors, the subject is decentred by the productive unconscious. The activity of desiring production is therefore not that of the subject (preconscious–conscious system), but that of unconscious desire. We should emphasize here that their definition of the unconscious is radically different from that of Lacan. For the latter, the unconscious is 'the discourse of *the Other*', which is found within the *personal field of the Other*. Lacan decentred the ego without succeeding in eliminating the personal field of the Other. For Deleuze and Guattari, on the other hand, the unconscious cannot be determined by the personal field of the self any more than by that of the Other: it is the field of *singularities*, namely the *impersonal* transcendental field.[93] The unconscious singularities do not constitute the activity of the subject, but that of *impersonal power* [puissance impersonnelle]. In *Anti-Oedipus*, this power is denoted by 'prepersonal singularities':

> The task of schizoanalysis is that of tirelessly taking apart egos and their presuppositions; liberating the prepersonal singularities they enclose and repress; mobilizing the flows they would be capable of transmitting, receiving, or intercepting; establishing always further and more sharply the schizzes and the breaks well below conditions of identity; and assembling the desiring-machines that countersect everyone and group everyone with others.[94]

---

93 Gilles Deleuze, *Logique du sens*, Minuit, 1969, 124; *The Logic of Sense*, Athlone Press, 1990, 102: 'We seek to determine *an impersonal and pre-individual transcendental field*, which does not resemble the corresponding empirical fields, and which nevertheless is not confused with an undifferentiated depth. This field cannot be determined as that of a consciousness. [. . .] we cannot retain consciousness as a milieu while at the same time we object to the form of the person and the point of view of individuation. A consciousness is nothing without a synthesis of unification, but there is no synthesis of unification of consciousness without the form of the I, or the point of view of the Self. What is neither individual nor personal are, on the contrary, emissions of *singularities* insofar as they occur on an unconscious surface and possess a mobile, immanent principle of auto-unification through a nomadic distribution, radically distinct from fixed and sedentary distributions as conditions of the syntheses of consciousness'. Our emphasis.

94 *L'Anti-Œdipe*, 434; *Anti-Oedipus*, 362.

The subject is certainly decentred. Nevertheless, an active power, such as singularities or impersonal power, is contained in the unconscious desire, which can realize the collective and machinic assemblage of subjects. It is this collective subjectivity de-subjected at the level of unconscious desire, namely the subject-group, which constitutes the originality of the Deleuzo-Guattarian notion of subject.

Since capitalism comprises a principle of decoding and liberation of the flows of impersonal power, the means of resisting power are immanent within it. This process is the consequence of the economic problematic which is based on productive desire. The Foucauldian notion of subject in *Discipline and Punish* lacks this power of resistance: the transcendental ego is only a simple agent of power, and therefore any power of resistance to power is erased. This is what we called the unicity of the transcendental instance. In Foucault's theory of power as he first formulated it, this power of resistance does not exist. His deconstruction of the Kantian (topical) subject by means of the primacy of power relations has in fact eliminated the active power of the subject. By contrast, in Deleuze and Guattari, the economic subject resides in the absolute productivity of unconscious desire. This productivity of the economic subject directly opens the way to the theorization of collective resistance to power. What then allows collective resistance is not the activity of the subject itself, but the activity of impersonal desiring power in the decentred subject (productive desire of the unconscious) and the multiplicity of the transcendental field, namely the machinic assemblage. And it is exactly this transcendental principle of becoming-other that enables the transformation of the subjected group into a subject-group.

3
Topic II, or Heterogeneous Thought (Foucault)

3.1 The arts of existence as a strategy of resistance

Between *The Will to Know* (the first volume of *The History of Sexuality*, 1976) and *The Use of Pleasure/The Care of the Self* (the second and third volumes of *The History of Sexuality*, 1984), we can discern a certain *Kehre* of Foucauldian theory. This turn is generally considered the shift from the genealogy of power to the aesthetic of existence. For example, for Paul Veyne, the turn of the last Foucault is to seek 'the idea of style of existence.'[1] For Richard Rorty, it is a return to the 'Romantic intellectual' who places importance on the 'search for private autonomy'.[2] For our part, we do not adopt such readings. Indeed, if we take a closer look at the meaning of the Foucauldian turn, we can interpret it as an attempt to introduce, within his theory, the problem of resistance to power. Foucault writes, for example, in the introduction to *The Use of Pleasure*:

---

1 Paul Veyne, « Le dernier Foucault et sa morale », *Critique* 471–2, 1986. However, we note that Veyne refuses to use the word 'aesthetic'. See also another article in the same volume, which discusses the Foucauldian turn from 'genealogical inquiry' to the 'aesthetic of existence': Mario Vegetti, « Foucault et les Anciens », *Critique* 471-2.

2 Richard Rorty, 'Moral Identity and Private Autonomy: The Case of Foucault', in *Essays on Heidegger and Others*, Cambridge University Press, 1991. Christopher Norris takes a critical stance on Rorty's article but sees, all the same, an abandonment of the nominalist position and of Nietzschean genealogical thought in the last Foucault. See Christopher Norris, '"What is Enlightenment?": Kant According to Foucault', in Gary Gutting, ed., *The Cambridge Companion to Foucault*, Cambridge University Press, 1994.

[I]n raising this very general question [how, why, and in what forms was sexuality constituted as a moral domain?], and in directing it to Greek and Greco-Roman culture, it occurred to me that this problematization [morality of sexual conduct] was linked to a group of practices that have been of unquestionable importance in our societies: I am referring to what might be called the 'arts of existence'. What I mean by the phrase are those intentional and voluntary actions by which men not only set themselves rules of conduct, but also seek to transform themselves, to change themselves in their singular being, and to make their life into an *oeuvre* that carries certain aesthetic values and meets certain stylistic criteria.[3]

The 'arts of existence' are practices by which men seek to transform themselves to 'meet certain stylistic criteria'. It is this practice — Foucault defines it elsewhere as an 'ethical' practice[4] — that Rorty considers as a 'search for private autonomy'. But what escapes him is the following question: for what purpose do men transform themselves or to meet what 'stylistic criteria'? In considering this question, we can understand that the ethical practice in question here relates directly to the political practice. In 'The Subject and Power' (1982), Foucault indeed suggests to '[take] the forms of resistance to the different types of power as a starting point' in order to 'go further towards a new economy of power relations'.[5] He continues as follows:

Maybe the target nowadays is not to discover what we are but to refuse what we are. We have to imagine and to build up what we could be to get rid of this kind of political 'double bind', which is the simultaneous individualization and totalization of modern power structures.

The conclusion would be that the political, ethical, social, philosophical problem of our days is not to try to liberate the individual from the state, and from the state's institutions, but to liberate us both from the state and from the type of individualization linked to the state. We have to promote new forms of subjectivity through the

---

3 Michel Foucault, *L'usage des plaisirs: Histoire de la sexualité 2*, Gallimard, 1984, 16–17; *The Use of Pleasure: The History of Sexuality, Vol. 2*, Pantheon Books, 1990, 10.

4 See, for example, ibid., 34; 27.

5 Michel Foucault, « Le sujet et le pouvoir », in *Dits et écrits*, T. IV, 225; 'The Subject and Power', in *Essential Works*, Vol. 3, 329.

refusal of this kind of individuality that has been imposed on us for several centuries.[6]

The practice to 'refuse what we are' is precisely that of transforming oneself to create 'a new economy of power relations'. This practice frees the subject from modern power structures (the 'double bind' of individualization and totalization realized by pastoral power) and transforms it into 'new forms of subjectivity'. In other words, ethical practices refer to 'the forms of resistance to different types of power' that rid individuals of 'who we are' — namely the actual economy of power relations. It is therefore not a simple 'search for private autonomy', but a political strategy of resistance to power.

3.2 Turn to the thematic of ethics

It is from this point of view that we will interpret the meaning of the Foucauldian *Kehre*. First, we must pay attention to the fact that the first volume of *The History of Sexuality* (1976) clearly intended to develop a critique of psychoanalysis. In this work, Foucault addresses the practice of confession. Since the institutionalization of Catholicism, confession has been associated with the practice of penance. But 'with the rise of Protestantism, the Counter Reformation, eighteenth-century pedagogy, and nineteenth-century medicine, it gradually lost its ritualistic and exclusive localization'.[7] It expanded its domain and 'it has been employed in a whole series of relationships: children and parents, students and educators, patients and psychiatrists, delinquents and experts'.[8] It was, so to speak, 'secularized'. According to Foucault, psychoanalysis is situated in this secularization of the confession. What, then, does this practice mean?

The confession is a ritual of discourse in which the speaking subject is also the subject of the statement; it is also a ritual that unfolds within a power relation, for one does not confess without the presence (or virtual presence) of a partner who is not simply the interlocutor but

---

6 Ibid., 232; 336.
7 *La volonté de savoir*, 84; *The History of Sexuality, Vol. 1*, 63.
8 Ibid., 84–5; 63.

the authority who requires the confession, prescribes and appreciates it, and intervenes in order to judge, punish, forgive, console, and reconcile.[9]

In the confession, the congruence between the subject of enunciation (the subject who speaks) and the subject of statement is ensured by the power relation between the one who confesses and the one who interprets the statement as 'the authority'. In psychoanalysis, this power relation corresponds to that of the analysand and the analyst, who ensures the 'truth' of the analysand's statement:

> The truth did not reside solely in the subject who, by confessing, would reveal it wholly formed. It was constituted in two stages: present but incomplete, blind to itself, in the one who spoke, it could only reach completion in the one who assimilated and recorded it. It was the latter's function to verify this obscure truth: the revelation of confession had to be coupled with the decipherment of what it said. The one who listened was not simply the forgiving master, the judge who condemned or acquitted; he was the master of truth. His was a hermeneutic function. With regard to the confession, his power was not only to demand it before it was made, or decide what was to follow after it, but also to constitute a discourse of truth on the basis of its decipherment.[10]

Whoever listens to the confession (the analyst) occupies the position of 'master of truth'. The one who confesses (the analysand) does not decide for himself the meaning of what he confesses. If the confession is the place where the subject of enunciation coincides with the subject of statement, it is the analyst who decides on the 'truth' of the analysand's statement. In this sense, the subject does not know the 'truth' of what he is saying — it is determined by the analyst as the analysand's Other. The subject's truth is then displaced outside the subject, in this case towards the Other. We can find a radical theorization of this relation between the subject and the Other in Lacanian theory:

---

9 Ibid., 82–3; 61–2. Translation modified.
10 Ibid., 89; 66–7.

As it draws to its end, interpretation points the desire [*pointe le désir*], with which, in a certain sense, it is identical. Desire, in fact, is interpretation itself.[11]

For Lacan, the subject's desire does not belong to the subject: it is 'the desire of the Other' which appears through the interpretation of the analyst. It only exists, so to speak, in analysis. Lacan introduced the technique of 'scansion' in order to articulate the analysand's statement. By 'scansion', the analyst suspends the analytical session when the subject says something important related to his unconscious. 'Point the desire [*pointer le désir*]' expresses this articulation of the statement by the analyst. And by this 'scansion', he articulates the 'truth' of desire. In this sense, desire is 'interpretation itself'. Here, the 'truth' of desire is radically shifted to the instance of the Other (the analyst). What Foucault criticizes is this intervention of power relation, which transforms the Other into a 'master of truth'. In other words, the subject is subjected to the Other by the practice of confession. This scheme has the same structure as the one he presented in *Discipline and Punish*: the subject is subjected to power by the power dispositives. It is precisely in this sense that the confession is an 'immense labour' to produce the subjection of men.[12] The practice of confession works to subject the subject to the Other; it is this mechanism that ensures subjection to power. Foucault thus criticizes the practice of confession and the structure of subjection in psychoanalytic practice. But at this point in his reflection, he cannot yet present a new concept of subject that would replace it.

To consider the 'history of sexuality' penetrated by power relations, Foucault uses the concept of 'dispositives of sexuality'. These dispositives aim to promote the body 'as an object of knowledge and an element in power relations' and the control of 'population'.[13] This configuration corresponds respectively to the 'anatomo-politics of the human body' and to the 'bio-politics of the population'.[14] These power dispositives have the particularity of not repressing sex but of making people talk about it and of producing a great deal of discourse about it ('the

---

11 Jacques Lacan, *Le séminaire*, Livre XI, « Les quatre concepts fondamentaux de la psychanalyse », Seuil, 1973, 161; *The Seminar*, Book XI, 'The Four Fundamental Concepts of Psychoanalysis', Norton, 1981, 176. Translation modified.

12 *La volonté de savoir*, 81; *The History of Sexuality, Vol. 1*, 60.

13 Ibid., 141; 107. Translation modified.

14 Ibid., 183; 139.

proliferation of discourse concerned with sex'[15]). Sex is therefore not repressed but, on the contrary, enormously 'produced' and put into discourse. This theory reminds us of the one Deleuze and Guattari presented in *Anti-Oedipus*, in which they criticize the Freudo-Marxist theory of sexual repression by power.

In this sense, a remark by Foucault on the work of Deleuze and Guattari is symptomatic of the turn he initiates towards the problem of ethics, closely linked to that of resistance. In the preface (1977) of the English translation of *Anti-Oedipus*, Foucault takes a unique perspective on this text. *Anti-Oedipus* is, he writes, an anti-fascist book: 'fascism' does not only denote the historical situation of the 1930s and 1940s; it also includes micro-fascism, 'the fascism in us all, in our heads and in our everyday behaviour, the fascism that causes us to love power, to desire the very thing that dominates and exploits us'.[16] Anti-fascism therefore means not wanting to subject oneself to power. Taking up the concepts of Deleuze and Guattari, Foucault expresses it in the following way: 'to "de-individualize" by means of multiplication and displacement, diverse assemblages [*agencements*]'.[17] Foucault reads *Anti-Oedipus* as a theory of resistance, which he calls 'ethics':

> I would say that *Anti-Oedipus* (may its authors forgive me) is a book of ethics, the first book of ethics to be written in France in quite a long time [. . .]: being anti-oedipal has become a life style, a way of thinking and living.[18]

Ethics means 'a life style, a way of thinking and of living'. If this 'way of thinking and living' designates a strategy of resistance to power, then we can assert that the Foucauldian *Kehre* towards the thematic of ethics is equivalent to the search for this strategy of resistance. Foucault takes a turn towards the problematic of resistance *as if he were inspired by the work of Deleuze and Guattari.*

---

15 Ibid., 26; 18.
16 Michel Foucault, « Préface », in *Dits et écrits*, T. III, 134; 'Preface', in *Anti-Oedipus*, xiii.
17 Ibid., 135–6; xiv. Translation modified.
18 Ibid., 134–5; xiii.

3.3 The soul is the prison of the body

In a letter to Foucault (1977), written a year after the publication of *The Will to Know*, Deleuze points out this problem of resistance and provides a critical point of view:

1) the one [direction] in *WK* [*The Will to Know*] (126–127) where phenomena of resistance would be like a reverse image of dispositives, where they would have the same characteristics, diffusion, heterogeneity . . . etc., where they would be vis-a-vis; but this direction seems to lead as much to a dead-end as to a way out of one; 2) the direction indicated in the interview in *Politique Hebdo*: if the power dispositives are constituents of truth, if there is a truth in power, there must be a kind of power of truth as a counter-strategy against powers. Hence the problem of the intellectual for Michel and his way of reintroducing the category of truth, since, in renewing it completely by making it dependent on power, he finds ammunition which can be turned against power? But I don't see how. We will have to wait for Michel to give his new conception of truth, on the micro analytical level; 3) the third direction, which would be that of pleasures, the body and its pleasures. Once again, I am in a state of waiting. How do pleasures animate counter-powers, and how does he conceive of this notion of pleasure?[19]

Deleuze asks two questions: first, what is the 'new conception of truth' that can resist the power dispositives producing the subject's 'truth'?; second, how can we resist it by using 'the body and its pleasures'? These two questions raised by Deleuze to Foucault allow us to begin to reflect on the latter's turn.

Let us deal with this question through the thematic of the body and the ego. In this perspective, we must return to an important sentence, to be found almost at the beginning of *Discipline and Punish*: 'The soul is the effect and instrument of a political anatomy; the soul is the prison of the body'.[20] This enigmatic sentence condenses the essential theoretical

---

19 Gilles Deleuze, « Désir et plaisir », in *Deux régimes de fous: textes et entretiens 1975–1995*, Minuit, 2003, 117–18; 'Desire and Pleasure', in *Two Regimes of Madness: Texts and Interviews 1975–1995*, Semiotext(e), 2007, 128–9. Translation modified.

20 *Surveiller et punir*, 34; *Discipline and Punish*, 30. For a critical interpretation of this sentence (from a Spinozist point of view), see Warren Montag, '"The Soul Is the Prison of the Body": Althusser and Foucault, 1970–1975', *Yale French Studies* 88, 1995.

dispositives of *Discipline and Punish*. But what does this expression mean?

In *Discipline and Punish*, Foucault insists that disciplinary power is realized in the investment of power over the body. He therefore begins his work with a chapter entitled 'The Body of the Condemned', where he writes:

> [W]e can surely accept the general proposition that, in our societies, the systems of punishment are to be situated in a certain 'political economy' of the body: even if they do not make use of violent or bloody punishment, even when they use 'lenient' methods involving confinement or correction, it is always the body that matters — the body and its forces, their utility and their docility, their distribution and their submission.[21]

The body is therefore the target of disciplinary power, and 'it is always the body that matters'. The disciplinary power acts on the body and on its forces, it ensures their usefulness, their docility, their distribution and their submission, which constitute together the 'docile body'. Through this process, disciplinary power 'increases the forces of the body (in economic terms of utility) and diminishes these same forces (in political terms of obedience)'.[22] This network of power investments on the body forms the mechanism of micropower. Foucault will express it in terms of 'the microphysics of power'.[23]

Let us refer here to *Bodies That Matter* by Judith Butler.[24] In the first chapter of the book, she analyses the Foucauldian formulation 'the soul is the prison of the body' through the Aristotelian concepts of matter and soul. According to her, '[f]or Aristotle the soul designates the actualization of matter, where matter is understood as fully potential and unactualized'.[25] In other words, matter does not appear without a scheme that defines it. This scheme corresponds, still according to her, to the soul in Foucault. She deduces then the following proposition:

---

21 *Surveiller et punir*, 30; *Discipline and Punish*, 25. Translation modified.

22 Ibid., 140; 138.

23 Ibid., 31; 28.

24 Judith Butler, *Bodies That Matter: On the Discursive Limits of Sex*, Routledge, 1993. This title recalls a phrase by Foucault in *Discipline and Punish*: 'it is always the body that matters [*c'est bien toujours du corps qu'il s'agit*]'.

25 Ibid., 32.

Foucault argues in *Discipline and Punish* that the 'soul' becomes a normative and normalizing ideal according to which the body is trained, shaped, cultivated, and invested; it is an historically specific imaginary ideal (*idéal spéculatif*) under which the body is effectively materialized.[26]

For Butler, the Foucauldian 'soul' becomes 'an historically specific imaginary ideal (*idéal spéculatif*)' which disciplines the body and materializes it as a social being.[27] This is what allows her to assert that the Foucauldian formulation is a reformulation of the Aristotelian concept.

However, while referring to Butler's theory, we can undertake a different analysis of Foucault's formulation. In *Bodies that Matter*, Butler evokes a passage from Freud's *The Ego and the Id*: 'The ego is first and foremost a bodily ego [*Das Ich ist vor allem ein körperliches*]; it is not merely a surface entity, but is itself the projection of a surface.'[28] Freud, in the same passage, explains the mechanism of the formation of the ego:

> Another factor, besides the influence of the system *Pcpt.*, seems to have played a part in bringing about the formation of the ego and its differentiation from the id. A person's own body, and above all its surface, is a place from which both external and internal perceptions may spring. It is seen like any other object, but to the touch it yields two kinds of sensations, one of which may be equivalent to an internal perception. Psychophysiology has fully discussed the manner in which a person's own body attains its special position among other objects in the world of perception. Pain, too, seems to play a part in the process, and the way in which we gain new knowledge of our

---

26 Ibid., 33.

27 See *La volonté de savoir*, 205; *The History of Sexuality, Vol. 1*, 155: 'sex is doubtless but an ideal point made necessary by the dispositive of sexuality and its operation. We must not make the mistake of thinking that sex is an autonomous agency which secondarily produces multiple effects of sexuality over the entire length of its surface of contact with power. On the contrary, sex is the most *speculative* [spéculatif], most *ideal* [idéal], and most internal element in a dispositive of sexuality organized by power in its grip on bodies and their materiality, their forces, energies, sensations, and pleasures'. Translation modified and our emphasis.

28 Sigmund Freud, *Das Ich und das Es*, in *Gesammelte Werke*, Bd. XIII, 253; *The Ego and the Id*, in *Standard Edition*, Vol. XIX, 26. Quoted in *Bodies That Matter*, 58–9.

organs during painful illnesses is perhaps a model of the way by which
in general we arrive at the idea of our body.[29]

For the ego to be different from the id, external perceptions (stimuli
from the outside world on the body) and internal perceptions of the
body (especially 'pain') must play a role. In Butler, this bodily 'pain',
which is psychically invested by prohibition and guilt, serves to produce
an idea of the body which delimits the bodily surface.[30] For our part, we
read this quote from Freud as a production of interiority, of the transcendental ego through the investment of regulatory power over the
body.

This reinterpretation of Freud's explanation authorizes another reading of the Foucauldian formulation: the ego which directs the body, this
'soul' which folds back onto the body, is formed by the investment of
disciplinary power over the body (stimuli of the outside world: surveillance, training, correction of the body) and by the reaction of the body
to this investment (the internal perceptions of the body: psychically
inscribed pain in the body). In other words, the reflective consciousness
of the ego is formed in the psychic inscription of pain through the training of the body. In *Discipline and Punish*, Foucault explains: 'it [the soul]
is produced permanently around, on, within the body by the functioning of a power that is exercised on those punished — and, in a more
general way, on those one supervises, trains and corrects, over madmen,
children at home and at school, the colonized, over those who are stuck
at a machine and supervised for the rest of their lives'.[31] The disciplinary
power supervises, trains, and controls the body of the individual and
establishes the reflective and regulatory ego that governs its body. In
other words, this investment of disciplinary power, psychically inscribing pain on the body, establishes the reflectivity of the ego, the 'empirico-transcendental doublet'. In this 'empirico-transcendental doublet',
the superior ego (the transcendental ego, the soul) watches and directs
the inferior ego (the empirical self, the body). We called the 'transcendental gaze' this reflective and regulatory gaze which directs the body.

---

29 Ibid., 253; 25–6.
30 *Bodies That Matter*, 63–4.
31 *Surveiller et punir*, 34; *Discipline and Punish*, 29. Butler reinterprets this
investment of power from the standpoint of prohibiting homosexuality and argues that
the guilt and pain induced by the prohibition produces the heterosexual 'ideal' of the
body. See *Bodies That Matter*, 63–5.

As we have already seen, it is difficult to find a possibility of resistance in this theoretical framework.[32]

If Foucault's turn takes place around the problem of resistance to power, we can interpret it as the inversion of the formulation that 'the soul is the prison of the body'. Foucault writes in *The Will to Know* as if he was announcing the direction of his coming turn:

> It is the instance of sex that we must break away from, if we aim —
> through a tactical reversal of the various mechanisms of sexuality —
> to counter the grips of power with the claims of bodies, pleasures, and
> knowledges, in their multiplicity and their possibility of resistance.
> The rallying point for the counterattack against the dispositive of
> sexuality ought not to be sex-desire, but bodies and pleasures.[33]

The 'dispositive of sexuality' normalizes the sexuality of each individual by their confession of the 'truth of desire'. The point of resistance to this dispositive resides, according to *The Will to Know*, in bodies and pleasures. We can legitimately wonder why.

If we remember that Foucault's concept of power was influenced by Nietzsche's conceptualization, we can refer to Deleuze's analysis in *Nietzsche and Philosophy*. 'We do not even know what a body can do', writes Deleuze, quoting Spinoza. He continues: 'we talk about consciousness and spirit and chatter on about it all, but we do not know what a body is capable of, what forces belong to it or what they are preparing for'.[34] However, the question here is not to neglect the problem of 'consciousness and spirit'. On the contrary, for Deleuze, it is necessary to deliberate on the consciousness and the spirit through the virtual power of the body.

From this, he defines what consciousness is: 'Like Freud, Nietzsche thinks that consciousness is the region of the ego affected by the external world'.[35] However, this definition is superimposed on the Freudian problem mentioned previously, on the formation of the ego by stimuli from the outside world and by the body's reactions to these stimuli.

---

32 See section 1.3.

33 *La volonté de savoir*, 208; *The History of Sexuality, Vol. 1*, 157. Translation modified.

34 Gilles Deleuze, *Nietzsche et la philosophie*, PUF, 1962; coll. « Quadrige », 1997, 44; *Nietzsche and Philosophy*, Continuum, 1986, 39.

35 Ibid.

Likewise, Nietzsche writes about the formation of consciousness:

> The role of 'consciousness'. — It is essential that one should not make a mistake over the role of 'consciousness': it is our *relation with the 'outer world'* that evolved it. On the other hand, the *direction* or protection and care in respect of the co-ordination of the bodily functions does not enter our consciousness; any more than spiritual *accumulation*: that a supreme instance rules over these things cannot be doubted — a kind of directing committee on which the various chief desires make their votes and power felt. 'Pleasure', 'displeasure' are signs from this sphere; also the act of will; also ideas. [. . .] Usually, one takes *consciousness* itself as the general sensorium and supreme court; nonetheless, it is only *a means of communication*: it is evolved through social intercourse and with a view to the interests of social intercourse — 'Intercourse [*Verkehr*]' here understood to include the influences of the outer world and the reactions they compel on our side; also our effect upon the outer world. It is *not* the directing agent, but *an organ of the directing agent.*[36]

Consciousness is therefore produced by 'the influences of the outer world', namely the relation of external forces and 'the reactions they compel on our side'. This relation of forces designates precisely the relation between the superior forces and the inferior forces, namely the active forces and the reactive forces. Deleuze writes:

> [C]onsciousness is defined less in relation to exteriority (in terms of the real) than in relation to *superiority* (in terms of values). This distinction is essential to a general conception of consciousness and the unconscious. In Nietzsche consciousness is always the consciousness of an inferior in relation to a superior to which he is subordinated or into which he is 'incorporated'. Consciousness is never self-consciousness, but the consciousness of an ego in relation to a self which is not itself conscious. It is not the master's consciousness but the slave's consciousness in relation to a master who is not himself conscious.[37]

---

36 Friedrich Nietzsche, *Nachlaß 1887–1889*, in *Kritische Studienausgabe*, Bd. 13, 67–8; *The Will to Power*, Vintage Books, 1968, 284. Translation modified.
37 *Nietzsche et la philosophie*, 44–5; *Nietzsche and Philosophy*, 39.

Consciousness is defined 'in terms of values'. It is 'always the consciousness of an inferior in relation to a superior'. Only the inferior holds
consciousness in relation to the superior: it is a 'slave's consciousness', so
'consciousness is essentially reactive'.[38] In Deleuze, this reactive
consciousness is called the 'ego', which is distinguished from the essentially unconscious 'self'. The 'ego' corresponds to 'the bad conscience' as
Nietzsche calls it in *On the Genealogy of Morals*. It signifies the reflectivity of the ego formed by reactive forces, the 'instinct for freedom pushed
back and repressed, incarcerated within and finally able to discharge
and vent itself only on itself'.[39]

If consciousness as ego is primarily reactive, how is the body defined
in relation to consciousness? In this regard, Deleuze asserts:

> Every force is related to others and it either obeys or commands.
> What defines a body is this relation between dominant and domi-
> nated forces. Every relationship of forces constitutes a body —
> whether it is chemical, biological, social or political. Any two forces,
> being unequal, constitute a body as soon as they enter into a relation-
> ship. This is why the body is always the fruit of chance, in the
> Nietzschean sense, and appears as the most 'astonishing' thing, much
> more astonishing, in fact, than consciousness and spirit.[40]

A body is made up of unequal forces, the dominant and the dominated,
and it is 'the fruit of chance', because the way in which the forces relate and
constitute it depends on historical contingency. In this sense, 'the body is
a multiple phenomenon, being composed of a plurality of irreducible
forces'.[41] Consciousness is essentially reactive, since it is 'always the
consciousness of an inferior in relation to a superior'. On the contrary, the
body is 'the "arbitrary" product of the forces of which it is composed';[42] in
other words, it is constituted under the contingency of the relation of
forces between them. As a result, the forces that flow through the body
exist as an irreducible multiplicity. In this sense, the body appears to be
'much more astonishing than consciousness and spirit'.

---

38 Ibid., 47; 41.
39 Friedrich Nietzsche, *Zur Genealogie der Moral*, in *Kritische Studienausgabe*, Bd.
5, 325; *On the Genealogy of Morals*, 87.
40 *Nietzsche et la philosophie*, 45; *Nietzsche and Philosophy*, 40.
41 Ibid.
42 Ibid.

In *Spinoza: Practical Philosophy*, Deleuze develops the same theme and draws from it an unexpected proposition: 'One seeks to acquire a knowledge of the powers of the body in order to discover, *in a parallel fashion* [parallèlement], the powers of the mind that elude consciousness'.[43] In other words, the discovery of the unknown powers of the body is equivalent to the discovery of the unknown powers of the mind. Through this discovery, the 'essentially reactive' consciousness meets the active forces and becomes itself active. Yet reactive forces never cease to be forces, so that what distinguishes reactive forces from active forces lies only in the qualifying difference of forces. So, the discovery of the active powers of the body is also that of the active powers that escape consciousness, by which the economy of the mind, dominated by the 'essentially reactive' consciousness, comes out transformed:

> The real problem is the discovery of active forces without which the reactions themselves would not be forces. What makes the body superior to all reactions, particularly that reaction of the ego that is called consciousness, is the activity of necessarily unconscious forces: 'This entire phenomenon of the body is, from the intellectual point of view, as superior to our consciousness, to our spirit to our conscious ways of thinking, feeling and willing, as algebra is superior to the multiplication table'. The body's active forces make it a self [*soi*] and define the self as superior and astonishing: 'A most powerful being, an unknown sage — he is called self. He inhabits your body, he is your body'.[44]

What is important for us is to discover the 'self [*soi*]' which inhabits the body and which is equivalent to the active forces totally different from the 'reaction of the ego that is called consciousness'. Discovering the self in the body will also transform the reactivity of the mind into activity. The 'consciousness of an ego [*conscience d'un moi*]' thus becomes the 'consciousness of self [*conscience de soi*]'[45] through the discovery of active powers that are not conscious. In Nietzschean terms, it is a question of transforming the 'bad conscience' 'pushed back and repressed, incarcerated within and finally able to discharge and vent itself only on

---

43 Gilles Deleuze, *Spinoza : Philosophie pratique*, Minuit, 1981, 29; *Spinoza: Practical Philosophy*, City Lights Books, 1988, 18. The word '*parallèlement*' tacitly designates Spinoza's 'parallelism'.

44 *Nietzsche et la philosophie*, 47; *Nietzsche and Philosophy*, 41–2.

45 Ibid., 44; 39. Translation modified.

itself', into a man who is 'like only to himself' and 'who has his own independent, protracted will and *the right to make promise*'.[46]

Let us now return to Foucault. The point of resistance to the dispositives of sexuality must lie in bodies and pleasures, wrote Foucault in *The Will to Know*. Indeed, after having made his turn, he will discuss the thematic of the 'self' as different from the 'ego', along with the use of the body and its pleasures. For example, in *The Use of Pleasure*, he writes: the main concern of the Greeks' thinking on sexual behaviour is 'to define the use of pleasures [. . .] in terms of a certain way of caring for one's body',[47] and 'the physical regimen ought to accord with the principle of a general aesthetics of existence in which the equilibrium of the body was one of the conditions of the proper hierarchy of the soul'.[48] Here, the care of the body and its pleasures is defined as a practice for providing the soul with 'the proper hierarchy', thereby transforming and delivering it. It is thus a question of transforming the reactive ego into an active 'self' by the discovery of the new economy of the body and its pleasures, or, again, of transfiguring the mode of 'essentially reactive' consciousness ('the soul is the prison of the body') through the unveiling of the self as a singularity that unconsciously inhabits the body. It is around this point that Foucauldian thought will be developed after the turn.

3.4 Ethical subjectivation and singularity

We can say that, schematically, in *Discipline and Punish* and *The Will to Know*, Foucault criticizes the subject's structure of decentration, in which the subject is passively determined by the disciplinary power as Other (subjection/*assujettissement*). On the other hand, in *The Use of Pleasure* and *The Care of the Self*, the issue is the 'relation to self [*rapport à soi*]', namely the self-creation of the subject himself (subjectivation). What, then, is at stake in this construction of the 'relation to self'? In *The*

---

46 *Zur Genealogie der Moral*, in *Kritische Studienausgabe* Bd. 5, 293; *On the Genealogy of Morals*, 59. For an interpretation of Nietzschean philosophy, the following of Judith Butler's essays were very suggestive to us: 'Circuits of bad conscience: Nietzsche and Freud', in *The Psychic Life of Power*; 'Ethical Ambivalence', in Marjorie Garber *et al.*, eds., *The Turn to Ethics*, Routledge, 2000.

47 *L'usage des plaisirs*, 112; *The Use of Pleasure*, 97.

48 Ibid., 118; 103–4.

Use of Pleasure, Foucault distinguishes several kinds of morality:

> Anyone who wishes to study the history of a 'morality [*morale*]' has to take into account the different realities that are covered by the term. [1] A history of 'moral behaviours [*moralités*]' would study the extent to which actions of certain individuals or groups are consistent with the rules and values that are prescribed for them by various agencies. [2] A history of 'codes [*codes*]' would analyse the different systems of rules and values that are operative in a given society or group, the agencies or mechanisms of constraint that enforce them, the forms they take in their multifariousness, their divergences and their contradictions. [3] And finally, a history of the way in which individuals are urged to constitute themselves as subjects of moral conduct would be concerned with the models proposed for setting up and developing relations to self, for self-reflection, self-knowledge, self-examination, self-decipherment by self, for the transformations that one seeks to accomplish with oneself as object. This last is what might be called a history of 'ethics [*éthique*]' and 'ascetics', understood as a history of the forms of moral subjectivation and of the practices of self that are meant to ensure it.[49]

In this quote, Foucault differentiates three 'moralities [*morales*]': 'moral behaviour [*moralité*]', 'code [*code*]', and 'ethics [*éthique*]'. In the first and second, it is a question of the adaptation of individuals to the given community or the coercion exerted within the framework of this adaptation (with punishment, in some cases); on the contrary, in the third, it is a question of the relation to self (self-reflection, self-knowledge, self-examination, self-decipherment by self). We propose to call 'morality' the first two types of morality, moral behaviour and code, to denote the relationship between the community and individuals, and 'ethics' the third type of morality, to denote the relation of self to self (via the relation to the other, which we will discuss later). Foucault does not necessarily distinguish these two terms in his works, but this distinction is, it seems to us, of great importance to interpret his texts.

By agreeing on this distinction, we can understand that Foucault does deal with the problem of ethics in *The Use of Pleasure* and *The Care*

---

49 Ibid., 36; 29. Translation modified. We added [1], [2] and [3] in this quote in order to clarify the context.

of the Self. This ethics treats the singularity of the subject, and not the normativity of a community's morality:

> We are a long way from a form of austerity that would tend to govern all individuals in the same way, from the proudest to the most humble, under a universal law whose application alone would be subject to modulation by means of casuistry. On the contrary, here everything was a matter of adjustment, circumstance, and personal position. The few great common laws — of the city, religion, nature — remained present, but it was as if they traced a very wide circle in the distance, inside of which practical thought had to define what could rightfully be done. And for this there was no need of anything resembling a text that would have the force of law, but rather, of a *technē* or 'practice', a *savoir-faire* that by taking general principles into account would guide action in its time, according to its context, and in view of its ends. Therefore, in this form of morality, the individual did not make himself into an ethical subject by universalizing the principles that informed his action; on the contrary, he did so by means of an attitude and a quest that individualized his action, modulated it, and perhaps even gave him a singular brilliance by virtue of the rational and deliberate structure his action manifested.[50]

Ethical subjectivation does not aim to conform the individual to the common law or norm; on the contrary, it individualizes its action and grants it a singular sign ('to change themselves in their singular being'[51]). If community's morality belongs to the 'generality–particularity' axis, ethics concerns the singularity that cannot be reduced to the 'generality–particularity' axis. Here, the singularity must be strictly distinguished from the particularity. Kojin Karatani offers the following distinction: unlike particularity, which is reduced to a case of generality, singularity concerns a kind of 'this-ness' which has no relation to generality; for example, the notion of 'I' only signifies the 'I' in general, thereby designating any 'I', but 'this I' is singular and 'irreplaceable' by some other 'I'.[52]

---

50 Ibid., 72–3; 62. Translation modified.
51 Ibid., 16; 10.
52 Kojin Karatani, *Tankyû II* [*Investigation II*], Kôdan-sha, 1989, 10, 128. His thematic on singularity is inspired by Deleuze's *Difference and Repetition*, which discusses repetition and singularity in Kierkegaard and Nietzsche (Gilles Deleuze, *Différence et répétition*, 8; *Difference and Repetition*, 1–2).

If we interpret the axis 'generality–particularity' in terms of the norm, then it is through certain norms that the individual as a particularity is reduced to a case of generality. For example, in Hegel, it is through the intermediary of objective morality [*Sittlichkeit*] that the individual as a particularity is *aufgehoben* and becomes a genus [*Gattung*] as a member of the state. In the Foucauldian sense, the individual as a particularity is nothing other than one who internalizes normality through the mechanism of disciplinary power. On the other hand, in ethics, the singularity of 'this I' is not reducible to generality, and it is 'irreplaceable' by another 'I'. Disciplinary power is a mechanism which imposes the norm as generality on the individual, but what Foucault seeks to find through ethical subjectivation is the singularity of the subject irreducible to normality as generality.

In this singularity of the subject, in this relation of self to self, the problem of resistance intervenes. In his lecture course at the Collège de France entitled *The Hermeneutics of the Subject* (1981–82), Foucault insists: 'there is no first or final point of resistance to political power other than in the relation of self to self' and continues as follows:

> [I]f we take the question of power, of political power, situating it in the more general question of governmentality understood as a strategic field of power relations in the broadest and not merely political sense of the term, if we understand by governmentality a strategic field of power relations in their mobility, transformability, and reversibility, then I do not think that reflection on this notion of governmentality can avoid passing through, theoretically and practically, the element of a subject defined by the relation of self to self. Although the theory of political power as an institution usually refers to a juridical conception of the subject of right, it seems to me that the analysis of governmentality — that is to say, the analysis of power as a set of reversible relationships — must refer to an ethics of the subject defined by the relation of self to self. Quite simply, this means that in the type of analysis I have been trying to advance for some time you can see that power relations, governmentality, the government of self and others, and the relation of self to self constitute a chain, a thread, and I think it is around these notions that we should be able to connect together the question of politics and the question of ethics.[53]

---

53 Michel Foucault, *L'herméneutique du sujet, Cours au Collège de France, 1981–1982*, Gallimard/Seuil, 2001, 241–2; *The Hermeneutics of the Subject,*

The 'analysis of power as a set of *reversible* relationships' denotes the problem of resistance: an 'ethics of the subject' as a relation of self to self opens up the possibility of resistance to governmentality. The singularity or the 'self' of the subject who escapes disciplinarization and can resist it forms the point of resistance to governmentality.

The question is then the following: how does Foucault seek to construct the ethical subject as a point of resistance? In *The Care of the Self*, he analyses Plato's *Alcibiades*:

> Socrates shows the ambitious young man [Alcibiades] that it is quite presumptuous of him to want to take charge of the city, manage its affairs, and enter into competition with the kings of Sparta or the rulers of Persia, if he has not first learned that which it is necessary to know in order to govern: he must first attend to himself — and right away, while he is young, for 'at the age of fifty, it would be too late'.[54]

In order to be a political subject, one must first take care of oneself and form an ethical subject. And in this care of the self, the self-reflective gaze is problematized again. In *The Hermeneutics of the Subject*, Foucault says, 'Socrates defined the fundamental modality of the care of the self. Essentially he described the practice of the care of the self as the exercise of looking, of a looking that focuses precisely on the self, on oneself. "One must be concerned about the self", [this was the translation] of *blepteon heauton*: [one must] look at oneself'.[55] This gaze of self on oneself makes the soul recognize the truth that it already knew from the depths of its memory. And it is through this recognition or reminiscence that the subject 'brings about his liberation; his return to his homeland and to his own being'.[56] We point out here that the reflectivity of the gaze does not function as a regulatory gaze which makes the subject obedient to himself, but as a gaze which transforms the subject's mode of being. The reflective gaze transforms the subject and forms the singularity of the 'self'. This suggests a new use of reflectivity: the transformation of the subjected subject into an ethical subject.

Lectures at the Collège de France, 1981–1982, Palgrave Macmillan, 2005, 252. Translation modified.

54 Michel Foucault, *Le souci de soi : Histoire de la sexualité 3*, Gallimard, 1984, 58; *The Care of the Self: The History of Sexuality, Vol. 3*, Pantheon Books, 1986, 44.

55 *L'herméneutique du sujet*, 436; *The Hermeneutics of the Subject*, 454.

56 Ibid., 442; 460.

This other use of the reflective gaze is more apparent in the following analysis of Seneca's text, in which Seneca closely examines his actions of the day before falling asleep:

> The words employed are significant. Seneca means to 'scrutinize' the entire day that has just unfolded (the verb *executere*, 'to shake out', 'to knock so as to make the dust fall', is used to denote the scrutiny by which one locates the errors in an account); he intends to 'inspect' it, to 'remeasure' the acts that were committed, the words that were spoken (*remetiri*, as one might do after a piece of work is finished, to see if it is up to the standards set for it). The subject's relation to himself in this examination is not established so much in the form of a judicial relationship in which the accused faces the judge; it is more like an act of inspection in which the inspector aims to evaluate a piece of work, an accomplished task. The word *speculator* (one needs to be a *speculator sui*) designates this role exactly. Further, the examination practiced in this manner does not focus, as if in imitation of the judicial procedure, on 'infractions'; and it does not lead to a verdict of guilty or to decisions of self-castigation.[57]

This relation to self through which the subject examines his acts of the day is formed in the reflective gaze in which the subject watches and examines himself. However, what is interesting here is that Foucault analyses this relation to self as one which 'is not established so much in the form of a judicial relationship in which the accused faces the judge'. In the previous paragraph, he points out that Seneca uses legal metaphors to express the form of this practice ('appear before the judge', 'give report of my own character', 'plead my cause'[58]). Despite these expressions, Foucault asserts that this examination of the self does not take 'the form of a juridical relationship' — that is, it does not function as a regulatory practice. Insofar as it is a 'labour of thought on itself',[59] it relies on the reflectivity of the subject. But the functioning of this reflectivity is completely different from that of regulatory reflectivity whereby, in establishing a system of self-surveillance and self-punishment, the subject internalizes the discipline. Here, the reflective gaze 'examines'

---

57 *Le souci de soi*, 78; *The Care of the Self*, 61–2.
58 Ibid., 78; 61.
59 Ibid., 79; 62.

the acts of the self and tries to transform the being into a rational and singular subject. Foucault thus concludes the paragraph cited above: 'The fault is not reactivated by the examination in order to determine a culpability or stimulate a feeling of remorse, but in order to strengthen, on the basis of the recapitulated and reconsidered verification of a failure, the rational equipment that ensures a wise behaviour'.[60]

We can thus clearly recognize the strategy of formation of the ethical subject, which consists of a transformation of the self through the reflective gaze. We will call this 'auto-affection',[61] borrowing the term from Deleuze, this use of reflectivity with a function other than regulatory. Auto-affection through the reflective gaze will then metamorphose the subjected modality of the subject and form the 'self' as an ethical subject. It is through this subjectivation that the point of resistance to disciplinary power is established. Subjectivation is therefore the other name for de-subjection [désassujettissement].

However, this relation of self to self is not established in a solitary practice. If the transformation of the subject means 'to become again what one never was',[62] the intervention of the other who leads it is essential. In *The Hermeneutics of the Subject*, Foucault explains it as follows:

> The individual should strive for a status as subject that he has never known at any moment of his life. He has to replace the non-subject with the status of subject defined by the fullness of the self's relationship to the self. He has to constitute himself as subject, and this is where the other has to intervene.[63]

In Socrates and Plato, this other is the philosopher as 'master' and, in the Roman Empire, the philosopher as 'friend'. Thus, it is through the

---

60 Ibid.

61 Gilles Deleuze, *Foucault*, Minuit, 1986, 115; *Foucault*, University of Minnesota Press, 1988, 107; *Qu'est-ce que la philosophie ?*, 35; *What is Philosophy?*, 32. The term 'auto-affection' is borrowed from Heidegger's interpretation of Kant. Heidegger defines the function of time in Kantian philosophy as 'pure auto-affection [*reine Selbstaffektion*]', which 'forms the essential structure of subjectivity'. See *Kant und das Problem der Metaphysik*, in *Gesamtausgabe* Bd. 3, 189; *Kant and the Problem of Metaphysics*, 132. Foucault also discusses, in a Heideggerian manner, the subject's auto-affection through the intermediary of 'truth'. See *L'herméneutique du sujet*, 233; *The Hermeneutics of the Subject*, 243.

62 *L'herméneutique du sujet*, 92; *The Hermeneutics of the Subject*, 95.

63 Ibid., 125; 129. Translation modified.

guidance of the other, who already knows the art of governing himself, that the subject learns to govern himself and becomes 'what one never was'. Therefore, 'the formation of a relation of self to self quite clearly connects up with the relationships of the self to the Other':[64] the relation to self necessarily passes the relation to the other. Here, we find traces of the Nietzschean problematic that subsists in Foucauldian thought: 'the thought of the outside'. Subjectivation cannot be realized without a relation to the outside. It is through the affection of the outside, of the other, that auto-affection is achieved (the process that we can define as 'auto-hetero-affection'[65]). And the knowledge which is born in the relation to the other, which affects the subject, establishes its singularity and has the effect of transforming it — Foucault considers this knowledge as playing the role of 'truth' in ancient spirituality. Here arises in Foucault the 'new conception of truth' awaited by Deleuze: knowledge 'whose effect and function are to change the subject's being. This truth must affect the subject'.[66]

The formation of the relation of self to self, namely ethical subjectivation, is linked to the relationship of the self and the other: 'The rationality of the government of others is the same as the rationality of the government of oneself', because 'it is in knowing how properly to conduct himself that he will be able to lead others properly'.[67] One who has formed himself as an ethical subject can establish an ethical relationship to others. And this relationship to others introduces the notion of singularity into the political field. The formation of the ethical subject who can resist governmentality is also a thought that finds the singularity of the self in relation to others. The subjectivation that Foucault mentions is a 'practice of freedom'[68] which allows the use of the singularity of the self in relation to others. This practice relates directly to non-slavery based on the self-knowledge or the care of the self, and it allows the reversibility of the power relation that necessarily intervenes in the relationship with others. Ensuring the reversible

---

64 Ibid., 150; 155. Translation modified.

65 We will return to the notion of 'auto-hetero-affection' in section 4.5.

66 L'herméneutique du sujet, 233; The Hermeneutics of the Subject, 243.

67 Le souci de soi, 109–10; The Care of the Self, 89.

68 On 'the care of the self' as an ontological condition for freedom in the field of politics and sexuality, see Michel Foucault, « L'éthique du souci de soi comme pratique de la liberté », in Dits et Écrits, T. IV; 'The Ethics of the Concern for Self as a Practice of Freedom', in Essential Works, Vol. 1, New Press, 1997.

power relation and not the fixed one — this is what is at the stake in the 'practice of freedom' in the formation of the ethical subject. In addition, in the field of sexuality, the practice of freedom would signify governing pleasures ('to dominate one's pleasures without ever being worsted'[69]), and using one's own body and its pleasures according to the singularity of the self. Dominating pleasures also means ethical care of others. The ethical relationship with the other is inseparable from the reversibility of the power relation and the singularity of the self and the other. It is precisely this relationship that turns pleasure into ethics.

3.5 Construction of immanence and anti-pastoral revolution

Foucault searched for the strategy of de-subjection by highlighting the practice of 'the care of the self' during the classical era. This search should therefore absolutely not be understood as a nostalgic 'return' to the Greco-Roman era, but it constitutes, on the contrary, an attempt to seek the strategy of resistance to power. It would also be an abuse to consider Foucault's turn as a simple 'return to the subject'. If subjectivation designates the formation of the subject's singularity to resist power, it is also an attempt at de-subjection. At the same time, through this ethico-political turn, Foucault presents a new concept of subject radically different from the modern concept. In what does this difference consist? It is essential to clarify this point if we want to understand the direction of his turn.

Several times during his turn, Foucault dealt with a small text by Kant entitled 'Was ist Aufklärung?' Why did he give such attention to this text? Let us refer to the lecture entitled 'What Is Critique?' (1978). In the Western society of the fifteenth and sixteenth centuries, there was 'a veritable explosion of the art of governing men'. If the question here is 'how to govern?', another question, 'how not to be governed like that?' — namely the attitude of resistance to a particular contemporary governmentality — derives directly from it.[70] In modern history, this question

---

69 L'usage des plaisirs, 82; The Use of Pleasures, 70. Quote from Diogenes Laertius, Lives of Eminent Philosophers. Translation modified.

70 Michel Foucault, « Qu'est-ce que la critique ? : Critique et Aufklärung », Bulletin de la société française de philosophie, 84ᵉ année 2, avril–juin 1990, 37; 'What Is Critique?', in The Politics of Truth, Semiotext(e), 1997, 27–8.

appears as a movement of 'return to the Scriptures' against the authority of the Church and as a natural law which determines the limit of sovereignty.[71]

If Foucault calls this question of 'how not to be governed *like that*?' a 'critical attitude',[72] then '*Was ist Aufklärung?*' reflects the development of this critical attitude. For Kant, the *Aufklärung* is a movement aimed at helping men who are still minors to become adults. Their minority is defined by its correlation with 'the exercise of an authority which maintains humanity in this minority condition', namely with the excess of power.[73] The Kantian *Aufklärung* thus appears as a means of resisting the excess of modern power.

What strategy of resistance to power does Foucault deduce from this text by Kant? Let us refer to 'What is Enlightenment?' (1984), where he defines the Kantian analysis of *Aufklärung* as a philosophy of 'actuality':

> Kant defines *Aufklärung* in an almost entirely negative way, as an *Ausgang*, an 'exit', a 'way out'. In his other texts on history, Kant occasionally raises questions of origin or defines the internal teleology of a historical process. In the text on *Aufklärung*, he deals with the question of contemporary reality alone. He is not seeking to understand the present on the basis of a totality or of a future achievement. He is looking for a difference: What difference does today introduce with respect to yesterday?[74]

In his historical reflections, Kant often introduces the questions of origin and end in a positive way (for example, in *Idea for a Universal History with a Cosmopolitan Aim*). On the other hand, in '*Was ist Aufklärung?*', he calls the *Aufklärung* movement 'pure actuality'. This implies that the actuality as a 'singular moment',[75] the singularity of the contemporary, becomes the philosophical object. In this sense, this text by Kant prefigures the new field of philosophy: that of actuality, which cannot be reduced to critical or historical reflection.

---

71 Ibid., 38–9; 29–31.
72 Ibid., 38; 28.
73 Ibid., 40; 33.
74 Michel Foucault, « Qu'est-ce que les Lumières ? », in *Dits et écrits*, T. IV, 564; 'What is Enlightenment?' in *Essential Works*, Vol. 1, 305.
75 Ibid., 568; 309. Translation modified.

Foucault calls this Kantian attitude on the *Aufklärung* an 'attitude of modernity' and derives from it 'a philosophical ethos' which he calls a 'historical ontology of ourselves', defined as follows:

> This philosophical ethos may be characterized as a *limit-attitude*. We are not talking about a gesture of rejection. We have to move beyond the outside-inside alternative; we have to be at the frontiers. Critique indeed consists of analysing and reflecting upon limits. But if the Kantian question was that of knowing what limits knowledge must renounce exceeding, it seems to me that the critical question today must be turned back into a positive one: In what is given to us as universal, necessary, obligatory, what place is occupied by whatever is singular, contingent, and the product of arbitrary constraints? The point, in brief, is to transform the critique conducted in the form of necessary limitation into a practical critique that takes the form of a possible crossing-over [*franchissement*].[76]

Historical ontology is characterized by a 'limit-attitude'. The term 'limit' immediately evokes the Kantian Critique: in *Critique of Pure Reason*, Kant prohibited the use of reason which goes beyond the limit of possible experience. In this sense, the Kantian 'limit' must not be crossed over and takes on a negative meaning. In his lecture course at the Collège de France entitled *Government of Self and Others* (1982–83), where he analyses '*Was ist Aufklärung?*', Foucault defines as 'analytic of truth' this 'question of the conditions under which true knowledge is possible'.[77] The strategy of historical ontology postulated by Foucault is therefore totally opposed to this Kantian attempt: he defines the 'limit-attitude' as 'a possible crossing-over'. It is not a question of the limit of reason, nor of staying within that limit; rather, it is a question of revealing the 'contingent' which determines us historically and of transgressing the limit of this 'contingent'.

It is at this point in the analysis that we can understand why Foucault was interested in the philosophy of actuality prefigured by '*Was ist Aufklärung?*' It grasps being from the historical perspective and

---

76 Ibid., 574; 315. Translation modified.

77 Michel Foucault, *Le gouvernement de soi et des autres, Cours au Collège de France, 1982–1983*, EHESS/Gammilard/Seuil, 2008, 21–2; *The Government of Self and Others, Lectures at the Collège de France, 1982–1983*, Graham Burchell, 2010, 20. Translation modified.

understands the mode of being under historical contingency. Being is, so to speak, always already 'projected' onto historical contingency; it is this contingency that determines the subject's mode of being. Foucault's position then approaches that of the Althusser of the 1980s ('aleatory materialism'), who aimed to grasp the historicity of the being in the 'facticity of contingency' or 'transcendental contingency'.[78]

In *Archaeology of Knowledge* (1969), Foucault opposes the formal *a priori* to the historical *a priori*. The first designates what determines the immanent condition of knowledge; the second designates the historical elements which determine it from the outside. In the context of 'What is Enlightenment?', the first corresponds to 'the analytics of truth' and the second to 'historical ontology'. In *Archaeology of Knowledge*, Foucault compares these two *a prioris*:

It [the historical *a priori*] cannot take account (by some kind of psychological or cultural genesis) of the formal *a prioris*; but it enables us to understand how the formal *a prioris* may have in history points of contact, places of insertion, irruption, or emergence, domains or occasions of operation, and to understand how this history may be not an absolutely extrinsic contingency, not a necessity of form deploying its own dialectic, but a specific regularity.[79]

The historical *a priori* does not relate to 'absolutely extrinsic contingency' but to 'specific regularity'; in this text, Foucault does not yet give importance to contingency. The specific problem of contingency will appear when he turns to the thematic of resistance to power. Foucault also designates this historical contingency by the term 'event', which leads the subject to becoming:

This entails an obvious consequence: that critique is no longer going to be practiced in the search for formal structures with universal value but, rather, as a historical investigation into the events that have led us to constitute ourselves and to recognize ourselves as subjects of what

---

78 Louis Althusser, « Le courant souterrain du matérialisme de la rencontre », in *Écrits philosophiques et politiques*, T. I, Stock/IMEC, 1994, 542–3; 'The Underground Current of the Materialism of the Encounter', in *Philosophy of the Encounter: Later Writing, 1978–87*, Verso, 2006, 170.

79 Michel Foucault, *L'archéologie du savoir*, Gallimard, 1969, 168–9; *Archaeology of Knowledge*, Routledge, 2002. 144. Translation modified.

we are doing, thinking, saying. In that sense, this critique is not transcendental, and its goal is not that of making a metaphysics possible:
it is genealogical in its design and archaeological in its method.
Archaeological — and not transcendental — in the sense that it will
not seek to identify the universal structures of all knowledge or of all
possible moral action, but will seek to treat the instances of discourse
that articulate what we think, say, and do as so many historical events.
And this critique will be genealogical in the sense that it will not
deduce from the form of what we are what it is impossible for us to do
and to know; but it will separate out, from the contingency that has
made us what we are, the possibility of no longer being, doing, or
thinking what we are, do, or think.[80]

Historical ontology historically criticizes 'events' as the basis for the
formation of knowledge, discourse and act, and it reveals the effects of
power inscribed in the subject. It is, therefore, an attempt to de-subject
the subject and to form the singular self. In this sense, de-subjection
means, so to speak, *becoming-self*. If the power relation is an effect of
'events', of historical contingencies, the subject's actual mode is purely
contingent and therefore open to the possibility of becoming. In other
words, 'the possibility of no longer being, doing, or thinking what we
are, do, or think' is always open. Historical ontology clears the contingent field of being. And it is this contingency that opens up the possibility of de-subjection or of 'becoming aleatory'[81] in the Althusserian
sense.

Historical ontology is oriented towards 'the actual limits of the
necessary'.[82] It reveals the historicity of the 'universal' and the 'necessary'
formed in contemporary power relations and it transgresses their 'actual
limits'. In this sense, this research is precisely Nietzschean. According to
Foucault, it is 'genealogical' and is 'not transcendental'. Certainly, it is
not transcendental 'in the sense that it will not seek to identify the
universal structures of all knowledge or of all possible moral action' —
that is to say, it will not seek the 'formal *a priori*' of knowledge and of the

---

80 « Qu'est-ce que les Lumières ? », in *Dits et écrits*, T. IV, 574; 'What is Enlightenment?'
in *Essential Works*, Vol. 1, 315–16. Translation modified.

81 Louis Althusser, « Le marxisme comme théorie 'finie' », in *Solitude de Machiavel*,
PUF, 1998, 286.

82 « Qu'est-ce que les Lumières ? », in *Dits et écrits*, T. IV, 572; 'What is Enlightenment?'
in *Essential Works*, Vol. 1, 313. Translation modified.

act. However, it presupposes the same reflectivity as that of the transcendental gaze, because it is based on the reflectivity as 'critique' of the subject on himself. If historical ontology asks 'what place is occupied by whatever is singular, contingent, and the product of arbitrary constraints' '[i]n what is given to us as universal, necessary, obligatory', it must be based on reflective thought or the reflective gaze. In a 1984 text, Foucault develops this point: critique 'brings to light transformable singularities. These transformations could not take place except by means of a working of thought upon itself; that is the principle of the history of thought as critical activity'.[83] Hence, it is through the reflective gaze ('a working of thought upon itself') that Foucauldian critique attempts to unveil the 'singularities' that constitute the subject himself and to transform his mode of being. Thus, the subject is always 'transformable', since the singularities that form the subject are determined by historical contingencies.

In this sense, Foucauldian critique is based on the strategy of the deconstruction of the Kantian subject by Nietzschean thought; it is therefore situated in the topical problematic. But we must remember that Foucault developed historical ontology as a strategy of resistance to power. In *Discipline and Punish*, the reflective gaze functioned as a regulatory gaze by which the subject disciplines itself. But in historical ontology, the reflective gaze functions as a power of resistance, since it extracts the effects of power inscribed in the subject and allows him to transform himself into a de-subjected self. In other words, the reflective gaze affects the subject himself, incites subjectivation and de-subjection and forms the ethical subject.

Three axes then coexist in the subject's reflectivity: 'the axis of knowledge, the axis of power, the axis of ethics'.[84] They correspond respectively to knowledge, domination and resistance. First, reflectivity forms the

---

83　Michel Foucault, « Préface à l'*Histoire de la sexualité* », in *Dits et écrits*, T. IV, 580; 'Preface to The History of Sexuality, Volume II', in Paul Rabinow, ed., *The Foucault Reader*, Pantheon Books, 1994, 335–6.

84　« Qu'est-ce que les Lumières? », in *Dits et écrits*, T. IV, 576; 'What is Enlightenment?' in *Essential Works*, Vol. 1, 318 : 'These practical systems stem from three broad areas: relations of control over things, relations of action upon others, relations with oneself. This does not mean that each of these three areas is completely foreign to the others. It is well known that control over things is mediated by relations with others; and relations with others in turn always entail relations with oneself, and vice versa. But we have three axes whose specificity and whose interconnections have to be analysed: the axis of knowledge, the axis of power, the axis of ethics'.

subject of knowledge: it objectifies the speaking subject, the working subject and the living subject as 'status of science'.[85] Second, it forms the subjected subject: it subjugates the subject itself and functions as an agent of power. Third, it forms the subject of resistance: it reveals the effects of power inscribed in the subject and allows him to criticize them. In the subject's reflectivity, these faculties coexist in a heterogeneous way.

The regulatory reflective gaze constitutes the transcendental instance as a mechanism of knowledge and domination. However, the intervention of the axis of resistance encourages the subject to criticize this normative and regulatory function and try to transform it. It is this reflectivity of the axis of resistance that forms the field of singularity capable of criticizing the disciplinarity of the transcendental instance. We call this field of singularity 'immanence'.[86] Subjectivation is therefore a practice that constructs immanence as a field of singularity.

However, if one grasps the transcendental instance in its formality, it is only a form of looking at oneself (reflectivity) and does not refer to any content. It is, so to speak, 'the zero sign', namely 'the nothingness that constitutes the structure of a system'.[87] And it can assume, as a pure formality, any content and can therefore make operate several axes: the axes of knowledge, domination and resistance. In the reflectivity of the subject, the disciplinarity of the transcendental and its critique by immanence coexist. In this sense, by making his turn, Foucault adds to reflectivity, the axis of resistance (immanence), in order to criticize the disciplinarity of the transcendental.

Note here the specificity of the axis of resistance. If the axis of knowledge and the axis of domination form respectively the subject of

---

85 Michel Foucault, « Le sujet et le pouvoir », in *Dits et écrits*, T. IV, 223; 'The Subject and Power', in *Essential Works*, Vol. 3, 326.

86 On the immanence as a field of singularity, see Deleuze's last text: Gilles Deleuze, « L'immanence : une vie . . . », in *Deux régimes de fous*; 'Immanence: a Life', in *Two Regimes of Madness*.

87 Kojin Karatani, *Transcritique: On Kant and Marx*, MIT Press, 2003, 78: 'the zero sign is a restatement of transcendental subjectivity — the nothingness that constitutes the structure of a system — and it is impossible to do away with it'. Here Karatani uses the notion of 'zero sign' in the sense of Jakobson and Lévi-Strauss, not in the Lacanian sense. According to him, structuralists believed it was possible to annihilate the 'subject' by introducing the 'zero sign', but in fact, they tacitly presupposed the 'transcendental subject' in the Kantian sense. See also, Kojin Karatani, *Architecture as Metaphor: Language, Number, Money*, MIT Press, 1995, Ch. 5: 'Structure and Zero'.

knowledge and the subjected subject, then they produce the very complex of 'power-knowledge'. The axis of resistance criticizes this complex of 'power-knowledge' in the subject. It therefore appears as the reflective critique of the 'transcendental'. In other words, critique by the axis of resistance is a *historical objectification of the transcendental*. If it is 'genealogical', as Foucault asserts, it is because the term 'genealogical' means exactly this *historical critique of the transcendental*.

In his last lecture course, entitled *The Courage of the Truth* (1983–84), Foucault considers this historical critique of the transcendental from the problematic of *parrhēsia* (truth-telling). *Parrhēsia* designates the subjective act of telling the truth against existing power, exposing the subject to danger. At the end of his long analysis of *parrhēsia*, to which he devoted two years of lectures, he treats Cynicism and notices Diogenes' precept '*parakharattein to nomisma* (change the value of the currency)', in which '*nomisma*, it is currency, but it is also *nomos*: the law, the custom'.[88] '*Parakharattein to nomisma*' therefore means 'to change the existing law or norm'. Foucault continues:

[T]he alteration of the currency, the change of its value, which is constantly associated with Cynicism, no doubt means something like: the forms and habits which usually stamp existence and give it its features must be replaced by the effigy of the principles traditionally accepted by philosophy. But by the very fact of applying these principles to life itself, rather than merely maintaining them in the element of the *logos*, by the fact that they give a form to life, just as the coin's effigy gives a form to the metal on which it is stamped, one thereby reveals other lives, the lives of others, to be no more than counterfeit, coin with no value. By adopting the most traditional, conventionally accepted and general principles of current philosophy, by making the philosopher's very existence their point of application, site of manifestation, and form of truth-telling, the Cynic life puts the true currency with its true value into circulation. The Cynic game shows that this life, which truly applies the principles of the true life, is other than the life led by men in general and by philosophers in particular.

88　Michel Foucault, *Le courage de la vérité : Le gouvernement de soi et des autres II, Cours au Collège de France, 1983–1984*, Gallimard/Seuil, 2009, 223; *The Courage of the Truth, Lectures at the Collège de France, 1983–1984*, Palgrave Macmillan, 2011, 227. Translation modified.

With this idea that the true life is the other life [*la vraie vie est la vie autre*], I think we arrive at a particularly important point in the history of Cynicism, in the history of philosophy, certainly in the history of Western ethics.[89]

The precept '*parakharattein to nomisma*' thus exposes the historical contingency of the existing law or norm; it prompts us to practice true life as 'other life [*vie autre*]' and reveals ordinary life as 'counterfeit, coin with no value'. Diogenes ate, masturbated and made love in public in order to expose the historical contingency of the law or norm; following these scandalous acts that exposed him to danger, he tried to overthrow existing values ('the true life is the other life'). In this sense, the Cynical practice is also the Nietzschean practice of reversing values: it transforms the way of living by reversing existing values. Cynical practice therefore constitutes a variant of the historical critique of the transcendental. And if this historical critique is realized collectively through the collective struggle (remember the militant character of the Cynical movement),[90] it will become an 'anti-pastoral revolution'.

In his lecture course *Security, Territory, Population* (1977–78), given during the same period as his lecture 'What Is Critique?' (1978), Foucault addresses this notion of 'anti-pastoral revolution'. Against pastoral power, which 'conducts the conduct' of individuals in order to integrate them into the totality of the state, arise the movements of 'wanting to be conducted differently', or 'movements that [...] seek [...] to escape direction by others and to define the way for each to conduct himself'.[91] Foucault calls pastoral governmentality 'conducting the conduct' and resistance to this governmentality 'counter-conduct'.[92] After discussing

89 Ibid., 225–6; 244. Translation modified.

90 Analysing *The Government of Self and Others* and *The Courage of the Truth*, Michael Hardt writes: 'The life the Cynics proposed is a militant life that struggles to change both ourselves and the world'. From this point of view, he affirms that Foucault, in these lectures, 'seeks not only to challenge traditional modes of political thought and action but to explore alternatives, even to the point of proposing a form of philosophical and political militancy'. See Michael Hardt, 'Militant Life: Review on Michel Foucault, *Le gouvernement de soi et des autres, Le courage de la vérité*', New Left Review 54, July–August 2010.

91 Michel Foucault, *Sécurité, territoire, population, Cours au Collège de France 1977–1978*, Gallimard/Seuil, 2004, 198; *Security, Territory, Population, Lectures at the Collège de France, 1977–1978*, Palgrave Macmillan, 2009, 194–5.

92 Ibid., 205; 201.

resistance as counter-conduct, he enigmatically asserts: 'There have been anti-feudal revolutions; there has never been an anti-pastoral revolution. The pastorate has not yet experienced the process of profound revolution that would have definitively expelled it from history'.[93] The 'anti-pastoral revolution' puts pastoral power 'definitively expelled from history': when the de-subjection is achieved collectively, it becomes the 'anti-pastoral revolution', in which *the subjects refuse to be governed in any way*.[94] In 'What Is Critique?', Foucault found in modern history a 'critical attitude': to refuse to be governed *in a particular way* ('how not to be governed *like that?*'). And here he pushes this critical attitude to the limit in order to propose the anti-pastoral revolution: to refuse to be governed *in any way*. This is how Foucauldian 'becoming-self' approaches Deleuzo-Guattarian 'becoming-other'. (i.e., the transformation of the subjected group to a subject-group).

Foucault sought, through his turn, to construct immanence as a field of singularity: in the heterogeneity of several reflective axes coexist the passivity of subjection and the activity of critique. He tried thus to overcome the aporia of his theory of power by making an ethico-political turn. What allows him to go beyond it is the very concept of historical contingency and the construction of immanence as a field of singularity.

---

93 Ibid., 153; 150.

94 On the anti-pastoral revolution, see Yoshihiko Ichida, *Kakumei ron* [*On the Revolution*], Heibon-sha, 2012; Yoshiyuki Koizumi, 'Fûkô no reisei [The Spirituality of Foucault]', in *Durûzu no reisei* [*The Spirituality of Deleuze*], Kawade-shobô-shinsha, 2019.

Appendix 1
Production of the Competitive Subject: Foucault and Neoliberalism

Since the 1980s, the world has been overwhelmed by neoliberal governmentality. Under the Thatcher government in the United Kingdom and the Reagan government in the United States, neoliberalism totally drove their economic policies. In Japan, neoliberalism was introduced by the Nakasone government in the 1980s and intensively developed by the Koizumi government in the 2000s.

As a result of market-based economic policies, such as public-sector privatization and deregulation, neoliberalism is often considered a return to classical liberalism (laissez-faire, in the sense of Adam Smith) or its modern application.[1] However, in his lecture course at Collège de France entitled *The Birth of Biopolitics* (1978–79),[2] Foucault offers a radically different analysis of the idea of neoliberalism formed since the 1930s in Germany and the United States. Paradoxically, he clarifies the significant role of 'state interventionism' in neoliberalism: in order to make the logic of the market penetrate the whole society, a state constructs institutional frameworks by means of legislative intervention. In order to criticize the overwhelming neoliberal governmentality seen around the world, and to seek means of resistance to this governmentality, we need to understand exactly the idea and the actual

---

1 See, for example, Douglas Greenwald, ed., *The McGraw-Hill Dictionary of Modern Economics*, McGraw-Hill, 1973, 397.

2 Michel Foucault, *Naissance de la biopolitique, Cours au Collège de France, 1978–1979*, Gallimard/Seuil, 2004; *The Birth of Biopolitics, Lectures at the Collège de France, 1978–1979*, Palgrave Macmillan, 2008.

development of neoliberalism. In this appendix, we will clarify the particularity of neoliberal governmentality and its subjectivity by following Foucault's analysis of neoliberalism.

1 Post-Fordist governmentality

Why did Foucault analyse neoliberalism in his 1978–79 course? In *Discipline and Punish* (1975), he proposed the notion of disciplinary power through analysing micropower. Disciplinary power normalizes subjects by mobilizing power dispositives in schools, prisons, hospitals and factories. It is power that disciplines and normalizes subjects. In contrast, in the first volume of *The History of Sexuality* (1976), Foucault proposes the notion of biopolitics, whose object is the life of the population. Biopolitics integrates 'an entire series of interventions and regulatory controls'.[3] It is a power that targets the totality of human life and all the mechanisms of life, but it does not intervene directly on the population as disciplinary power does; biopolitics apprehends it statistically and optimizes its environment in order to govern it. In this sense, as Foucault shows in his lecture course on *Security, Territory, Population* (1977–78), it is essentially liberal governmentality, which he calls 'dispositives of security'.[4]

Foucault sees modern governmentality as biopower, which is a combination of disciplinary power and biopolitics. From the first volume of *The History of Sexuality* to the early 1980s, his research focused on the study of biopolitics and its governmental techniques. What should we understand in this theoretical shift? According to our hypothesis, it shows that governmental technique was transforming from disciplinary governmentality to neoliberal governmentality in the late 1970s. The crisis of the welfare state was already evident in the second half of the 1970s. In many developed countries that had adopted welfare state politics, the two oil crises in the 1970s deteriorated national economies and caused financial deficits that encroached on the economic foundations of public services. This degradation of the economy and financial difficulties of the welfare states prepared a shift into neoliberal

---

3 *La volonté de savoir : Histoire de la sexualité 1*, 183; *The History of Sexuality*, Vol. 1, 139.

4 See *Security, Territory, Population*, lectures on 11, 18, 25 January 1978.

governmentality that insisted on a drastic reduction of the public sector.[5] What interests us here is that Foucault's lecture course about neoliberalism ended just before the victory of the English Conservative Party that appointed Margaret Thatcher as British prime minister (in May 1979).[6] Thus, by 1978, the governmentality of the welfare state was already in crisis, and another governmentality was being formed. Foucault was no doubt aware of this transformation in governmentality. It is this diagnosis on actuality that led him to analyse biopolitics in the late 1970s.

If the governmentality of the welfare state was in crisis in the second half of the 1970s, and if the shift into neoliberal governmentality began at the end of the 1970s, what is the concrete difference between these two types of governmentality? On this point, let us refer to Nancy Fraser's article entitled 'From Discipline to Flexibilization?' Interpreting the Foucauldian notion of disciplinary power as 'the Fordist mode of social regulation',[7] Fraser examines the transformation in disciplinary Fordist governmentality as society had become more intensely globalized since 1989, the year of the fall of socialism. She identifies 1989 as the shifting point from disciplinary to neoliberal governmentality, while we assume that the second half of the 1970s was the shifting point. But her hypothesis is not contradictory to ours, if we understand that her formulation identifies a breaking point in 1989 in order to describe the post-Fordist system under globalization and that the symptoms of this break had accumulated since the period of the crisis of the welfare state in the 1970s.

Fordism is an economic system characterized by massive production, high wages and massive consumption. It functioned alongside Taylorism (a system of scientific control of labour) and the Keynesian welfare state (a governmental system that creates welfare — what Jacques Donzelot calls 'the social'[8] — through income redistribution such as redistributive taxation and social security), two systems established in the 1930s

---

5 David Harvey, *A Brief History of Neoliberalism*, Oxford University Press, 2005, 12.

6 Colin Gordon, 'Governmental Rationality: An Introduction', in Graham Burchell *et al.* eds., *The Foucault Effect: Studies in Governmentality*, Harvester Wheatsheaf, 1991, 6.

7 Nancy Fraser, 'From Discipline to Flexibilization?: Rereading Foucault in the Shadow of Globalization', *Constellations* 10: 2, 2003, 160.

8 See Jacques Donzelot, *L'invention du social*, Fayard, 1984; Seuil, coll. « Points », 1994.

and 1940s. Superimposing Fordist governmentality upon disciplinary governmentality in the Foucauldian sense, Fraser defines three characteristics of this governmentality:

1) Fordist discipline was totalizing, aimed at rationalizing all major aspects of social life, including many never before subject to deliberate organization. It sought to rationalize not only factory production but also the family and community life of their workers.

2) If Fordist discipline was totalizing, it was nevertheless socially concentrated within a national frame. Various previously discrete disciplines converged upon a new societal space within the nation-state. Called 'the social' by Hannah Arendt and Jacques Donzelot, this was a dense nexus of overlapping apparatuses where institutions of social control became interconnected.

3) This Fordist mode of social ordering worked largely through individual self-regulation. As Foucault emphasized, advocates of social control sought to foster self-activating subjects capable of self-governance. Wagering that such subjects would be more rational, cooperative, and productive than those directly subordinated to external authority, Fordist reformers devised new organizational forms and management practices. The overall thrust was to 'subjectify' individuals and thereby to augment their capacities for self-policing.[9]

According to Fraser, the attributes of disciplinary Fordist power dispositives are the totalization of social life, social concentration within nation-state and self-control. What, then, distinguishes the post-Fordist power dispositives that replace disciplinary Fordist power dispositives? Let us refer again to Fraser's article:

1) In the post–89 era or post-Fordist globalization, social interactions increasingly transcend the borders of states. As a result, the ordering of social relations is undergoing at major shift in scale, equivalent to denationalization and transnationalization. In the case of public health, policing, banking regulation, labour standards, environmental regulation, and counter-terrorism, country-based agencies are increasingly expected to harmonize their policies with those at the transnational and international levels. Although national ordering is

---

9 Ibid., 163–4. Summarized by us.

not disappearing, it is in the being decentred as its regulatory mechanisms become articulated with those at other levels. What is emerg-
ing, therefore, is a new type of regulatory structure, a multi-layered
system of globalized governmentality whose full contours have yet to
be determined.

2) In the same time, regulation is also undergoing a process of deso-
cialization. In today's hegemonic neoliberal variant of globalization,
massive, unfettered, transnational flows of capital are derailing the
Keynesian project of national economic steering. The tendency is to
transform the Fordist welfare state into a post-Fordist 'competitive
state'. Politics such as deregulation and privatization of social services
destructures the zone of 'the (national) social', formerly the heartland
of Fordist discipline.

3) As Fordist discipline wanes in the face of globalization, its orientation to self-regulation tends to dissipate too. In addition, the enfeeblement of Keynesian state steering means more unemployment and less
downward redistribution, hence increased inequality and social
instability. The resulting vacuum is more likely to be filled by outright
repression than by efforts to promote individual autonomy.[10]

Fraser characterizes the particularity of post-Fordist governmentality as a
multi-layered globalized system, destruction of 'the (national) social', the
enfeeblement of self-regulation and the return of violent repression. It is
from this perspective that we must read Foucault's lecture course about
neoliberalism as an attempt to analyse post-Fordist governmentality.

2 Neoliberal governmentality

Before analysing the neoliberal governmentality problematized in *The
Birth of Biopolitics*, we must define governmentality itself. This notion
was introduced in the previous year's course, *Security, Territory,
Population*, in order to analyse the governmental technique of the state
in classical liberalism.[11] In *The Birth of Biopolitics*, Foucault writes:
'what I have proposed to call governmentality, that is to say, the way in

---

10 Ibid., 165–6. Summarized by us.
11 See *Sécurité, territoire, population*, 111–13; *Security, Territory, Population*,
108–10.

which one conducts the conduct of men, is no more than a proposed analytical grid for [the] power relations'.[12] From this definition, we define governmentality as *the way in which state power conducts individual conduct through controlling socio-economic relations.*

In *The Birth of Biopolitics*, Foucault analyses two sorts of neoliberalism: one is the German neoliberalism practised in West German politics between 1948 and 1962; the other is the neoliberal theory developed by the second generation of the Chicago School in the 1960s and 1970s. In the German neoliberal politics of the post-war period, Foucault finds 'a new art of government' or 'a renewal of the liberal art of government'.[13] What is this 'new art of government'? Foucault explains:

> In fact, in contemporary Germany, the economy, economic development and economic growth, produces sovereignty; its political sovereignty through the institution and institutional game that, precisely, makes this economy work. The economy produces legitimacy for the state that is its guarantor. In other words, the economy creates public law, and this is an absolutely important phenomenon, which is not entirely unique in history to be sure, but is nonetheless a quite singular phenomenon in our time.[14]

Foucault affirms that a state's economic development produces its political sovereignty and political legitimacy in neoliberal governmentality. The political instance then loses its autonomy and is eroded by the economic.

Let us compare this neoliberal governmentality with that of the Keynesian welfare state. According to Jacques Donzelot in *L'invention du social*, Keynesianism created 'the social' through interventionist policies, such as social security and income redistribution, in order to reduce the opposition between capital and labour. In other words, by constantly intervening in the economic instance, the state as an autonomous political instance has generated society by articulating the economic to the social.[15] For Keynesianism, the market always includes irrationality ('market failure'), and the contradictions that this irrationality produces

---

12 *Naissance de la biopolitique*, 192; *The Birth of Biopolitics*, 186. Translation modified.
13 Ibid., 181–2; 176.
14 Ibid., 85–6; 84.
15 *L'invention du social*, 174.

must be modified by political intervention to produce the social. On the other hand, in neoliberal governmentality, the autonomy of political instance does not exist, because the political is subjected to and eroded by the economic. The social produced by the welfare state is reduced or erased. The disappearance of the autonomy of political instance, the reduction of the social — in other words, governance by the economic — is a global tendency after 1989.

We now examine the theory of German neoliberalism and relate it to the actual neoliberal situation. Between 1948 and 1962, an economic theory called 'ordoliberalism' determined economic policy in West Germany.[16] Ordoliberalism was established by Walter Eucken and Franz Böhm, who taught at the University of Freiburg in the 1930s and founded the journal *Ordo* in 1948. Their ordoliberalism was strongly influenced by the theory of Wilhelm Röpke, Alexander Rüstow and Friedrich Hayek, who were exiled from Germany or Austria after the rise of Nazism.

How does their theory differ from the classical liberalism? To answer this question, we must first of all define classical liberalism. Referring to the theories of physiocrats and Adam Smith, Foucault summarizes it as follows.

First, the market obeys 'natural' mechanisms. By virtue of its price control mechanism, it gives a 'natural' and 'normal' price to the exchanged object. In this sense, it functions as 'a site of veridiction' that forms 'natural' prices.[17]

Second, government does not intervene in the market (per the principle of laissez-faire). If it does intervene, it is only insofar as the intervention produces interests. In other words, government does not deal with 'the things in themselves of governmentality' such as individuals, things, wealth and land.[18]

On these premises, Foucault clarifies the difference between classical liberalism and ordoliberalism. In the former, the market signifies free exchanges that generate an exchange value between two products. These exchanges produce the 'natural' price in the market. On the other hand, what does the market mean to German neoliberalism? It means

---

16 In *The Birth of Biopolitics*, Foucault consults Bilger's work in order to analyse the theory of German ordoliberalism. See François Bilger, *La pensée économique libérale dans l'Allemagne contemporaine*, Librairie générale de droit et de jurisprudence, 1964.

17 *Naissance de la biopolitique*, 33–4; *The Birth of Biopolitics*, 31–2.

18 Ibid., 47; 45.

'competition'. Nevertheless, for the ordoliberals, competition is not the 'natural' given found in the market. Foucault elaborates:

> This is where the ordoliberals break with the tradition of eighteenth and nineteenth century liberalism. They say: Laissez-faire cannot and must not be the conclusion drawn from the principle of competition as the organizing form of the market. Why not? Because, they say, when you deduce the principle of laissez-faire from the market economy, basically you are still in the grip of what could be called a 'naïve naturalism', that is to say, whether you define the market by exchange or by competition you are thinking of it as a sort of given of nature, something produced spontaneously which the state must respect precisely inasmuch as it is a natural datum. But, the ordoliberals say — and here it is easy to spot the influence of Husserl — this is naive naturalism. For what in fact is competition? It is absolutely not a given of nature. The game, mechanisms, and effects of competition which we identify and enhance are not at all natural phenomena; competition is not the result of a natural interplay of appetites, instincts, behaviour, and so on. In reality, the effects of competition are due only to the essence that characterizes and constitutes it. The beneficial effects of competition are not due to a pre-existing nature, to a natural given that it brings with it. They are due to a formal privilege. Competition is an essence. Competition is an *eidos*. Competition is a principle of formalization. Competition has an internal logic; it has its own structure. Its effects are only produced if this logic is respected.[19]

Foucault refers here to a theory of Eucken. Eucken met Husserl and learned phenomenology while teaching at the University of Freiburg. We can thus find Husserl's influence in his theory.[20] Following his phenomenological method, Husserl refrained from taking a 'naturalist' stance (which perceives the world as given) and tried to construct the phenomenal world through internal perception. In the same manner, for neoliberalism, 'competition' cannot be the 'natural' given or the spontaneous phenomenon that *a priori* exists in the market. In classical

---

19 Ibid., 123–4; 119–20.
20 See Walter Eucken, 'Was leistet die nationalökonomische Theorie?', in *Kapitaltheoretische Untersuchungen*, Fischer, 1934; Mohr/Polygraph, 1954, 20.

liberalism, the market signifies free exchanges, through which 'natural' values or equal prices are generated. On the other hand, to ordoliberals, the market signifies competition. Competition does not spontaneously exist, but it must be 'produced' in a way that respects the 'internal logic' — that is to say, by regulating the activities of individuals and organizing society. In other words, competition must be produced as a result of a government's constructive efforts: it is a *principle of government of society*:

> Basically, [neoliberal government] has to intervene on society so that competitive mechanisms can play a regulatory role at every moment and every point in society and by intervening in this way its objective will become possible, that is to say, a general regulation of society by the market. So this will not be the kind of economic government imagined by the physiocrats, that is to say, a government which only has to recognize and observe economic laws; it is not an economic government, it is a government of society.[21]

Neoliberal government constructs competitive mechanisms in every domain of society. If neoliberalism tries to organize competition that does not spontaneously exist in the market, it is not 'laissez-faire' government, but one that intervenes in the market in order to construct competition. Hayek clarifies this neoliberal principle:

> It is important not to confuse opposition against this kind of planning with a dogmatic *laissez-faire* attitude. The liberal argument is in favour of making the best possible use of the forces of competition as a means of co-ordinating human efforts, not an argument for leaving things just as they are. It is based on the conviction that where effective competition can be created, it is a better way of guiding individual efforts than any other.[22]

According to Hayek, the neoliberal principle never resides in 'laissez-faire' as classical liberalism intended ('the liberal argument is [. . .] not an argument for leaving things just as they are'). Neoliberalism creates the 'effective competition', namely the competition 'by which our

---

21 *Naissance de la biopolitique*, 151; *The Birth of Biopolitics*, 145–6.
22 Friedrich A. Hayek, *The Road to Serfdom* (1944), Routledge, 2001, 37.

activities can be adjusted to each other' and which organizes a society.[23] In this sense, unlike classical laissez-faire liberalism, neoliberalism is a 'positive liberalism' or 'intervening liberalism' that intentionally builds competition into society.[24]

But if neoliberalism emphasizes the market principle, Keynesian intervention (for example, public investment, social security and income redistribution) which distorts the market mechanism must be rigorously excluded. Ordoliberalism has intensely criticized Keynesian planning as well as socialist and Nazi planning for their destruction of the market mechanism. What kind of 'intervention', then, does ordoliberalism propose? Foucault clarifies:

> As a good Kantian, Eucken says: How should government intervene? It should intervene in the form of regulatory actions, that is to say, it must intervene in fact on economic processes when intervention is imperative for conjunctural reasons. 'The economic process always leads to temporary frictions, to modifications which risk giving rise to exceptional situations with difficulties of adaptation and more or less serious repercussions on some groups'. It is necessary then, he says, not to intervene on the mechanisms of the market economy, but on the conditions of the market.[25]

Neoliberal government does not intervene directly in the market mechanism. In other words, it does not intervene in the Keynesian manner, such as public investment and social security, but it intervenes on the 'conditions' or 'framework' of the market by establishing rules and institutions in order to regulate economic processes.[26]

In this respect, let us refer to Hayek's theory. For Hayek, intervention in the 'conditions of the market' means producing the 'rules of the game', namely the legal and institutional frameworks in order to create 'effective' competition. Hayek writes:

> The functioning of competition not only requires adequate organization of certain institutions like money, markets, and channels of

---

23 Ibid.
24 *Naissance de la biopolitique*, 138; *The Birth of Biopolitics*, 133.
25 Ibid., 143–4; 138.
26 Ibid., 145; 140.

information — some of which can never be adequately provided by private enterprise — but it depends above all on the existence of an appropriate legal system, a legal system designed both to preserve competition and to make it operate as beneficially as possible.[27]

For Hayek, intervention in the 'conditions of the market' signifies producing an 'appropriate legal system' in order to make competition work 'as beneficially as possible'. Neoliberal governmentality as 'intervening liberalism' is thus a governmental technique that produces effective competition in the market by intervening in juridical and institutional systems.

We can reformulate Hayek's thesis from the Foucauldian point of view: neoliberal governmentality intervenes in the 'environment' or 'milieu' as an institutional framework: it controls individuals' activities by designing the environment (namely, by constructing 'effective' competition). In this sense, it is a governmental technique which tries to 'plan a milieu in terms of events or series of events or possible elements, of series that will have to be regulated within a multivalent and transformable framework'.[28] We can call this the 'power of environmental intervention', which controls individual's desire and activities by constructing competition in the environment.

In reading *The Birth of Biopolitics*, François Ewald points out that neoliberal governmentality produces control by producing liberty: 'We have to remember that Foucault makes an important distinction: liberalism, or this kind of governmentality, is a way by means of which to produce liberty and also to produce security and control. It is absolutely not *laissez-faire*. And liberty, he explains, is not something to be observed like a quality or a property of man, no, liberty is what this kind of government has to produce to govern the people: "I make you free, because if you are free I can better govern you". Perhaps you think that this is a very liberal sentence, but that is not so evident to me'.[29] If we interpret this 'liberty' as 'competition', we can understand that neoliberal governmentality controls the population by producing competition in the environment.

---

27 *The Road to Serfdom*, 39.

28 *Sécurité, territoire, population*, 22; *Security, Territory, Population*, 20.

29 François Ewald, 'François Ewald on Foucault & Neoliberalism', Foucault 13/13, 24 January 2016, blogs.law.columbia.edu.

In this process, neoliberal governmentality also produces inequality between economic agents:

> Practically since the end of the nineteenth century, more or less all liberal theory has accepted that the most important thing about the market is competition, that is to say, not equivalence but on the contrary *inequality*. It is the problem of competition and monopoly, much more than that of value and equivalence, that forms the essential armature of a theory of the market. On this point therefore the ordoliberals do not depart in any way from the historical development of liberal thought. They take up this classical conception and the principle that competition, and only competition, can ensure economic rationality.[30]

For neoliberal governmentality, 'the most important thing about the market is competition, that is to say, not equivalence but on the contrary *inequality*', affirms Foucault. Through this inequality, it imposes on the subject the categorical imperative to win the competition in the market, and it controls the subject's desire by this imperative.

Let us note here three crucial problems caused by such a neoliberal governmental technique. The first problem relates to competition. Presupposing that competition does not exist spontaneously in the market, neoliberal government intervenes in the market in order to produce competition and inequality. For example, the abolition of lifetime employment, the increase of precarious employment and the introduction of a performance-related salary system have produced competition that did not formerly exist in the labour market. With these institutional changes, individual objectives and evaluation permanently control employees, and the labour environment is structurally precarized through the possibility of dismissal. 'Positive liberalism' or 'intervening liberalism' thus produces competition and inequality and thereby creates mechanisms of permanent control.

The second problem is that of unemployment and the 'flexibilization' (precarization) of labour. Neoliberal governmentality does not hold full employment as an objective. An unemployed person is thus interpreted as 'a worker in transit between an unprofitable activity and a more profitable activity'. The problem is that neoliberal governmentality accepts a

---

30 *Naissance de la biopolitique*, 122; *The Birth of Biopolitics*, 119. Our emphasis.

certain rate of unemployment in order to produce 'flexibility' of labour (i.e., professional mobility). In other words, neoliberalism intentionally produces flexibility or precarity by creating temporary employment and fixed-term contract labour in order to promote cheap labour power. This situation intensifies social divisions and instability. The social vacuum that originates in this situation could be filled by direct repression or by racist and populist politics (such as the exclusion of foreign labourers).

The third problem concerns social policy. One of the objectives of the Keynesian welfare state was income redistribution through a tax system and social security. However, neoliberal governmentality rejects this objective. The idea of relative equalization of individuals in the welfare state has been replaced by the idea of minimum income guarantees.[31] Such policy results in the privatization of the social. For example, in the welfare state, social insurance protects individuals from risks such as illness, accidents, or unemployment. Donzelot calls this policy 'the socialization of risk'.[32] But neoliberal governmentality refuses to socialize the risk of individuals. Instead of social insurance, private as well as mutual insurance is recommended (recall Thatcher's expression criticizing people's 'dependence' on social security: 'There is no such thing as society'[33]). It is 'an individualization of social policy'.[34] The social that covered the society in the welfare state is thus reduced to the minimum. A wave of reduction of the social is extended not only to social security, but to other social services (including the privatization of public enterprises, public hospitals, public cultural facilities, national education and universities). Privatization of the social introduces the principle of competition in every domain of society, forcing the market principle even on those sectors where the pursuit of profits is not a priority.[35] All

---

31 See, for example, *The Road to Serfdom*, Ch. 9 'Security and Freedom'.

32 *L'invention du social*, 138–9.

33 'I think we have gone through a period when too many children and people have been given to understand "I have a problem, it is the Government's job to cope with it!" or "I have a problem, I will go and get a grant to cope with it!" "I am homeless, the Government must house me!" and so they are casting their problems on society and who is society? There is no such thing! There are individual men and women and there are families and no government can do anything except through people and people look to themselves first' ('Interview for *Woman's Own*', 31 October 1987, margaretthatcher.org.

34 *Naissance de la biopolitique*, 149; *The Birth of Biopolitics*, 144.

35 In 2004, the Japanese government semi-privatized all national universities and

of these aspects demonstrate the neoliberal governmental technique, which fills every societal domain with the principles of competition and precarity.

3 Neoliberal subjectivity

To conclude, we will examine the structure of neoliberal subjectivity by referring to the Foucauldian interpretation of Chicago School theory. In his lecture course on neoliberalism, Foucault discusses the second generation of the Chicago School, particularly the theory of 'human capital' by Gary Becker and Theodore Schultz. Their theory can be directly connected to the ordoliberal ideal that attempts to completely fill society with the economic.

The theory of human capital is founded on an economic analysis of labour that had not been explored by classical economics. If classical economics pays attention to capital, investment and production, the theory of human capital chooses labour as the object of economic analysis. In this theory, economic analysis is not concerned with production processes but with 'human behaviour'. For example, Becker defines economics by citing Lionel Robbins: 'Economics is the science of human behaviour as a relationship between ends and scarce means which have mutually exclusive uses'.[36] It is therefore the analysis of an individual's strategy of rational behaviour: it determines how an economic agent or a worker chooses means from among scarce choices to achieve their ends.

To analyse workers' behaviour strategies, the theory of human capital distinguishes capital from income. Capital refers to the worker's ability or skill as a source of income. Income means the wage attributed to this capital. For example, Schultz defines human capital as follows: 'The distinctive mark of human capital is that it is a part of man. It is *human* because it is embodied in man, and *capital* because it is a source of future

---

transformed them into 'National University Corporations' in order to intensively introduce the principle of competition in this sector.

36 Lionel Charles Robbins, *Essay on the Nature and Significance of Economic Science*, Macmillan, 1932, 16; Gary S. Becker, *The Economic Approach to Human Behavior*, University of Chicago Press, 1976, 4, note 3. Quoted in *Naissance de la biopolitique*, 228; *The Birth of Biopolitics*, 222.

satisfactions or of future earnings, or of both'.[37] Foucault analyses this
definition of labour as follows:

> We should therefore view the whole as a machine/flow complex
> [labour machine as a worker who has aptitude or competence, and
> wage flow], say the neo-economists [. . .], it is therefore a machine-
> flow ensemble, and you can see that we are at the opposite extreme of
> a conception of labour power sold at the market price to a capital
> invested in an enterprise. This is not a conception of labour power; it
> is a conception of capital-ability which, according to diverse variables,
> receives a certain income that is a wage, an income-wage, so that the
> worker himself appears as a sort of enterprise for himself.[38]

In the theory of human capital, work does not refer to the labour power
sold to a capitalist for company production, but rather a 'capital-ability'
as a worker's ability or skill. Income denotes the wage paid for this 'capital-ability'. A worker is then considered an agent who has his own 'capital-ability' and who invests it in his work in order to receive a wage. The
worker thus defined is a kind of 'enterprise for himself'.

Human capital as 'capital-ability' consists of innate and acquired
elements. The former are hereditary and the latter acquired through
education. The formation of human capital is especially related to the
latter — that is, to education or educational investments. What does this
investment consist of? Foucault explains:

> Experimentally, on the basis of observations, we know it is consti-
> tuted by, for example, the time parents devote to their children outside
> of simple educational activities strictly speaking. We know that the
> number of hours a mother spends with her child, even when it is still
> in the cradle, will be very important for the formation of an abilities-
> machine, or for the formation of a human capital, and that the child
> will be much more adaptive if in fact its parents or its mother spend
> more rather than less time with him or her. This means that it must be
> possible to analyse the simple time parents spend feeding their

---

37 Theodore W. Schultz, *Investment in Human Capital: The Role of Education and of
Research*, Free Press, 1971, 48.

38 *Naissance de la biopolitique*, 231; *The Birth of Biopolitics*, 225. Translation
modified.

children, or giving them affection as investment which can form human capital. Time spent, care given, as well as the parents' education — because we know quite precisely that for an equal time spent with their children, more educated parents will form a higher human capital than parents with less education — in short, the set of cultural stimuli received by the child, will all contribute to the formation to those elements that can make up a human capital.[39]

Educational 'investments' are not purely economic; even *non-economic* acts such as feeding and giving parental affection to children are interpreted as 'investments'. This interpretation is based on the idea of substitutable choices between scarce resources. For example, these 'investments' allocate the limited time and energy of the parents (scarce resources) to the education of their children. The theory of human capital thus applies economic analysis to non-economic acts. It is, so to speak, a theory that considers all human acts as objects of economic analysis.

The theory of human capital values mobility as a constituent of human capital. There are nevertheless many negative factors in mobility. For example, there are physical and psychological costs associated with moving from one company to another or from one occupation to another. In spite of these negative factors, why does the theory of human capital give importance to mobility? What is the function of these costs? Foucault analyses these questions as follows:

In the elements making up human capital should also include mobility, that is to say, an individual's ability to move around, and migration in particular. Because migration obviously represents a material cost, since the individual will not be earning while he is moving, but there will also be a psychological cost for the individual establishing himself in his new milieu. There will also be at least a loss of earnings due to the fact that the period of adaptation will certainly prevent the individual from receiving his previous remunerations, or those he will have when he is settled. All these negative elements show that migration has a cost. What is the function of this cost? It is to obtain an improvement of status, of remuneration, and so on, that is to say, it is an investment. Migration is an investment; the migrant is an investor.

39 Ibid., 235–6; 229.

He is an entrepreneur of himself who incurs expenses by investing to obtain some kind of improvement.[40]

In the theory of human capital, every individual is considered an 'entrepreneur of himself' who invests in himself and controls costs in order to improve his social status and attain high remuneration. Referring to Fraser's argument, we said previously that disciplinary self-regulation weakens in neoliberal post-Fordist governmentality. However, following this Foucauldian analysis, we can say that the disciplinary subject who controls himself through internalizing social norms is now replaced by the 'entrepreneur of himself' — namely, the subject of self-management who regards himself as an object of investment. In other words, it is an economic subject who controls himself by internalizing the market principle or the principle of competition.

Relating this economic subject to the economic concept of *homo œconomicus*, Foucault asserts: 'neoliberalism appears under these conditions as a return to *homo œconomicus*'.[41] In economics, *homo œconomicus* designates a model of a rational man who organizes his acts in the most reasonable way to obtain the largest profit. In neoliberal governmentality, *homo œconomicus* appears as an 'entrepreneur of himself, being for himself his own capital, being for himself his own producer, being for himself the source of his earnings'.[42] *Homo œconomicus*, in this sense, corresponds to an economic agent who transforms himself according to environmental changes. Foucault evaluates this form of neoliberal subjectivity as follows:

> [I]n Becker's definition which I have just given, *homo œconomicus*, that is to say, the person who accepts reality or who responds systematically to modifications in the variables of the environment, appears precisely as someone manageable, someone who responds systematically to systematic modifications artificially introduced into the environment. *Homo œconomicus* is someone who is eminently governable.[43]

---

40 Ibid., 236; 230.
41 Ibid., 231; 225.
42 Ibid., 232; 226.
43 Ibid., 274; 270.

Foucault defines *homo œconomicus* in neoliberal governmentality as 'the person who accepts reality or who responds systematically to modifications in the variables of the environment'. This type of subject is eminently 'manageable' and 'governable' insofar as he transforms himself in accordance with environmental changes (for example, marketization and intensified competition).

In this sense, *homo œconomicus* is the interface between power and the individual, which neoliberal power needs in order to intervene indirectly in the subject and govern it: when neoliberal governmentality constructs the principle of competition in the environment, *homo œconomicus* tries to transform himself into a competitive subject according to his 'natural' desire to win the competition. In this process, 'the individual becomes governmentalizable, that power gets a hold on him to the extent, and only to the extent, that he is a *homo œconomicus*. That is to say, the surface of contact between the individual and the power exercised on him, and so the principle of the regulation of power over the individual, will be only this kind of grid of *homo œconomicus*. *Homo œconomicus* is the interface of government and the individual'.[44]

Under this neoliberal governmentality, we are asked to internalize the principle of competition and to manage ourselves following the principle of 'entrepreneur of himself'. We can call this a neoliberal 'competitive subjectivity'. As we have seen, neoliberal governmentality does not intervene directly on the subject as disciplinary power does in order to normalize it, but it intervenes on the environment in order to build the principle of competition and promotes the formation of a competitive subject. This governmental technique, which we called the 'power of environmental intervention', adopts therefore a lower-cost mechanism than disciplinary power.

The structural precarization of labour and the reduction of the social promote this type of competitive subject or subject of self-management, one who internalizes the market principle, manages his career and increases his human capital in order to ameliorate his social status. In neoliberal governmentality, those who can adapt to the imposed imperative of the market climb up the social ladder, and those who cannot do so are dismissed from society. From this point of view, we can reformulate a Foucauldian definition of modern biopolitics proposed in *'Society Must Be Defended'*: neoliberal governmentality 'makes live' those who

---

44 Ibid., 257–8; 252–3.

can adapt to the imperative of the market, and 'lets die' those who cannot do so.[45] It thus introduces a *break line* between those who can live in society and those who must exist precariously.[46]

How can we then resist this neoliberal governmentality that individualizes and divides us through the principle of competition? We will try to answer this question in the conclusion to Part I.

45 See Michel Foucault, « *Il faut défendre la société* », *Cours au Collège de France, 1975–1976*, Gallimard/Seuil, 1997, 214; *'Society Must Be Defended'*, *Lectures at the Collège de France, 1975–1976*, Picador, 2003, 241: 'The right of sovereignty was the right to make die or let live. And then this new right is established: the right to make live and to let die'. Translation modified.

46 Bernard Harcourt critiques a latent tendency of the theory of human capital to divide a population between those who deserve to be invested in and those who do not. See Gary S. Becker, François Ewald, Bernard E. Harcourt, 'Becker on Ewald on Foucault on Becker American Neoliberalism and Michel Foucault's 1979 "Birth of Biopolitics" Lectures', Coase-Sandor Institute for Law & Economics Working Paper 614, University of Chicago Law School, 2012, chicagounbound.uchicago.edu.

Conclusion to Part I
Becoming-other and Becoming-self

We started from an aporia of 'structuralist' theories of power, namely from the impossibility of thinking about resistance to power. This impossibility meant suppressing the subject's productivity in relation to power and the virtual concentration of power in the formal structure as an 'object' or, to put it another way, the radical decentration of the subject by the internalization of power. We have found two strategies to resolve this aporia. The first strategy is the economic problematic of Deleuze and Guattari and the second strategy is the topical problematic of Foucault.

Deleuze and Guattari's strategy consists in deconstructing the activity of the subject and giving impersonal power [*puissance impersonnelle*] to the machinic unconscious. In *Anti-Oedipus*, they ruthlessly criticize Lacanian theory but never annihilate Lacan's revolutionary thesis, the 'decentration of the subject'. For these authors, the subject is radically decentred, and the activity given by modern philosophy to the subject belongs to the unconscious. However, the unconscious is not deter-mined, in their theory, by the 'desire of the Other'; it is the field of imper-sonal desire never reducible to the personal as the ego or the Other. By detaching the unconscious from the personal, they free it from the Hegelo-Lacanian dialectic — that is, from the dialectic of the subject and the Other which persists in Lacanian psychoanalytic theory.

Pushing structuralist thought to its limit, they open up a path for resistance to power through the concept of the economic subject — namely the subject as multiplicity. If the movement of capitalism represses the dynamics of the production and consumption of energy flows through family repression, thereby seeking to construct the Oedipal topical subject, then the means of resistance to capitalism would be the following: in order to achieve de-subjection collectively, the proletarians must find the productivity of desire through their struggle of interests and transform the hierarchical and vertical subjected group into a horizontal and transversal subject-group. This subject-group formation will achieve 'the reversal of power such that desiring-production subjects social production and yet does not destroy it.'[1] Deleuze and Guattari's strategy of resistance is thus based on *becoming-other*, namely the transformation of the subjected group into a subject-group, and on the economic problematic of impersonal desire.

In contrast, the Foucauldian strategy of resistance to power involves pushing the topical problematic to its limits — and remaining there — and in making the transcendental instance heterogeneous (coexistence and intersection of domination and resistance). Through his *Kehre* towards an ethical thematization, Foucault redefines the transcendental system as a heterogeneity in which immanence (the field of singularity) and internalized power coexist; only then will the former be able to criticize the disciplinarity of the latter. This modification of the definition allows the subjected subject to criticize power relations. However, since the subject is produced and reproduced by power dispositives, he cannot be completely freed from power relations. The practice of de-subjection will therefore consist in constantly criticizing actual power relations in order to transform the subjected ego into an ethical self. We have called this attempt 'becoming-self'.

In this sense, Foucault's strategy of resistance to power designates a persistent historico-reflective critique: the philosophy of 'actuality' and the notion of 'historical contingency' allow the becoming of the subject. For Deleuze and Guattari, it is the economic problematic of impersonal desire that can theorize the impersonal power of becoming. Foucault, for his part, remains in the topical problematic by ensuring the becoming in another way, namely by introducing historical contingency.

In contemporary neoliberal society, power forces us to accept the total competitive environment; through this neoliberal governmentality, it individualizes us in order to deprive us of the possibility of

---

1 *L'Anti-Œdipe*, 456–7; *Anti-Oedipus*, 380. Translation modified.

solidarity. Keynesian capitalism, established in the 1930s, gave workers the food, housing and medicine to continue working, and for those who could not work, it gave social security to support them collectively. It thus reproduced workers and kept them alive in order to exploit them. In contrast, neoliberal capitalism, which has covered the whole world since the end of socialism in 1989, has no intention of supporting workers in order to exploit them. Neoliberalism cuts wages and indebts workers, and it seeks profit even through this indebtedness (the financialization of capitalism); it thus pushes the workers to the point where the reproduction of labour power is no longer possible. It therefore does not profit from *exploitation*, but from *expropriation*. In this economico-political situation, we must choose *both* the Foucauldian strategy *and* the Deleuzo-Guattarian strategy: by revealing the effects of neoliberal power (individualization and competition) in the subjected subject in a reflective manner, we must organize the collective anti-neoliberal struggle, and through this struggle of interests, we must form the de-subjected subject-group of the schizos that detaches their desiring production from the pursuit of interests.[2]

In his lecture course *Security, Territory, Population*, devoted to a meticulous analysis of liberal governmentality, Foucault enigmatically asserted: 'there has never been an anti-pastoral revolution.'[3] If pastoral power means the power that 'conducts the conduct' of individuals in order to integrate them into totality like the state and the market (Foucault called this way of government 'omnes et singulatim'[4]), resistance to power should not be a simple individual resistance, but an anti-pastoral revolution which transforms the pastoral structure into a collective autonomous subjectivity. In Part II, we examine the theory of structural transformation as social revolution in Althusser and Derrida. Althusser reflected on the 'becoming' of social formation itself, relying on an actual contingency. In a 1978 text, he asserts that Marxist theory

---

2 On the strategy of collective resistance in the era of neoliberalism, see the following two important works: Judith Butler, *Notes Toward a Performative Theory of Assembly*, Harvard University Press, 2015; Michael Hardt/Antonio Negri, *Assembly*, Oxford University Press, 2019.

3 *Sécurité, territoire, population*, 153; *Security, Territory, Population*, 150.

4 Ibid., 132; 128. Michel Foucault, « Omnes et singulatim : vers une critique de la raison politique », in *Dits et écrits*, T. IV; 'Omnes et singulatim: Towards a Criticism of 'Political Reason', in *The Tanner Lectures on Human Values*, Vol. II, University of Utah Press, 1981.

is 'inscribed within and limited to the *actual phase*'[5] and continues as follows:

> Only a 'finite' theory can be really *open* to contradictory tendencies, which it detects in capitalist society, and open to their aleatory becoming, open to the unforeseeable 'surprises' which have never ceased to mark the history of the workers' movement, open therefore attentive, and capable of taking seriously and accounting *in time* the incorrigible imagination of history.[6]

If the 'aleatory becoming' of social formation is caused by contradictions and contingency in social formation, we can interpret this theory of contingency as that of the causality of structural change. To examine it, we will consider, in Part II, the question of contingency and structural alteration.

---

5 « Le marxisme comme théorie 'finie' », in *Solitude de Machiavel*, 285.
6 Ibid., 286.

Part II

Becoming of the Structure: Althusser and Derrida

4

Death Drive, Contingency, and Resistance (Derrida)

Introduction to Part II

One of the theoretical contributions of structuralism is the renewal of the theory of temporality, which understands historical time no longer in terms of linear continuity but in terms of radical discontinuity. For example, Michel Foucault presents, in *The Order of Things*, the concept of episteme and suggests rethinking the history of ideas as a succession of epistemes, between which exists a radical rupture. He calls such rupture a 'mutation' of the episteme, or quite simply an 'event' — but he says nothing about the causality of this 'mutation' or 'event'. At the end of the eighteenth century, for example, the 'representative discourse' which dominated knowledge in the classical age was suddenly replaced by 'man', who became the 'object to know' and the 'subject who knows'. One episteme disappears and another appears, that is all.

In contrast, Althusser tried to theorize the causality of structural becoming. Discussing the problem of the 'irruption' of the new structure, he explains, in a 1966 text, that the new structure, once it has irrupted by rupture with the previous one, reproduces itself 'atemporally'; it 'operates in a closed circuit, in the mode of atemporality, [. . .] far from being subject to the temporality of "chronology", that is, of simple temporal succession, or historicity in the common sense'. Althusser calls this reproduction of the structure 'synchronic reproduction'.[1] This theorization is closely related to

1 Louis Althusser, « Lettre à D . . . », in *Écrits sur la psychanalyse*, Stock/IMEC, 1993, 93; 'Letter to D . . ', in *Writing on Psychoanalysis: Freud and Lacan*, Columbia University Press, 1999, 62–3: 'Marx does indeed propose to explain the mode of *irruption* of a new

his famous theory of ideology, according to which the dominant ideology subjects the subject by suppressing his power of resistance, reproducing social relations 'atemporally'. In this sense, 'synchronic' reproduction refers to the fixation of social relations, and the subjection of the subject by the dominant ideology inculcated in it by the ideological apparatuses of the state.[2] But how, then, can the social structure provided by this 'synchronic' reproduction be altered?

Under this problematic, we examine, in this second part, the question of structural transformation and contingency in Althusser and Derrida. According to our hypothesis, they share certain theoretical motifs: first, they reflect on the question of rupture and structural change in relation to contingency; second, they theorize through the critical alteration of psychoanalytic theory. This is not a simple critique, but a *deconstruction* and *alteration* of psychoanalytic theory in order to conceptualize the relationship between rupture and contingency. Our reflection on this attempt will lead us to the crucial problems for psychoanalysis.

In this fourth chapter, we address the problem of structural alteration in Derrida in its relation to the 'death drive'. Why integrate this notion of the death drive into our reflection? Because in Derrida, the question of resistance (recall the double meaning of the word '*Widerstand*' — political and psychoanalytic 'resistance'[3]) is theorized around the two

---

reality, but he can do it, despite several formulations of a Hegelian or evolutionist stamp, only by rejecting, in the practice of his theoretical work, the concepts of genesis (the Hegelian concepts); he thus does indeed propose to resolve a problem that you call (and that we can call provisionally for heuristic reasons) *diachronic*. And at the same time, once the *new* structure has *irrupted*, it functions *atemporally, exactly like* the unconscious. Marx says precisely that every mode of production is *"eternal"*, [. . .] When he says that the mode of production is "eternal", he means that it functions in a closed circuit, in the mode of atemporality, and that far from being subject to the temporality of "chronology", that is, of simple temporal succession, or of historicity in the common sense, it is independent of it; *exactly like* the unconscious, it *reproduces itself* endlessly, and that atemporal "synchronic" reproduction is the absolute condition of its "production" in the economic sense as in all other senses'. Translation modified.

2 In this sense, ideology functions as a repetitive process of the synchronic reproduction of the social structure. See, for example, Alain Badiou's definition of ideology in an article on the work of Althusser: Alain Badiou, « Le (re)commencement du matérialisme dialectique », *Critique* 240, 1967, 449: 'If science is a process of *transformation*, ideology, as the unconscious comes to constitute and form itself there, is a process of *repetition*'.

3 Jacques Derrida, « Résistances », in *Résistances — de la psychanalyse*, Galilée, 1996, 13–15; 'Resistances', in *Resistances of Psychoanalysis*, Stanford University Press, 1998, 1–3.

completely antinomic aspects of the death drive: the death drive that threatens human life (cruelty) and the death drive that defends the subject against this cruelty of the drive itself (resistance). To deal with the problem of resistance and contingency in Derrida, we cannot avoid reflecting on these two antinomic aspects.

In exploring the difference between Lacan and Derrida on the interpretation of the Freudian notion of drive, we first note that the Lacanian theorization constitutes an 'obstacle' (in the sense of Bachelard) to the conceptualization of the question of contingency and structural alteration. We then demonstrate that, in Derrida, the deconstruction of the Lacanian theory of the drive is essential to present the notions of resistance and rupture, even the strategy of resistance. This chapter therefore mainly develops the notion of contingency and its relationship with rupture. In the fifth and sixth chapters, this Derridean deconstruction of psychoanalysis is superimposed — with certain differences — on the critique of ideology and on the attempt to produce Althusser's 'general theory' of structural becoming.

4.1 Lacanian Thing

In 'Seminar on "The Purloined Letter"' (1957), Lacan, in examining the problem of memorization, recollection and the compulsion to repeat, refers to the Freudian theoretical path that develops from *Project for a Scientific Psychology* (1895) through *Beyond the Pleasure Principle* (1920) to 'A Note upon the Mystic Writing-Pad' (1925). This reference to Freudian texts, which were relatively unknown at the time, coincides curiously with that of Derrida in 'Freud and the Scene of Writing' (1966).[4] The fact that Derrida had not then read this Lacan's Seminar[5] arouses all the more our curiosity.[6] But, in fact, this coincidence

---

4 « Le séminaire sur 'La Lettre volée' », in *Écrits*, 42, 44–6; 'Seminar on "The Purloined Letter"', in *Écrits: The Complete Edition*, 31, 33–5.

5 In this chapter, the capitalized Seminar designates 'Seminar on "The Purloined Letter"' by Lacan, which inaugurates his *Écrits* and to which he granted 'the privilege of opening their suite despite its diachrony [*le privilège d'ouvrir leur suite en dépit de la diachronie de celle-ci*]') (« Ouverture de ce recueil », in *Écrits*, 9).

6 See Jacques Derrida, *Positions*, Minuit, 1972, 113, note 33; *Positions*, 108, note 44: 'At the time of my first publications Lacan's *Écrits* had not been collected and published. When *De la grammatologie* and "Freud et la scène de l'écriture" were published I had

illuminates the radical difference in their theoretical positions around the Freudian notion of drive. It is, first of all, this theoretical difference that we seek to elucidate (sections 4.1 and 4.2). This perspective requires reflection on the notion of the death drive and its two antinomic aspects in Freud and Derrida (sections 4.3 and 4.4). This examination will finally lead us to the thematic of resistance to state cruelty and rupture in Derrida (sections 4.5 and 4.6).

We start with Lacan, who writes in the Seminar:

For it is his inaugural discovery that Freud reaffirms in it: namely, the conception of memory implied by his 'unconscious'. The new facts provide him with an occasion to restructure that conception in a more rigorous manner by giving it a generalized form, but also to reopen his problematic to combat the decline, which one could sense already at that time, seen in the fact that people were taking its effects as a simple pregiven.

What is revamped here was already articulated in the 'Project' [*Project for a Scientific Psychology*], in which Freud's divination traced the avenues his research would force him to go down: the ψ system, a predecessor of the unconscious, manifests its originality therein, in that it is unable to satisfy itself except by *refinding an object that has been fundamentally lost* [retrouver l'objet foncièrement perdu].[7]

The 'ψ system, a predecessor of the unconscious', writes Lacan, manifests in *Project for a Scientific Psychology* 'its originality therein, in that it is unable to satisfy itself except by *refinding an object that has been fundamentally lost*'. According to *Project*, the ψ system, 'impermeable neurons (loaded with resistance and holding back quantity (Qη))', is the 'vehicle [*Träger*] of memory, and so probably of psychic processes [*psychischen Vorgänge*] in general'. It is opposed to both the φ system, 'permeable neurons (offering no resistance and retaining nothing), in the service of perception [*Wahrnehmung*]', and to the ω system, 'which is excited along with perception, but not along with reproduction, and whose states of excitation give rise to the various qualities, that is to say, *conscious sensations* [bewußte

read only "Fonction et champ de la parole et du langage en psychanalyse" and "L'instance de la lettre dans l'inconscient ou la raison depuis Freud'".

7 « Le séminaire sur 'La Lettre volée' », in *Écrits*, 45; 'Seminar on "The Purloined Letter"', in *Écrits: The Complete Edition*, 34.

Empfindungen]'.[8] Unlike the φ system (system of perception) and ω system (system of conscious sensation), the ψ system is the 'vehicle of psychic processes in general', because it corresponds to the archives of unconscious memory. The latter therefore has a close relationship with the experience of satisfaction [Befriedigungserlebnis] or the image of object memory [Objekterinnerungsbild] that produced it. In the chapter on Befriedigung-serlebnis, Freud clearly affirms the relation between the mechanism of the ψ system and that of the experience of satisfaction.[9] But, curiously, we do not find the expression 'refinding an object that has been fundamentally lost'. The very word 'wiederzufinden' — Lacan designates it, in a text, as being the original term for 'refind [retrouver]'[10] — does not exist in the Project. What, then, does this Lacanian thesis mean?

Let us refer to the seminar 'The Ethics of Psychoanalysis' (1959–60). In a session entitled 'Rereading of the Entwurf', Lacan deals with the Freudian concept of 'Nebenmensch' (the fellow human being):[11] 'the subject's experience of satisfaction is entirely dependent on the other, on the one whom Freud designates in a very beautiful expression [. . .], the Nebenmensch. [. . .] it is through the intermediary of the Nebenmensch as speaking subject that everything that has to do with the thought processes is able to take shape in the subjectivity of the subject'.[12] The Nebenmensch desig-nates the mother as the other, who is, writes Freud, 'simultaneously the [subject's] first satisfying object and further his first hostile object, as well as his sole helping power'.[13] From this point of view, Freud approaches the problem of the establishment of judgment and recognition:

---

8 Sigmund Freud, Entwurf einer Psychologie, in Gesammelte Werke, Nachtragsband, 392, 401; Project for a Scientific Psychology, in Standard Edition, Vol. I, 299–300, 309. Translation modified.

9 See ibid., 410–12; 317–19.

10 Le séminaire, Livre VII, « L'éthique de la psychanalyse », 72; The Seminar, Book VII, 'The Ethics of Psychoanalysis', 58: 'Das Ding has, in effect, to be identified with the Wiederzufinden, the impulse to refind [retrouver], that for Freud establishes the orientation of the human subject to the object'. Translation modified.

11 In his seminar on 'The Ethics of Psychoanalysis', Lacan never translates the term 'Nebenmensch' to keep this 'very beautiful expression'. In the translation of the Project that we quote (in Standard Edition), the 'Nebenmensch' is translated as a 'fellow human being'.

12 Le séminaire, Livre VII, « L'éthique de la psychanalyse », 50; The Seminar, Book VII, 'The Ethics of Psychoanalysis', 39. Translation modified.

13 Entwurf einer Psychologie, in Gesammelte Werke, Nachtragsband, 426; Project for a Scientific Psychology, in Standard Edition, Vol. I, 331.

Thus the complex of the *Nebenmensch* falls apart into two components, of which one makes an impression by its constant structure and
stays together as Thing [*als Ding*], while the other can be *understood*
by the activity of memory [*Erinnerungsarbeit*] — that is, can be traced
back to information from [the subject's] own body.[14]

The *Nebenmensch* is divided into two components: a part that the subject
can recognize 'by the activity of memory' and another part which evades
judgment. Freud calls the latter the 'Thing [*Ding*]': 'What we call things
[*Dinge*] are residues which evade being judged'.[15] Lacan comments on
this passage from Freud:

> The *Ding* is the element that is initially isolated by the subject in his
> experience of the *Nebenmensch* as being by its very nature alien,
> *Fremde*. The complex of the object is in two parts; there is a division,
> a difference in the approach to judgment. Everything in the object
> that is quality can be formulated as an attribute; it belongs to the
> investment of the ψ system and constitutes the primitive *Vorstellungen*
> around which the destiny of all that is controlled according to the
> laws of *Lust* and *Unlust*, of pleasure and unpleasure, will be played out
> in what might be called the primary emergences of the subject. *Das
> Ding* is something entirely different.[16]

According to Lacan, the *Ding* is the alien, the *Fremde* for the subject in
his experience of the *Nebenmensch*. By isolating this *Fremde*, the subject
constitutes the primitive representations that motivate desire. What
controls desire is therefore this 'original division of the experience of
reality'.[17] Lacan goes on to quote another text by Freud, 'Negation'
(1925):

> The first and most immediate goal of the test of reality is not to find in
> a real perception an object which corresponds to the one which the

---

14 Ibid., 426–7; 331. Translation modified. Part of this sentence is translated and
quoted by Lacan (*Le séminaire*, Livre VII, « L'éthique de la psychanalyse », 64), and we
consult here that translation.

15 Ibid., 429; 334.

16 *Le séminaire*, Livre VII, « L'éthique de la psychanalyse », 64–5; *The Seminar*, Book
VII, 'The Ethics of Psychoanalysis', 52. Translation modified.

17 Ibid., 65; 52.

subject represents to himself at that moment, but to *refind* [wiederzu-finden] it, to confirm that it is still present in reality.[18]

The question here is whether what is represented really exists (reality-testing: *Realitätsprüfung*). 'What is unreal, merely represented and subjective, is only internal; what is real is also there outside'.[19] The purpose of the reality-testing therefore consists in judging whether the Thing — Freud defines it, in this text, as an object of satisfaction [*Befriedigungsobjekt*][20] — exists not only as a representation, but also in reality. Freud continues: 'it is evident that a precondition for the setting up of reality-testing is that objects shall have been lost which once brought real satisfaction'.[21] This precise point finally allows us to understand Lacan's thesis 'the ψ system is unable to satisfy itself except by *refinding an object that has been fundamentally lost*'. He comments on Freud's previous quote as follows:

The whole progress of the subject is then oriented around the *Ding* as *Fremde*, strange and even hostile on occasion, or in any case the first outside. It is clearly a probing form of progress that seeks points of reference, but with relation to what? — with the world of desires. It demonstrates that something is there after all, and that to a certain extent it may be useful. Yet useful for what? — for nothing other than to serve as points of reference in relation to the world of wishes and expectations; it is turned toward that which helps on certain occasions to reach *das Ding*. That object will be there when in the end all conditions have been fulfilled — it is, of course, clear that what is supposed to be found cannot be refound. It is in its nature that the object as such is lost. It will never be refound. Something is there while one waits for something better, or worse, but which one wants. The world of our experience, the Freudian world, assumes that it is

---

18 Sigmund Freud, 'Die Verneinung', in *Gesammelte Werke*, Bd. XIV, 14; 'Negation', in *Standard Edition*, Vol. XIX, 237–8. We consult here Lacan's translation (*Le séminaire*, Livre VII, « L'éthique de la psychanalyse », 65; *The Seminar*, Book VII, 'The Ethics of Psychoanalysis', 52).

19 Ibid., 13; 237. Translation modified.

20 Ibid., 13–14; 237: 'Experience has shown the subject that it is not only important whether a thing (an object of satisfaction for him) possesses the 'good' attribute and so deserves to be taken into his ego, but also whether it is there in the external world, so that he can get hold of it whenever he needs it'.

21 Ibid., 14; 238.

this object, *das Ding*, as the absolute Other of the subject, that one is supposed to refind. It is to be found at the most as something missed. One doesn't find it, but only its pleasurable associations. It is in this state of wishing for it and waiting for it that, in the name of the pleasure principle, the optimum tension will be sought; below that there is neither perception nor effort.[22]

According to Lacan, the subject's desire is determined and motivated by the original experience of the satisfaction ('primitive *Vorstellungen*') that the other brings as *Ding*. But this experience is 'fundamentally lost' by the prohibition of incest (symbolic castration). The subject is therefore forced into seeking to 'refind' 'the object of satisfaction' in the other object. Yet, it 'will always be missing something'.[23] This 'lack' will motivate the desire 'in the name of the pleasure principle'. It is therefore the 'lack' that forces the subject to repeat in vain the search for the 'lost object' ('the principle of repetition', says Lacan[24]). In *Project*, Freud defined the Thing as an unrecognizable part of the object, of the other. But Lacan interprets the Thing as other (here, 'absolute Other') which indeed is the object of desire but remains unapproachable. It will appear as 'lack of being [*manque-à-être*]' in the subject. Lacan also calls the Thing 'the real':

> If the Thing were not fundamentally veiled, we wouldn't be in the kind of relationship to it that obliges us, as the whole of psychic life is obliged, to encircle it or bypass it in order to conceive it. Wherever it affirms itself, it does so in domesticated spheres. That is why the spheres are defined thus; it always presents itself as a veiled entity.
>
> Let's say today that if the Thing occupies the place in the psychic constitution that Freud defined on the basis of the thematics of the pleasure principle, this is because the Thing is that which in the real, the primordial real, I will say, suffers from the signifier — and you should understand that it is a real that we do not yet have to limit, the real in its totality, both the real of the subject and the real he has to deal with as exterior to him.[25]

---

22 *Le séminaire*, Livre VII, « L'éthique de la psychanalyse », 65; *The Seminar*, Book VII, 'The Ethics of Psychoanalysis', 52.
23 Ibid., 52; 41.
24 Ibid.
25 Ibid., 142; 118.

This is how the Thing belongs to the real as the radical exteriority of the subject. 'It always *presents itself* as a *veiled* entity' insofar as it is the traumatic that one can neither represent nor internalize. It is around this unrepresentable 'lack' that the subject's desire is organized and the subject itself is formed.

In 'Seminar on "The Purloined Letter"', Lacan tried to explain the dialectic of desire and lack through the theory of the signifier (of the 'letter'), which is summarized as follows: 'a letter always arrives at its destination'.[26] Derrida clearly interprets this enigmatic phrase in '*Le facteur de la vérité*' (1975). In Lacan's Seminar, the 'letter', writes Derrida, corresponds to the 'phallus' as a signifier of lack, or to the veiled 'castration-truth'.[27] The Lacanian thesis regarding the 'letter' therefore designates the formation of the subject by the lack ('hole'), in other words, the 'itinerary of the detour which leads from hole to hole, from the hole to itself, and which therefore has a *circular* form'.[28] Thus, the signifier of lack, 'signifier of signifiers', affirms the unity of the signifying chain, namely the unity of desire. It is a 'transcendental signifier' that organizes all the signifiers around the lack.[29] The organization of desire by the transcendental signifier is an extremely refined formalization of the second Freudian topic developed around the Oedipal relationship. What Derrida calls 'the most rigorous philosophy of psychoanalysis today', 'the most rigorous Freudian philosophy'[30] refers exactly to this formalization of Freudian theory, to this transcendental system of lack. The route followed by the reasoning of the seminar on 'The Ethics of Psychoanalysis' can therefore be summarized as follows: Lacan begins with an economic point of view (reading the *Project*), discusses the problem of the compulsion to repeat (*Beyond the Pleasure Principle*) and finally grafts it on the Oedipal relationship ('Negation'). The course of this seminar clearly shows the characteristics of Lacanian theory in the

---

26 « Le séminaire sur 'La Lettre volée' », in *Écrits*, 41; 'Seminar on "The Purloined Letter"', in *Écrits: The Complete Edition*, 31.

27 Jacques Derrida, « Le fauteur de la vérité », in *La carte postale : de Socrate à Freud et au-delà*, Flammarion, 1980, 469; 'Le facteur de la vérité', in *The Post Card: From Socrates to Freud and Beyond*, University of Chicago Press, 1980, 441.

28 Ibid., 465; 437.

29 Ibid., 493; 465.

30 Ibid., 494, note 16; 466, note 38: 'What we are analysing here is the most rigorous philosophy of psychoanalysis today, more precisely the most rigorous Freudian philosophy, doubtless more rigorous than Freud's philosophy, and more strictly controlled in the exchanges with the history of philosophy'. Translation modified.

1950s and 1960s in which the economic point of view is finally reduced
to the transcendental system of lack.

4.2 Economics of *différance*

Let us move on to the case of Derrida. In 'Freud and the Scene of Writing',
he deals with the Freudian problem of 'memory' as it develops from
Project to 'A Note upon the Mystic Writing-Pad' via *The Interpretation of
Dreams*. What he finds there is the theme of 'writing' — not of the signifier — and of the 'trace'. We will deliberate mainly on his reading of
Project, where Freud reflects on the question of the inscription of
memory in neurons. What Derrida notices is precisely the 'breaching
[*Bahnung*]' between neurons and the 'resistance [*Widerstand*]' that it
produces:

> Breaching, the tracing of a trail, opens up a conducting path. Which
> presupposes a certain violence and a certain resistance to effraction.
> The path is broken, cracked, *fracta*, breached. Now there would be
> two kinds of neurones: the permeable neurones (φ), which offer no
> resistance and thus retain no trace of impression, would be the
> perceptual neurones; other neurones (ψ), which would oppose
> contact-barriers to the quantity of excitation, would thus retain the
> printed trace: they 'thus afford a possibility of representing (*darzustel-
> len*) memory' (*SE*, I, 299). This is the first representation, the first
> staging of memory. [. . .] Freud attributes psychical quality only to
> these latter neurones. They are the 'vehicles of memory and so prob-
> ably of psychical processes in general' (*SE*, I, 300). Memory, thus, is
> not a psychical property among others; it is the very essence of the
> psyche: resistance, and precisely, thereby, an opening to the effraction
> of the trace.[31]

The permeable neurons (the φ system: system of perception) offer no
resistance and do not retain any trace of impressions; on the other hand,
the impermeable neurons (the ψ system: system of memory)

---

31 Jacques Derrida, « Freud et la scène de l'écriture », in *L'écriture et la différence*,
Seuil, 1967; coll. « Points », 1979, 298–9; 'Freud and the Scene of Writing', in *Writing and
Difference*, Routledge, 2001, 252.

accompany, by their 'contact-barriers [*Kontaktschranken*]', resistance during the breaching of excitation.[32] The mechanism of the inscription of memory consists of this 'breaching', which Freud will later call the 'memory-trace [*Erinnerungsspur*]'.[33] The essence of memory, even of 'psychic events', therefore resides in this system of breaching and resistance. But in addition to this process, a difference between the breachings must intervene so that memory is established:

> An equality of resistance to breaching, or an equivalence of the breaching forces, would eliminate any preference in the choice of itinerary. Memory would be paralyzed. It is the difference between breaches which is the true origin of memory, and thus of the psyche. Only this difference enables a 'pathway to be preferred (*Wegbevorzugung*)': 'Memory is represented (*dargestellt*) by the differences in the facilitations of the ψ neurones' (*SE*, I, 300). We then must not say that breaching without difference is insufficient for memory; it must be stipulated that there is no pure breaching without difference. Trace as memory is not a pure breaching that might be reappropriated at any time as simple presence; it is rather the ungraspable and invisible difference between breaches. We thus already know that psychic life is neither the transparency of meaning nor the opacity of force but the difference within the exertion of forces.[34]

Memory makes the difference between the breachings. In other words, the difference between the resistances, which the breechings bring about, produces the psyche itself. There is no memory, nor even a psyche, without resistance when the exciting quantity is transferred between neurons. For if no difference is established between resistances or breachings, there can be no difference between memories. The essence of the psyche therefore resides in 'the difference within the exertion of forces'. This proposition allows Derrida to reinterpret the 'difference' in the psyche in terms of *différance*:

---

32 *Entwurf einer Psychologie*, in *Gesammelte Werke*, Nachtragsband, 391; *Project for a Scientific Psychology*, in *Standard Edition*, Vol. I, 298.

33 See, for example, *Die Traumdeutung*, in *Gesammelte Werke*, Bd. II/III, 543; *The Interpretation of Dreams*, in *Standard Edition*, Vol. V, 538.

34 « Freud et la scène de l'écriture », in *L'écriture et la différence*, 299; 'Freud and the Scene of Writing', in *Writing and Difference*, 252–3.

All these differences in the production of the trace may be reinterpreted as moments of deferring. In accordance with a motif which will continue to dominate Freud's thinking, this movement is described as the effort of life to protect itself by *deferring* a dangerous investment, that is, by constituting a reserve (*Vorrat*). The threatening expenditure or presence are deferred with the help of breaching or repetition. Is this not already the detour (*Aufschub*) which institutes the relation of pleasure to reality (*Beyond [the Pleasure Principle]*, already quoted)? Is it not already death at the origin of a life which can defend itself against death only through an *economy* of death, through deferment, repetition, reserve? For repetition does not *happen* to an initial impression; its possibility is already there, in the resistance offered *the first time* by the psychical neurones. Resistance itself is possible only if the opposition of forces lasts and is repeated at the beginning.[35]

For Lacan, repetition is produced by the 'lack of being', while for Derrida, it is the *resistance* during the breaching that leads to the repetition. Resistance limits the permeability of the exciting amount, defers the investment, and causes repetition. Derrida finds here a dominant motif in *Beyond the Pleasure Principle* in which Freud writes: 'the aim of all life is death', but 'the living organism struggles most energetically against events (dangers, in fact) which might help it to attain its life's aim rapidly — by a kind of short-circuit [*auf kurzem Wege (durch Kurzschluß sozusagen)*]'. Here we recognize 'a lengthening of the road to death [*eine Verlängerung des Todesweges*]'.[36] Deferral of investment under the effect of resistance is 'the effort of life to protect itself by *deferring* a dangerous investment'. In this sense, the *différance* 'constitutes the essence of life'.[37]

It is now possible for us to understand Derrida's fundamental strategy in his interpretation of Freud: reading Freudian economics according to that of *différance* and resistance. To qualify this Freudian system, he would later use the term 'restance' (= rest and resistance). The system of inscription such as writing and trace signifies, for Derrida, that of *différance* and resistance. The 'lack' is not to be found in this system. Life

---

35 Ibid., 300–1; 253–4. Translation modified.

36 *Jenseits des Lustprinzips*, in *Gesammelte Werke*, Bd. XIII, 41–2; *Beyond the Pleasure Principle*, in *Standard Edition*, Vol. XVIII, 38–40.

37 « Freud et la scène de l'écriture », in *L'écriture et la différence*, 302; 'Freud and the Scene of Writing', in *Writing and Difference*, 255.

resists death, and death is deferred. Memory as memory-trace resists
'lack', and meaning is deferred. It is from this perspective that we will
interpret Derrida's 'Le facteur de la vérité'.

In this extremely dense text, Derrida constantly questions Lacan's
thesis that 'a letter always arrives at its destination'. But why does the
letter *always* arrive at its destination? What supports the effectiveness of
this thesis is the 'singularity' and 'materiality' of the signifier, namely the
indivisibility of the letter ('Cut a letter in small pieces, and it remains the
letter that it is'[38]):

> Now, for the signifier to be kept in its letter and thus to make its
> return, it is necessary that in its letter it does not admit 'partition', that
> one cannot say *some* letter [de la lettre], but only a letter, letters, the
> letter (p. 23–24). If it were divisible, it could always be lost en route.
> To protect against this possible loss the statement about the 'material-
> ity of the signifier', that is, about the signifier's indivisible singularity,
> is constructed. *This 'materiality', deduced from an indivisibility found
> nowhere, in fact corresponds to an idealization.* Only the ideality of a
> letter resists destructive division. 'Cut a letter in small pieces, and it
> remains the letter it is': since this cannot be said of empirical material-
> ity, it must imply an ideality (the intangibility of a self-identity displac-
> ing itself without alteration). This alone permits the singularity of the
> letter to be maintained. If this ideality is not the content of meaning,
> it must be either a certain ideality of the signifier (what is identifiable
> in its form to the extent that it can be distinguished from its empirical
> events and re-editions), or the *'point de capiton'* which staples the
> signifier to the signified. The latter hypothesis conforms more closely
> to the system. This system is in fact the system of the ideality of the
> signifier.[39]

The 'materiality of the signifier' designates the 'signifier's indivisible singularity', which is not 'empirical materiality', but in fact an 'ideality' ('lack'). It
is the singularity and indivisibility of the signifier that allows the letter to
maintain a transcendental position, which allows it to organize all the

38 « Le séminaire sur 'La Lettre volée' », in *Écrits*, 24; 'Seminar on "The Purloined
Letter"', in *Écrits: The Complete Edition*, 16.
39 « Le facteur de la vérité », in *La carte postale*, 492; 'Le facteur de la vérité', in *The
Post Card*, 464.

other signifiers under the effect of 'lack'. In this sense, the 'phallus' is, as a transcendental signifier, the '*point de capiton*' which hooks all signifiers to the signifier of 'castration-truth'. On the other hand, if the letter is 'divisible', the organization of desire by the 'singular' signifier is not established. The signifying chain then becomes multiple and the transcendental system of lack dissolves. Derrida writes as follows:

> The remaining structure of the letter is that — contrary to what the Seminar says in its last words ('what the "purloined letter", that is, the not delivered letter [*lettre en souffrance*] means is that a letter always arrives at its destination') — a letter can always not arrive at its destination. Its 'materiality' and 'topology' are due to its divisibility, its always possible partition. It can always be fragmented without return, and the system of the symbolic, of castration, of the signifier, of the truth, of the contract, etc., always attempts to protect the letter from this fragmentation [. . .]. Not that the letter never arrives at its destination, but it belongs to the structure of the letter to be capable, always, of not arriving. And without this threat (breach of contract, division or multiplication, the separation without return from the phallus which was begun for a moment by the Queen, i.e. by every 'subject'), the circuit of the letter would not even have begun. But with this threat, the circuit can always not finish. Here dissemination threatens the law of the signifier and of castration as the contract of truth. It *broaches/breaches* [*entame*] the unity of the signifier, that is, of the phallus.[40]

Here Derrida opposes the Lacanian thesis against another: 'a letter can always not arrive at its destination'. By sticking to the *metaphoricity* of the sentence,[41] we can interpret it at least in two different ways.

---

40 Ibid., 472; 443–4. Translation modified.

41 On the role of metaphor in philosophical discourse, see Jacques Derrida, « La mythologie blanche », in *Marges — de la philosophie*, Minuit, 1972; 'White Mythology', in *Margins of Philosophy*, Harvester Press, 1982. In this text, Derrida evokes a 'self-destruction of metaphor': the 'self-destruction of metaphor thus resembles the philosophical one to the point of being taken for it. [. . .] This self-destruction still has the form of a generalization, but this time it is no longer a question of extending and confirming a philosopheme, but rather, of unfolding it without limit, and wresting its borders of propriety from it. And consequently to explode the reassuring opposition of the metaphoric and the proper, the opposition in which the one and the other have never done anything but reflect and refer to each other in their radiance' (323; 270–1). In this chapter, we will see that Derrida varies the metaphor of the post ('letter',

1) The (anti-)Lacanian interpretation[42]

If the Lacanian thesis is based on the indivisibility of the letter, what supports the Derridian thesis is the divisibility of the letter, 'its always possible partition'. The divisibility of the letter or of the 'phallus' threatens the stability of the transcendental system itself that organizes desire through the singular signifier (lack). In 'Envois' (1980), Derrida designates the 'fatal partition' or the 'capacity not to arrive [*pouvoir-ne-pas-arriver*]'[43] of the letter as a 'chance' or '*tukhē*':

> Finally a chance, if you will, if you yourself can, and if you have it, the chance (*tukhē*, fortune, this is what I mean, good fortune, good fate: us). The mischance (the mis-address) of this chance is that in order *to be able* not to arrive [pouvoir *ne pas arriver*], it must bear within itself a force and a structure, a straying of the destination, such that it *must* also not arrive in any way. Even in arriving (always to some 'subject'), the letter takes itself away *from the arrival / at arrival* [*se soustrait* à l'arrivée]. It arrives elsewhere, always several times. You can no longer take hold of it. It is the structure of the letter (as post card, in other words the fatal partition that it must support) which demands this, I have said it elsewhere, delivered to a *facteur* subject to the same law. The letter demands this, right here, and you too, you demand it.[44]

Recall that *tukhē* signifies, in Lacan, a traumatic encounter with 'the unassimilable' (the real), which brings the 'lack' to the subject.[45] In this sense, the Lacanian *tukhē* constitutes a motor capable of constructing the transcendental system of lack, namely the subject

---

'destination') in many ways. It is not just a philosophical game. By 'unfolding it without limit' the metaphor of the post and by tearing off 'its borders of property', he deconstructs 'the most rigorous philosophy of psychoanalysis', namely that of Lacan. It is a philosophical practice to shake it from the interior of the transcendental system of lack.

42 This reading is suggested by the following decisive work: Hiroki Azuma, *Sonzaironteki, Yūbinteki: Jakku Derida ni tsuite* [*Ontological, Postal: On Jacques Derrida*], Shinchō-sha, 1998. Here we develop his reading of Derrida under the aspect of the 'inscription' of drive.

43 « Le facteur de la vérité », in *La carte postale*, 517; 'Le facteur de la vérité', in *The Post Card*, 489.

44 « Envois », in *La carte postale*, 135; 'Envois', in *The Post Card*, 123–4.

45 See *Le séminaire*, Livre XI, « Les quatre concepts fondamentaux de la psychanalyse », 54–5; *The Seminar*, Book XI, 'The Four Fundamental Concepts of Psychoanalysis', 55.

itself. On the other hand, the Derridian *tukhē* threatens, as a 'chance' or a 'capacity not to arrive', this transcendental system under the effect of the 'fatal partition' of the letter, of the 'phallus'. It is precisely the *Unheimliche* which threatens the stability of the transcendental system.[46] Here, we must ask a more fundamental question: what is the 'signifier' in Lacan?

In his seminar on 'The Ethics of Psychoanalysis', Lacan compares the signifier to the representative-representation [*Vorstellungsrepräsentanz*].[47] According to his own reference, let us consult Freud's 'The Unconscious' (1915): 'A drive can never become an object of consciousness — only the representation that represents the drive can [*nur die Vorstellung, die ihn repräsentiert*]. Even in the unconscious, moreover, a drive cannot be represented otherwise than by a representation. If the drive did not attach itself to a representation or manifest itself as an affective state, we could know nothing about it'.[48] The *Vorstellungsrepräsentanz* thus 'represents' the drive in the unconscious. In other words, it 'inscribes' the drive in the unconscious.[49] The drive only exists through this inscription, this 'representation', since it is neither psychic nor somatic: it is the concept of demarcation between the psychic and the somatic.[50] On the other hand, this inscription is at the very origin of the formation of the unconscious. Here is what Freud writes on this subject in 'Repression' (1915): 'We have reason to assume that there is a primal repression [*Urverdrängung*], a first phase of repression, which consists in the psychical (representative-) representation of the drive [*(Vorstellungs-) Repräsentanz des Triebes*] being denied entrance into the conscious. With this a *fixation* is established; the representation in question persists unaltered from then

---

46 On the importance of the *Unheimliche* in Derridian philosophy, See Sarah Kofman, « Un philosophe 'unheimlich' », in *Lectures de Derrida*, Galilée, 1984.

47 *Le séminaire*, Livre VII, « L'éthique de la psychanalyse », 75–6; *The Seminar*, Book VII, 'The Ethics of Psychoanalysis', 61.

48 Sigmund Freud, 'Das Unbewußte', in *Gesammelte Werke*, Bd. X, 275–6; 'The Unconscious', in *Standard Edition*, Vol. XIV, 177. Translation modified.

49 *Vocabulaire de la psychanalyse*, 414.

50 Sigmund Freud, *Drei Abhandlungen zur Sexualtheorie*, in *Gesammelte Werke*, Bd. V, 67; *Three Essays on Sexuality*, in *Standard Edition*, Vol. VII, 168: 'By a "drive" is provisionally to be understood the psychic representation [*die psychischen Repräsentanz*] of an endosomatic, continuously flowing source of stimulation, as contrasted with a "stimulus", produced by sporadic and external excitations. The drive is therefore one of the concepts of demarcation between the psychic and the somatic [*Trieb ist so einer der Begriffe der Abgrenzung des Seelischen vom Körperlichen*]'. Translation modified.

onwards and the drive remains attached to it.'[51] The mechanism of the organization of the unconscious (the primal repression) therefore means repressing the representative-representation of the drive and inscribing it in the unconscious. From there, we could say that Lacan considers as a 'castration' this primal inscription [*Niederschrift*] of the drive in the unconscious by calling 'phallus' the representative-representation inscribed there. However, for Derrida, there is not a single primal inscription, but, rather, multiple *inscriptions* [*Niederschriften*].[52] These multiple inscriptions will threaten the singularity of the 'phallus' and can disrupt the order of the transcendental system of lack. He calls these inscriptions 'dissemination'.[53] It is strictly in this sense that dissemination '*broaches/ breaches* [*entame*] the unity of the signifier, namely, of the phallus'. It is the 'change', the contingency or the *Unheimliche* which threatens the stability of the system itself and which can disturb it. With this perspective, we will return later to the problem of the alteration of structure as a static system.[54]

2) The Freudian interpretation

The Derridean thesis ('a letter can always not arrive at its destination') signifies the 'remaining structure of the letter' or its 'internal drifting'.

---

51 Sigmund Freud, 'Die Verdrängung', in *Gesammelte Werke*, Bd. X, 250; 'Repression', in *Standard Edition*, Vol. XIV, 148. Translation modified.

52 See, for example, « Envois », in *La carte postale*, 73–4; 'Envois', in *The Post Card*, 66: 'If the post (technology, position, "metaphysics") is announced at the "first" *envoi*, then there is no longer A metaphysics, etc. (I will try to say this one more time and otherwise), nor even AN *envoi*, but *envois* without destination. For to coordinate the different epochs, halts, determinations, in a word the entire history of Being with a destination of Being is perhaps the most outlandish postal lure. There is not even the post or the *envoi*, there are posts and *envois*'.

53 Jacques Derrida, « La double séance », in *La dissémination*, Seuil, 1972, 300, note 56; 'The Double Session', in *Dissemination*, Athlone Press, 1981, 268, note 67. René Major tries to find the Derridian thematic of 'dissemination' in Lacan's seminar on '*Encore*' (see René Major, *Lacan avec Derrida*, Flammarion, coll. « Champ », 2001, in particular 142–5), but the privileged position of the signifier never changes in Lacan, even after the introduction of the formula of sexual difference ('there is no sexual relation'). For example, as Major reminds us (142), Lacan said in his seminar: 'it would have been better to qualify the signifier with the category of the contingent' (*Le séminaire*, Livre XX, « Encore », Seuil, 1975, 41; *The Seminar*, Book XX, 'Encore', Norton, 1988, 40. Translation modified); however, this 'category of the contingent' designates nothing other than the creation *ex nihilo* (from nothing, namely from the lack) of the signifier. In other words, *the signifier is never disseminated in Lacanian theory.*

54 We will discuss this problem in sections 4.5 and 4.6.

The letter can remain as 'restance' (rest and resistance) in its journey and drift ('its capacity not to arrive torments it with an internal drifting').[55] This is a mechanism by which the letter's path is diverted and delayed. We must interpret here the 'destination' to mean 'destiny', and the 'Schicken [envoi/sending]' 'Geschick [destiny]': 'to speak of post for Geschick, to say that every envoi is postal, that the destinal posts itself'.[56] In other words, we must read the term 'destiny' as 'death':

> Genet said that his theatre was addressed to the dead and I take it like that on the train in which I am going writing you without end. The addressees are dead, the destination is death: no, not in the sense of S. or p.'s predication, according to which we would be destined to die, no, not in the sense in which to arrive at our destination, for us mortals, is to end by dying. No, the very idea of destination includes analytically the end of death, like a predicate (p) included in the subject (S) of destination, the addressee or the addressor. And you are, my love unique
> the proof, the living proof precisely, that a letter can always not arrive at its destination, and that therefore it never arrives. And this is really how it is, it is not a misfortune, that's life, living life, beaten down, tragedy, by the still surviving life.[57]

If the destination of the letter 'is death', we can therefore affirm that the 'remaining structure of the letter' or its 'internal drifting' is the mechanism of 'resistance' and 'différance' which defers death as 'destination' and 'dangerous investment'. 'To post is to send by "counting" with a halt, a relay, or a suspensive delay, the place of a mailman, the possibility of going astray and of forgetting (not of repression, which is a moment of keeping, but of forgetting)',[58] writes Derrida. Posting is therefore the mechanism of delay and différance of the drive, of relay and connection between drives. Based on this metaphorical series, we are going to reinterpret Beyond the Pleasure Principle.

---

55 « Le facteur de la vérité », in La carte postale, 517; 'Le facteur de la vérité', in The Post Card, 489.
56 « Envois », in La carte postale, 72; 'Envois', in The Post Card, 64.
57 Ibid., 39; 33–4.
58 Ibid., 73; 65.

4.3 Primacy of masochism

In *Beyond the Pleasure Principle* (1920), Freud develops a 'speculation [*Spekulation*]': the hypothesis of the death drive. But why does he call it 'speculation'? This certainly does not mean that the death drive is reduced to a simple unobservable and unverifiable hypothesis, since it is based on 'observed material'[59] — that is, on the compulsion to repeat. In 'The Economic Problem of Masochism' (1924), he identifies the death drive with masochism:

> The existence of a masochistic tendency in the human life of drive [*menschlichen Triebleben*] may justly be described as mysterious from the economic point of view [*als ökonomisch rätselhaft*]. For if psychic processes [*seelischen Vorgänge*] are governed by the pleasure principle in such a way that their first aim is the avoidance of unpleasure and the obtaining of pleasure, masochism is incomprehensible. If pain and unpleasure can be not simply warnings but actually aims, the pleasure principle is paralysed — it is as though the watchman over our mental life were put out of action by a drug.
>
> Thus masochism appears to us in the light of a great danger, which is in no way true of its counterpart, sadism. We are tempted to call the pleasure principle the watchman over our life rather than merely over our mental life. But in that case we are faced with the task of investigating the relationship of the pleasure principle to the two classes of drives which we have distinguished — the death drives and the erotic (libidinal) life drives; and we cannot proceed further in our consideration of the problem of masochism till we have accomplished that task.[60]

According to Freud, the masochistic tendency is 'economically enigmatic', since it is contrary to the pleasure principle that is said to dominate 'psychic processes'. Within the framework of his first theory of drives (formulated in the years 1910–15), Freud relied on a dichotomy: ego drives and sexual drives. He defined the former as self-preservation

---

59 *Jenseits des Lustprinzips*, in *Gesammelte Werke*, Bd. XIII, 64; *Beyond the Pleasure Principle*, in *Standard Edition*, Vol. XVIII, 59.

60 Sigmund Freud, 'Das ökonomische Problem des Masochismus', in *Gesammelte Werke*, Bd. XIII, 371; 'The Economic Problem of Masochism', in *Standard Edition*, Vol. XIX, 159. Translation modified.

drives and the latter as object-directed libidinal drives[61] and saw both as under the mastery [*Herrschaft*] of the pleasure principle from the perspective of desire fulfilment [*Wunscherfüllung*]. Even sadism is found, from this same perspective, under the pleasure principle (the fulfilment of the drive for mastery). However, in the death drive and masochism, pain and displeasure can be 'aims'. Freud constructs his psychoanalytic theory under the mastery of the pleasure principle, which is, so to speak, the 'first principle' of psychoanalysis. But masochism totally contradicts this proposition. It therefore appears 'in the light of a great danger' for psychoanalytic theory itself. We must then reflect on the 'destiny' of the 'enigmatic [*rätselhaften*]' phenomenon of masochism in Freudian theory.

In '*Triebe und Triebschicksale* [Drives and their Destiny]' (1914), Freud characterizes the 'reversal into the opposite' and the 'turning round upon the subject's own self' as the 'destiny of drive'. In sadism and masochism, the 'reversal into the opposite' corresponds to that of a drive 'from activity to passivity', and the 'turning round upon the subject's own self' corresponds to the 'change of object' and the reversal on the subject's own self. Masochism is precisely 'sadism turned round upon the subject's own ego'.[62] Freud describes these two processes thusly:

> In the case of the pair of opposites, sadism–masochism, the process may be represented as follows:
>
> (a) Sadism consists in the exercise of violence or power upon some other person as object.
>
> (b) This object is abandoned and replaced by the subject's self. With the turning round upon the self the change from an active to a passive aim of drive is also effected.
>
> (c) An extraneous person is once more sought as object; this person, in consequence of the alteration which has taken place in the aim, has to take over the role of the subject.
>
> Case (c) is what is commonly termed masochism. Here, too, satisfaction follows along the path of the original sadism [*auf dem Wege*

---

61 *Vocabulaire de la psychanalyse*, 380–1.

62 Sigmund Freud, 'Triebe und Triebschicksal', in *Gesammelte Werke*, Bd. X, 219–20; 'Instincts and Their Vicissitudes', in *Standard Edition*, Vol. XIV, 126–7. Translation modified.

des ursprünglichen Sadismus], the passive ego placing itself back in phantasy in its first role, which has now in fact been taken over by the extraneous subject. Whether there is, besides this, a more direct masochistic satisfaction is highly doubtful. An original masochism, not derived from sadism in the described manner, seems not to be met with [*Ein ursprünglicher Masochismus, der nicht auf die beschriebene Art aus dem Sadismus entstanden wäre, scheint nicht vorzukommen*].[63]

Freud specifies that masochism is 'derived from sadism' in such a way that the 'object is abandoned and replaced by the subject's self' and that 'the turning round upon the self the change from an active to a passive aim of drive is [. . .] effected'. From this, he deduces that an original masochism, not derived from sadism, does not seem to exist. We must emphasize here that this deduction has a precise meaning: by taking masochism for a phenomenon derived from sadism, he can keep mastery of the pleasure principle as the first principle of his psychoanalytic theory.

However, in 'The Economic Problem of Masochism' (1924), Freud proposes a completely opposite hypothesis to the former: he asserts that 'an original masochism' exists:

If one is prepared to overlook a little inexactitude, it may be said that the death drive which is operative in the organism — original sadism [*Ursadismus*] — is identical with masochism. After the main portion of it has been transposed outwards on to objects, there remains inside, as a residuum of it, the original erotogenic masochism [*eigentlich erogene Masochismus*], which on the one hand has become a component of the libido and, on the other, still has the self as its object. This masochism would thus be evidence of, and a remainder from, the phase of development in which the coalescence, which is so important for life, between the death drive and Eros took place. We shall not be surprised to hear that in certain circumstances the sadism, or destruction drive, which has been directed outwards, projected, can be once more introjected, turned inwards, and in this way regress to its earlier situation. If this happens, a secondary masochism is produced, which is added to the original masochism [*Er ergibt dann

---

63 Ibid., 220–1; 127–8.

den sekundären Masochismus, der sich zum ursprünglichen hinzuaddiert].[64]

Here, Freud calls the death drive 'original masochism' — 'if one is prepared to overlook a little inexactitude'.[65] The 'original masochism' can be turned outwards (sadism), and again introjected, turned inwards, thus regressing to its previous situation (secondary masochism). In this modification of the hypothesis, the assumption of a 'beyond' of the pleasure principle plays a determining role. In *Beyond the Pleasure Principle*, Freud affirms: 'masochism could also be a primary [*der Masochismus könnte auch (. . .) ein primärer sein*]'.[66] In other words, the 'speculative' hypothesis of the primacy of masochism is invoked by the very supposition of a 'beyond' — that is, of the death drive. This drive will therefore be found 'beyond' the first principle of psychoanalytic theory, beyond the mastery of the pleasure principle. It is, so to speak, 'beyond' psychoanalytic theory. It is in this sense that Freud calls the death drive a 'speculation'.

The introduction of the concept of the 'death drive' makes it possible to formulate the hypothesis of the primacy of masochism. But what exactly does 'original masochism' or the primacy of masochism mean?

---

64 Sigmund Freud, 'Das ökonomische Problem des Masochismus', in *Gesammelte Werke*, Bd. XIII, 377; 'The Economic Problem of Masochism', in *Standard Edition*, Vol. XIX, 164. Translation modified.

65 One could say, to be more precise, that the 'original masochism' consists of the death drive. In this text, Freud defines the death drive as a return to 'inorganic stability [*anorganischen Stabilität*]' which does not involve any sexuality; and 'original masochism' is rather identical to 'erotogenic masochism'. The death drive, 'with the help of the sexual co-excitation [. . .] becomes libidinally bound there. It is in this portion that we have to recognize the original, erotogenic masochism [*ursprünglichen, erogene Masochismus*]' (ibid., 376; 163-4. Translation modified). This 'original erotogenic masochism' is strictly differentiated from secondary masochism, which is sadism 'regress[ed] to its earlier situation'. We define here 'original masochism' as an original self-destruction drive, corresponding to erotogenic masochism, which is therefore accompanied by sexuality and which is composed of the death drive. For example, quoting 'The Economic Problem of Masochism', Jean Laplanche remarks this 'co-excitation' produces sexuality 'if it is true that "we are never dealing with the death drives or the life drives in the pure state, but always in various mixtures of these drives [. . .]". It is indeed one of these alloys, the "original erotogenic masochism", that is first for us, and this erotogenic masochism emerges through the phenomenon of "co-excitation"' (Jean Laplanche, *Vie et mort en psychanalyse*, Flammarion, 1970, 147; *Life and Death in Psychoanalysis*, 96. Johns Hopkins University Press, 1976, Translation modified).

66 *Jenseits des Lustprinzips*, in *Gesammelte Werke*, Bd. XIII, 59; *Beyond the Pleasure Principle*, in *Standard Edition*, Vol. XVIII, 55. Translation modified.

Or, to put it another way, why can self-aggression be 'primary' in the human subject?

Let us now reflect on the phenomenon of the 'compulsion to repeat'. According to Freud, 'the compulsion to repeat also recalls [*wiederbringt*] from the past experiences *which include no possibility of pleasure*, and which can never, even long ago, have brought satisfaction even to drive impulses which have since been repressed'.[67] It obliges the subject to passively 'repeat [*wiederholen*] the repressed material as a contemporary experience instead of [. . .] remembering [*erinnern*] it' voluntarily.[68] In relation to the compulsion to repeat, Freud discusses the 'protection against stimuli [*Reizschutz*]' in Chapter IV of *Beyond*. The living organism 'is supplied with its own store of energy and must above all endeavour to preserve the special modes of transformation of energy operating in it against the effects threatened by the enormous energies at work in the external world — effects which tend towards a levelling out of them and hence towards destruction'.[69] To this end, it possesses protection against stimuli and defends itself from 'destructive' external energies. However, 'traumatic excitations' are 'powerful enough to break through the protection'; and 'an event as an external trauma is bound to provoke a disturbance on a large scale in the functioning of the organism's energy and to set in motion every defensive measure'. In such cases, 'the pleasure principle is for the moment put out of action [*außer Kraft gesetzt*]'.[70] When 'every defensive measure' is set in motion, control of the pleasure principle is *momentarily suspended* ('put out of action: *außer Kraft gesetzt*'). We can detect here a reserve on Freud's part: even if the beyond of the pleasure principle is released, mastery of the pleasure principle, this first principle of psychoanalysis, is only suspended and does not collapse. But 'every defensive measure' certainly refers to the force of the 'beyond' as compulsion to repeat. By what mechanism, though, is 'every defensive measure' constituted against traumatic excitations? We will find that in the course of developing this reflection, Freud gradually removes the limit between the notions of pleasure/unpleasure.[71]

---

67 Ibid., 18; 20. Translation modified and our emphasis.

68 Ibid., 16; 18.

69 Ibid., 27; 27.

70 Ibid., 29; 29. Translation modified.

71 What is curious is that Freud's definition of 'pleasure' is itself very uncertain. The sensation of pleasure and unpleasure is, he writes, 'the most obscure and inaccessible region of psychic life': 'we would readily express our gratitude to any philosophical or

In Chapter II of *Beyond*, he deals with the famous theme of the *'fort: da'*: a little child (his grandson) throws a reel over the edge of his curtained cot, where it disappears, while that he pronounces *'fort* [gone]'), he then pulled the reel out of the cot again by the string and hailed its reappearance with a joyful *'da* [there]'.[72] Interpreting this child's play scene, Freud continually returns to the pleasure principle. He notices, identifying the reel with the mother of the child, that *'fort'* means the 'painful experience', namely the mother's absence, and *'da'* means the mother's 'joyful return'. At that point, he asks: 'How then does his repetition of this distressing experience as a game fit in with the pleasure principle?'.[73] His response is the following: the child 'was in a *passive* situation — he was overpowered by the experience; but, by repeating it, unpleasurable though it was, as a game, he took on an *active* part'.[74] In other words, the *'fort: da'* is the voluntary and active repetition of the 'painful experience'. He deduces then that this game would come from the 'drive for mastery [*Bemächtigungstrieb*]' (of the painful experience) or from the 'drive to revenge [*Racheimpuls*]' his mother ('All right, then, go away! I don't need you. I'm sending you away myself').[75] From this, Freud concludes: 'the child may [. . .] only have been able to repeat his unpleasant experience in play because the repetition carried along with it *a yield of pleasure of another sort but none the less a direct*

---

psychological theory which was able to inform us of the signification [*Bedeutung*] of the feelings of pleasure and unpleasure [. . .]. But on this point we are, alas, offered nothing to our purpose' (i.e., the absence of a qualitative definition of 'pleasure'). He continues: 'since we cannot avoid contact with it, the least rigid hypothesis [*die lockerste Annahme*], it seems to me, will be the best'. Hence he decides to 'relate pleasure and unpleasure to the quantity of excitation that is present in the mind but is not in any way 'bound'; and to relate them in such a manner that unpleasure *corresponds* to an increase in the quantity of excitation and pleasure to a diminution'. He uses the word 'correspond', which does not mean a 'directly proportional' relation: 'What we are implying by this is not a *simple relation* between the strength of the feelings of pleasure and unpleasure and the corresponding modifications in the quantity of excitation; least of all [. . .] are we suggesting any *directly proportional* ratio' (ibid., 3–4; 7–8. Translation modified and our emphasis). In other words, in this text, even in Freudian theory, neither the 'qualitative' definition (philosophical or psychological), nor the 'qualitative' (from the economic point of view) of 'pleasure' are guaranteed. See Jacques Derrida, « Spéculer — sur Freud », in *La carte postale*, 294–5; 'To Speculate — on Freud', in *The Post Card*, 275–6.

72 *Jenseits des Lustprinzips*, in *Gesammelte Werke*, Bd. XIII, 12; *Beyond the Pleasure Principle*, in *Standard Edition*, Vol. XVIII, 15.

73 Ibid., 13; 15.

74 Ibid., 13; 16.

75 Ibid., 14; 16. Translation modified.

one.[76] This 'yield of pleasure of another sort but none the less a direct one' comes from the fulfilment of the 'drive for mastery' or the 'drive to revenge', namely from the drive to aggression turned outwards. Freud insists here on the idea that this repetition of the game is reconciled 'with the pleasure principle'. However, if we apply the schema of 'The Economic Problem of Masochism' to it, what appears here is rather the outwardly turned death drive thus becoming a sadistic drive.

The compulsion to repeat is distinguished from the '*fort: da*' game insofar as it passively repeats the painful experience. In this repetition, the death drive, which is 'more original [*ursprünglicher*]' than mastery of the pleasure principle, operates without reserve. After discussing the protection against stimuli, Freud puts forward a hypothesis in Chapter IV:

> If dreams of accident neurosis so regularly lead patients back to the situation of the accident, they are certainly not thereby at the service of the fulfilment of wishes, even if the hallucinatory production of wishes became their function under the domination of the pleasure principle. We may assume, rather, that dreams are here helping to carry out another task, which must be accomplished before the dominance of the pleasure principle can even begin. These dreams are endeavouring to master the stimulus retrospectively, by developing the anxiety whose omission was the cause of the traumatic neurosis. They thus afford us a view of a function of the psychic apparatus which, though it does not contradict the pleasure principle, is nevertheless independent of it and seems to be more original [*ursprünglicher*] than the purpose of gaining pleasure and avoiding unpleasure.[77]

Dreams of accident neurosis (i.e., the compulsion to repeat) 'are endeavouring to master the stimulus retrospectively, by developing the anxiety'. In Chapter II, Freud distinguishes 'anxiety [*Angst*]' from 'fright [*Schreck*]'. The term 'anxiety [*Angst*]' refers to 'a particular state of expecting the danger or preparing for it, even though it may be an unknown one'; the term 'fright [*Schreck*]' refers to 'the state a person gets into when he has run into danger without being prepared for it'; '[t]here is something

---

76 Ibid. Our emphasis.
77 Ibid., 32; 32. Translation modified.

about anxiety that protects its subject against fright and so against fright-neuroses'.[78] In other words, it is because the subject is not preparing for a dangerous situation (a lack of anxiety) that he is seized with fear, with traumatic impressions. Against these impressions, the compulsion to repeat seeks to form anguish retroactively: it therefore aims to ensure 'the psychic binding [*psychischen Bindung*] of traumatic impressions'.[79]

In Chapter V, Freud finally recognizes that the game of '*fort: da*' responds to the same mechanism as the compulsion to repeat: 'In the case of children's play we seemed to see that children repeat even unpleasant experience [*auch das unlustvolle Erlebnis*] for the additional reason that they acquire a much more radical mastery of strong impression [*eine weit gründlichere Bewältigung des starken Eindruckes*] thoroughly by being active than they could by merely experiencing it passively. Each new repetition seems to strengthen the mastery they are in search of '.[80] The repetition of '*fort: da*' seeks to actively bind the 'strong impression' that comes from the 'unpleasant experience' (the absence of the mother). In other words, the repetition of the unpleasant experience itself acts to protect the subject against traumatic impressions. What is unleashed here is an *original* and *radical* function of the repetition itself,[81] which has nothing to do with the 'yield of pleasure of another sort but none the less a direct one'.

The compulsion to repeat in traumatic neurosis signals the appearance of the death drive — it is the death drive as 'original masochism'. Here, we are led to point out a curious thing: it is by forming 'anxiety' and by binding traumatic impressions that the compulsion to repeat, an appearance of the death drive, defends the subject against traumatic excitations. This means that the death drive 'protects' the subject. But what mechanism makes this paradoxical function possible?

Let us refer to *The Freudian Body* by Leo Bersani. In this essay, he notices a passage in *Three Essays on Sexuality* concerning 'The Sources of Infantile Sexuality': 'It is easy to establish, whether by contemporary observation or by subsequent research, that all comparatively intense

---

78 Ibid., 10; 12–13.
79 Ibid., 33; 33. Translation modified.
80 Ibid., 36; 35. Translation modified.
81 On the radical power of repetition itself which is absolutely independent of direct pleasure, see Gilles Deleuze, *Présentation de Sacher-Masoch*, 104; 'Coldness and Cruelty', in *Masochism*, 120.

affective processes, including even frightening excitations [*die schreck-haften Erregungen*], spill over into sexuality [*auf die Sexualität übergreifen*]';[82] he then quotes another passage from the conclusive Summary: 'sexual excitation arises as a by-product [*als Nebenprodukt*], as it were, of a large number of processes that occur in the organism, as soon as they reach a certain degree of intensity, and most especially of any relatively powerful emotion, even though it is of a distressing nature [*painlicher Natur*]'.[83] This means that intensive affections such as 'frightening excitations' [*die schreckhaften Erregungen*], or even traumatic impressions become sources of sexual excitations ('libidinal co-excitation when there is tension due to pain and unpleasure [*libidinöse Miterregung bei Schmerz- und Unlustspannung*]').[84] In *Beyond*, Freud illustrates this proposition as follows: 'the mechanical violence of the trauma would liberate a quantity of sexual excitation which, owing to the lack of preparation for anxiety, would have a traumatic effect'.[85] From this perspective, Bersani interprets the Freudian thesis:

> In passages such as these, Freud appears to be moving toward the position that the pleasurable unpleasurable tension of sexual excitement occurs when the body's 'normal' range of sensation is exceeded, and when the organization of the self is momentarily disturbed by sensations or affective processes somehow 'beyond' those compatible with psychic organization. [. . .] Sexuality would be that which is intolerable to the structured self. [. . .] Sexuality is a particularly human phenomenon in the sense that its very genesis may depend on a *décalage*, or gap, in human life between the quantities of stimuli to which we are exposed and the development of ego structures capable of resisting, or, in Freudian terms, of binding those stimuli. The *mystery* of sexuality is that we seek not only to get rid of this shattering tension but also to repeat, even to increase it. [. . .] Sexuality — at

---

82 *Drei Abhandlungen zur Sexualtheorie*, in *Gesammelte Werke*, Bd. V, 104; *Three Essays on Sexuality*, in *Standard Edition*, Vol. VII, 203. Translation modified. Quoted in Leo Bersani, *The Freudian Body*, Columbia University Press, 1986, 37.

83 Ibid., 134; 233. Quoted in *The Freudian Body*, 38.

84 'Das ökonomische Problem des Masochismus', in *Gesammelte Werke*, Bd. XIII, 375; 'The Economic Problem of Masochism', in *Standard Edition*, Vol. XIX, 163. Translation modified.

85 *Jenseits des Lustprinzips*, in *Gesammelte Werke*, Bd. XIII, 34; *Beyond the Pleasure Principle*, in *Standard Edition*, Vol. XVIII, 33.

least in the mode in which it is constituted — could be thought of as a tautology for masochism.[86]

Thus, 'that which is intolerable to the structured self' produces a pleasure/displeasure tension ('libidinal co-excitation'), namely 'sexuality', which seeks to repeat and increase itself. Bersani calls 'masochism' this process of sexual proliferation.[87] This allows us to interpret the mechanism of the compulsion to repeat: what produces the repetition of traumatic impressions is the mechanism of masochistic sexuality, which binds them. We can then understand why Freud called the death drive 'the original masochism'. Bersani affirms: 'masochism serves life'.[88] From this expression, we can say that *the death drive serves life*. 'Masochistic' sexuality, like the death drive, propels the compulsion to repeat; by this mechanism, the subject seeks to survive the trauma. It is a 'psychical strategy'[89] that adopts the subject threatened by the unforeseeable and inevitable traumatic excitations of the outside world.

But this 'psychical strategy' is extremely dangerous for the subject: it can bring death insofar as the subject seeks *jouissance* in the drive for self-destruction itself. However, it is necessary for the subject to survive the trauma. Here we are faced with an antinomy of the death drive. *The death drive is necessary for the survival of the subject, but it can give death to the subject* [donner la mort au sujet][90]. How can we resolve this antinomy?

---

86 *The Freudian Body*, 38–9.

87 In Lacanian theory, it corresponds to '*jouissance*'. In Lacan, '*jouissance*' is experienced in the 'second death' which appears in the drive for (self-)destruction and which one can never access. By interpreting the death drive as a destruction drive and not as a 'return to the inorganic', Lacan situates *jouissance* 'beyond the tendency to return to the inanimate' (*Le séminaire*, Livre VII, « L'éthique de la psychanalyse », 251; *The Seminar*, Book VII, 'Ethics of Psychoanalysis', 212. Translation modified). In other words, *jouissance* seeks the 'satisfaction' of the death drive, which can never be reached: 'The problem involved is that of *jouissance*, because *jouissance* presents itself as buried at the centre of a field and has the characteristics of inaccessibility, obscurity and opacity; moreover, the field is surrounded by a barrier which makes access to it difficult for the subject to the point of inaccessibility, because *jouissance* appears not purely and simply as the satisfaction of a need but as the satisfaction of a drive' (ibid., 247–8; 209). We appreciate most positively the Lacanian theory of 'second death' as well as that of '*jouissance*', a theorization at which Freud, who persisted in the mastery of the pleasure principle, could not arrive.

88 *The Freudian Body*, 39.

89 Ibid.

90 This expression, originally used by Derrida (*se donner la mort*: giving oneself death), has a double meaning: 'committing suicide' and 'sacrificing oneself for the other'. See Jacques Derrida, *Donner la mort*, Galilée, 1999, 26-7; *The Gift of Death*, University of Chicago Press, 1995, 10.

4.4 Detours of the drive

Let us go back to Derrida. In 'To Speculate — on Freud' (1975), he reflects on the relationship between the pleasure principle, the reality principle, and the death drive. In *Beyond*, he highlights the system of detour [*Umweg*] and the chain of drives.

Let us first examine the relationship between the pleasure principle and the reality principle. Freud writes in Chapter I of *Beyond*: 'We know that the pleasure principle is proper to a primary method of working on the part of the mental apparatus, but that, from the point of view of the self-preservation [*Selbstbehauptung*] of the organism among the difficulties of the external world, it is from the very outset inefficient and even highly dangerous. Under the influence of the ego's drives of self-preservation, the pleasure principle is relayed [*abgelöst*] by the *reality principle*. This latter principle does not abandon the intention of ultimately obtaining pleasure, but it nevertheless demands and carries into effect the delay of satisfaction [*Aufschub der Befriedigung*], the abandonment of a number of possibilities of gaining satisfaction and the temporary toleration of unpleasure as a step on the long indirect road to pleasure [*auf dem langen Umwege zur Lust*]'.[91] The pleasure principle is 'the method of working employed by the sexual drives, which are so hard to "educate [*erziehbaren*]"'[92] and whose satisfaction is often doomed to failure. The pleasure principle is then 'relayed by the reality principle'. It is in reading Freud that Derrida finds the movement of '*différance*' and 'detour':

> The reality principle imposes no definitive inhibition, no renunciation of pleasure, only a detour in order to defer enjoyment, the relay of a *différance* (*Aufschub*). On this 'long detour' (*auf dem langen Umwege zur Lust*) the pleasure principle submits itself, provisionally and to a certain extent, to its own lieutenant. The latter, as representative, slave, or informed disciple, the disciplined one who disciplines also plays the role of the preceptor in the master's service. As if the latter produced a *socius*, put in 'motion' an institution by signing a contract with 'discipline', with the assistant master or foreman who nevertheless does nothing but

---

91 *Jenseits des Lustprinzips*, in *Gesammelte Werke*, Bd. XIII, 6; *Beyond the Pleasure Principle*, in *Standard Edition*, Vol. XVIII, 10. Translation modified.
92 Ibid. Translation modified.

represent him. A false contract, a pure speculation, the simulacrum of an engagement which binds the lord only to himself, to his own modifica- tion, to himself modified. The master addresses to himself the text or the corpus of this simulated engagement via the detour of an institutional telecommunication. He *writes himself, sends himself* [*s'envoie*]; but if the length of the detour can no longer be mastered, and rather than its length its structure, then the return to (one)self is never certain, and without return to sender the engagement is forgotten to the very extent that it becomes undeniable, unshakable.[93]

The reality principle does not impose a renunciation of pleasure, but it 'defers' and 'diverts' the fulfilment of pleasure. Since the pleasure principle is 'extremely dangerous' for psychic life, it must be 'relayed' by the reality principle, by which the fulfilment of pleasure will be deferred, taking a 'long detour'. We note here the intervention of the Derridean thesis: 'a letter can always not arrive at its destination'. By relaying or modifying the pleasure principle to the reality principle, the 'destination' as the fulfil- ment of pleasure is infinitely deferred: the 'capacity not to arrive' of the letter (i.e., of the pleasure) always intervenes. For example, in 'Envois', the 'Pleasure Principle' (*Principe de Plaisir*: PP) is defined as the 'Postal Principle' (*Principe Postal*: PP), and the 'Reality Principle' (*Principe de Réalité*: PR) as the 'Poste Restante' (PR). The 'Poste Restante' denotes this 'capacity to not arrive' of the letter — that is, of the pleasure.[94]

We are now arriving at the death drive. Freud interpreted the compul- sion to repeat as an appearance of the death drive. The manifestations of a compulsion to repeat 'exhibit to a high degree a character of drive and, when they act in opposition to the pleasure principle, the demoniac character [*dämonischen Charakter*]'.[95] Regarding this 'demoniac' charac- ter of the compulsion to repeat, Derrida writes:

---

93 « Spéculer — sur Freud », in *La carte postale*, 301–2; 'To Speculate — on Freud', in *The Post Card*, 282–3. Translation modified.

94 « Envois », in *La carte postale*, 124; 'Envois', in *The Post Card*, 113: 'And of course, there is not only the *facteur de la verité, du tout*, there is not only the family scenes, the scene of inheritance, and the questioning of the "cause" of the analytic movement, etc., there is also, as you pointed out to me right away, the chance that must not be abused: the Reality Principle [*Principe de Realité*] (and who knows this better than us?) is the poste restante (PR) of the Postal Principle, I mean of the Pleasure Principle (PP). And this is demonstrable, with death at both ends'.

95 *Jenseits des Lustprinzips*, in *Gesammelte Werke*, Bd. XIII, 36; *Beyond the Pleasure Principle*, in *Standard Edition*, Vol. XVIII, 35.

The return of the demoniac, not far from the 'perpetual recurrence of the same thing' is in convoy with repetition beyond the PP. This will recur regularly from now on.

Truly speaking, there is not a return *of the* demoniac. The demon is that very thing which *returns* [revient] without having been called by the PP. The demon is the *revenance* which repeats its entrance, returning from one knows not where ('early infantile influences', says Freud), inherited from one knows not whom, but already persecutory, by means of the simple form of its return, indefatigably repetitive, independent of every apparent desire, *automatic*. Like Socrates' demon [. . .] this automaton returns without returning to anyone, it produces effects of ventriloquism without origin, without emission, and without addressee. It is only posted, the post in the 'pure' state, a kind of mailman [*facteur*] without destination. Tele — without telos. Finality without end, the beauty of the devil. It no longer obeys the subject whom it persecutes with its return. It no longer obeys the master, the name of the master being given to the subject constructed according to the economy of the PP, or to the PP it(him)self.[96]

The 'return of the demoniac' (death drive as a compulsion to repeat) is 'inherited from one knows not whom': it returns 'without returning to anyone', and it returns 'without origin, without emission and without addressee'. Derrida calls it 'the post in its "pure" state, a kind of mailman [*facteur*] without destination'. The post in the "pure" state without a destination will disturb the psychic apparatus which contains its own destination (fulfilment of desire) — even if it is deferred. The death drive as the return of the demoniac is the *Unheimliche*, which disturbs the psychic system. Derrida does not reduce this return of the demoniac to either the 'early infantile influences' (Freud) or 'castration' (Lacan), because the inscriptions [*Niederschriften*] of the drive in the unconscious are multiple: the *Unheimliche* is overdetermined by multiple inscriptions.

The death drive is the post in the 'pure' state, and the second *Umweg* intervenes to defer this dangerous drive. In Chapter V of *Beyond*, Freud discusses 'excitations from within', against which the protection against

---

96 « Spéculer — sur Freud », in *La carte postale*, 363; 'To Speculate — on Freud', in *The Post Card*, 341–2. Translation modified.

stimuli is powerless: 'The most abundant sources of this internal excitation are what are described as the organism's drives'. Protections against stimuli cannot defend the psychic apparatus against these drives; therefore, 'these transmissions of stimuli [*diese Reizübertragungen*] [. . .] often occasion economic disturbances comparable with traumatic neuroses'.[97] The problem of the death drive is extended here to that of drive in general. Elaborating on the relationship between drive and the compulsion to repeat, Freud writes: 'It seems that a drive is an urge [*Drang*] inherent in organic life to restore [*zur Wiederherstellung*] an earlier state of things'.[98] The 'earlier state of things' means 'the inorganic [*das Anorganische*]' — namely death. In other words, it is death which constitutes the final goal of the drive.[99] The mechanism of the 'detour' identified here (detours leading to death: *Umwege zum Tode*)[100] defers death as 'the aim of all life'. As Freud details in Chapter V of *Beyond*:

> Since all drive impulses have the unconscious systems as their point of impact, it is hardly an innovation to say that they obey the primary process. Again, it is easy to identify the primary psychical process with Breuer's freely mobile investments and the secondary process with changes in his bound or tonic investment. If so, it would be the task of the higher strata of the psychic apparatus to bind [*binden*] the drive excitation reaching the primary process. A failure to effect this binding would provoke a disturbance analogous to a traumatic neurosis; and only after the binding has been accomplished would it be possible for the dominance of the pleasure principle (and of its modification, the reality principle) to proceed unhindered. Till then the other task of the mental apparatus, the task of mastering or binding excitations [*die Erregung zu bewältigen oder zu binden*], would have precedence — not, indeed, in opposition to the pleasure principle, but independently of it and to some extent in disregard of it.[101]

The drives follow a primary process, identified with the unbound 'freely mobile investments', that the secondary process attempts to bind

---

97 *Jenseits des Lustprinzips*, in *Gesammelte Werke*, Bd. XIII, 35; *Beyond the Pleasure Principle*, in *Standard Edition*, Vol. XVIII, 34. Translation modified.
98 Ibid., 38; 36. Translation modified.
99 Ibid., 40; 38.
100 Ibid., 41; 39. Translation modified.
101 Ibid., 36; 34–5. Translation modified.

[*binden*] and change into a tonic investment: 'A failure to effect this binding would provoke a disturbance analogous to a traumatic neurosis'. Under the effect of the binding of the primary process by the secondary process, the dangerous investment is deferred and the mastery of the pleasure principle is established. Derrida calls this binding mechanism the 'supplement', the 'stricture', and the 'post':

> In the same statement, describing one and the same operation, one and the same function, Freud says that it consists of binding (*binden*) the primary process (*pp*) and of replacing (*ersetzen*) the *pp* which has mastery (*herrschenden*) over the life of the drives with the secondary process: displacement, replacement of mastery, stricture as supplementary detachment. The secondary is the supplementary *sending* [*envoi*]. It transforms freely mobile investment energy into immobile investment energy, it *posits* and *posts*.[102]

The binding of the primary process by the secondary process corresponds to the 'supplement'. In this binding, free investment is transformed into bound investment ('stricture'). We can finally identify two detours [*Umwege*] in the movement of the psychic. The first *Umweg* modifies the pleasure principle into the reality principle and defers the achievement of pleasure; the second *Umweg* binds the primary process and defers the dangerous investment. The second is a condition of the

---

102 « Spéculer — sur Freud », in *La carte postale*, 420; 'Speculate — on Freud', in *The Post Card*, 394. Translation modified. Derrida expresses 'primary processes' by the abbreviation *pp*. The *pp* could also be interpreted as 'the post in the "pure" state': post as the demoniac, or post as the *Unheimliche*, which disrupts the psychic system. And the condition for mastering the pleasure principle is to bind [*binden*] this 'post in the "pure" state' which threatens human life. Interpreting Freud's former citation, Derrida writes: 'The essential characteristic of these processes of internal origin (drives and their representatives) is that they are *not bound*. In the *Traumdeutung* Freud had given these unconscious processes the name primary process. They correspond to a free, non-bound, non-tonic charge. The work of the higher layers of the psychic apparatus is to tie into the "secondary" process the drive excitations issuing from the *pp*. Now, and this is what is most important, the PP (or its modified form, the PR) can affirm its dominance only by binding the *pp*.

PP (+ PR): this is the *generation of the master* and the condition for rightful pleasure'
  PP
(ibid., 372; 350).

Thus the *binding* of the demoniac 'post in the pure state' (second *Umweg*) is the *sine qua non* for mastering the pleasure principle and its modification to the reality principle (first *Umweg*).

first. It is this movement of supplement that will resolve what we have called *the antinomy of the death drive*. The death drive is ·necessary for the survival of the subject, but it can give death to the subject. *It must therefore be deferred by the economic movement of the supplement.*

We affirm here that the supplementary relay of the drives cannot be reduced to either the Lacanian dialectic or the Hegelian dialectic: 'The graphics of the strictural supplement are not dialectical, do not proceed by oppositions in the last analysis. If they necessarily produce dialectical *effects*, for example the entire dialectic said to be of the master and the slave, they do not know negativity, lack, opposition.'[103] First, the mechanism of supplement is not reduced to a Hegelian dialectic, which is a movement of contradiction, opposition and relief [*Aufhebung, relève*] and in which the oppositional terms are suppressed (movement of negation) under the effect of *Aufhebung*[104] — for example, the opposition between the death drive and the pleasure principle would be cancelled and relieved [*aufgehoben, relevé*] by the reality principle. Contrary to this dialectical theory, the drives are only bound and deferred in their additional movement. They 'resist', as 'the remaining of the rest [*la restance du reste*]',[105] the dialectic of removal and suppression. The death drive is never suppressed by the opposition. Second, the supplementary movement has nothing to do with the Lacanian dialectic. In Lacan, the death drive is reduced to the Thing as the object of desire, but it remains unapproachable and its negativity, the 'lack of being', motivates desire in the subject. What Derrida notices in *Beyond* is a supplementary relay of the drives and the mechanism by which the drives seek to defer their own 'destination' (death). The death drive never produces lack in *Beyond*: 'desire is there without "without", is of a *without* without *without*'.[106]

The mechanism of *différance* and supplement is, at the same time,

---

103 Ibid., 428; 401.

104 On the relationship between the Derridian theory and the Hegelian *Aufhebung* [*relève*], see Jacques Derrida, *Glas*, Galilée, 1974, in particular 42–4; *Glas*, University of Nebraska Press, 1986, in particular 34–5.

105 Jacques Derrida, « Résistances », in *Résistances — de la psychanalyse*, 40; 'Resistances', in *Resistances of Psychoanalysis*, 26. In this article, we read: 'to think this resistance as the remaining of the rest [*la restance du reste*], which is to say, in a way that is not simply ontological (neither analytic nor dialectical), since the remaining of the rest is not *psychoanalytic*. Above all because, very simply, it is not. The rest *is* not or *est* not [*Le reste n'est ou n'este pas*]'. This is how the 'remaining of the rest' resists dialectic and psychoanalysis at the same time.

106 Ibid., 428; 401.

that of the connection of the drive, of the self-chaining of the drive. It is not mastery through 'lack' but 'self-mastery [*maîtrise de soi*]' of the drive.[107] The pleasure principle asserts its mastery 'by limiting the possible intensity of pleasure or unpleasure' 'by limiting the possible intensity of pleasure or displeasure'[108] (binding of the primary process, of the free investment). In other words, the pleasure principle unbinds pleasure only by binding it. We could here evoke the Freudian strategy: '*Wo Es war, soll Ich werden*'. But the Derridian strategy is slightly different from the Freudian. The issue for Freud is mastery of the dangerous investment in the primary process (*Es*: id), insofar as the dangerous id must become the rational self: it is, so to speak, the 'teleology of a progress'.[109] Unlike Freud, Derrida insists on 'self-mastery' in the dangerous investment of the id. The Derridian thesis will therefore be formulated as follows: 'Id limits itself in order to increase itself [*Ça se limite pour s'accroître*]'.[110] Let us remember, for example, the case of the compulsion to repeat, the process in which it delivers masochistic sexuality and, at the same time, binds the dangerous investment of the death drive. This is how 'post' means the structure of 'self-mastery' in the life of a drive; this 'self-mastery' likewise relies on the contradictory process of binding/unbinding. How, then, will Derrida interpret the Freudian concept of the 'drive for mastery [*Bemächtigungstrieb*]'?

4.5 Resistance of non-resistance

In 'Speculate — on Freud', Derrida discusses the 'drive for mastery':

> In the Freudian corpus, the guiding thread of such a problematic, one of its threads at least, intersects with a word and a concept that we have encountered. Coming back [*revenant*] to the scene of the *fort: da*, one might attribute all the grandson's efforts, in the repetition of the game, to a 'drive for mastery [*pulsion de maîtrise*]' (*Bemächtigungstrieb*). [. . .]
> In question, then, is a simple allusion, but what the allusion

---

107 Ibid., 430; 403. Translation modified.
108 Ibid., 427; 400.
109 Jacques Derrida, *États d'âme de la psychanalyse*, Galilée, 2000, 75.
110 « Spéculer — sur Freud », in *La carte postale*, 428; 'Speculate — on Freud', in *The Post Card*, 401.

designates calls upon the singularity of a drive that would not permit itself to be reduced to any other. And it interests us all the more in that, being irreducible to any other, it seems to take part in all the others, in the extent to which the entire economy of the PP and its beyond is governed by relations of 'mastery'. One can envisage, then, a quasi-transcendental privilege of this drive for mastery, drive for power, or drive for domination [*cette pulsion de maîtrise, pulsion de puissance ou pulsion d'emprise*]. The latter denomination seems preferable: it marks more clearly the relation to the other, even in domination *over oneself* [*emprise* sur soi]. And the word immediately places itself in communication with the lexicon of *giving, taking, sending*, or *destining* that is inciting us here from a distance, and that soon will concern us more directly. The drive to dominate must also be the drive's relation to itself: there is no drive not driven to bind itself to itself and to assure itself of self-mastery [*maîtrise de soi*] as a drive. Whence the transcendental tautology of the drive to dominate: it is the drive as drive, the drive of the drive, the drivenness of the drive. Again, it is a question of a relation to oneself as a relation to the other, the auto-affection of a *fort: da* which gives, takes, sends and destines itself, distances and approaches itself by its own step, the other's.[111]

He interprets the 'drive for domination' as the 'transcendental' drive of the drive: it is the drive to dominate the drive itself. By binding the lethal investment and delaying it, the drive controls itself (auto-affection of the drive). But at the same time, it is also the drive to dominate the other: 'especially in the passages relative to sadism. The sadistic component can come to "dominate [*beherrschen*]" all of sexuality'.[112] The drive is the 'drive for domination' in its transcendental nature: it is the drive of the drive, the drivenness of the drive. What the drive carries is power and domination over oneself and the other: 'The "posts" are always posts of power'.[113]

Does the death drive identify itself with the drive for domination as the drivenness of the drive? Of course not. To the extent that the drive for domination functions as 'domination over oneself', it serves to maintain the stability of the organism's drive system. Rather, the death drive

---

111 Ibid., 430; 403.
112 Ibid., 431; 404.
113 Ibid.

is the 'failure' or 'limit' of this domination over oneself, to the extent that it is fatally exerted on oneself or on the other. At the same time, it comes from 'power', from the 'origin' of the drive itself. So, if there is no drive for domination as 'the drivenness of the drive', the death drive does not exist. In the failure or limit of the drive's 'domination over oneself', the death drive appears as an aggressive drive that leads oneself or the other to death.

In *États d'âme de la psychanalyse* (2000), Derrida seeks to articulate this 'cruelty' of the drive to the political problem in general. He interprets 'cruelty', which is the destruction drive 'turned outwards on to objects' (Freud), as 'a cruelty inherent in the drive for power or for sovereign mastery [*la pulsion de pouvoir ou de maîtrise souveraine*] (*Bemächtigungstrieb*)'.[114] We must notice that the *Bemächtigungstrieb* is translated here as 'the drive for sovereign mastery'. When the *Bemächtigungstrieb* is articulated with the political question, it becomes 'the drive for sovereign mastery' or even 'the drive for empowerment [*la pulsion de l'habilitation*]' of the state, which monopolizes violence and thus organizes sovereign order. This drive affirms, as 'performative power', the stability of the 'symbolic' or sovereign order.[115] To this stability, Derrida opposes 'the irruptions which can and must rout' the sovereign order.[116] At the beginning of *États d'âme de la psychanalyse*, he states the problem as follows:

This [ultimate] question will not be: is there a death drive (*Todestrieb*), that is to say, and Freud regularly associates them, a cruel drive for destruction or annihilation? Or again: is there also a cruelty inherent in the drive for power or sovereign mastery (*Bemächtigungstrieb*) beyond or below principles — for example the principles of pleasure or of reality? My question will rather be the following: is there, for thought, for psychoanalytic thought to come, another beyond, if I may say, a beyond that stands beyond these *possibles* which are still the pleasure and reality principles *and* the death drive or the drive for sovereign mastery which seem to be exercised wherever cruelty is announced? In other words, in totally other words, can we think of this apparently impossible thing, but otherwise impossible, namely a

---

114 *États d'âme de la psychanalyse*, 14.
115 Ibid., 47–8.
116 Ibid., 87.

beyond of the death drive or the drive for sovereign mastery, therefore
the beyond of a cruelty, a beyond which would have nothing to do
neither with drives nor with principles?[117]

Derrida identifies here what could disrupt and alter the sovereign order
organized by the drive for sovereign mastery as 'a beyond of the death
drive or the drive for sovereign mastery, therefore the beyond of a
cruelty'. This other 'beyond' is also called 'beyond of the beyond' (of the
pleasure principle) or 'an unconditional without sovereignty, and therefore without cruelty':

> I will say that there is, there must be some reference to the uncondi-
> tional, an unconditional without sovereignty, and therefore without
> cruelty, something that is doubtless very difficult to think of. [. . .]
> This [original affirmation] is not a principle, a reign [*principat*], a
> sovereignty. It therefore comes from beyond of the beyond, and there-
> fore from the beyond of the economy of the possible. It is linked to a
> life, of course, but to a life other than that of the economy of the possi-
> ble, an im-possible life perhaps, a *sur-vie*, and not symbolizable, but
> the only one that is *worth* living, without alibi, once and for all, the
> only one from which (I mean *from* which) a thought of life is possible.
> [. . .]
>   This original affirmation from the beyond of the beyond is given
> from many figures of the impossible unconditional. I have studied a
> few elsewhere: hospitality, gift, forgiveness — and first of all the
> unforeseeability, the 'maybe', the 'what if' of the event, the coming and
> the coming of the other in general, its arrival. Their possibility always
> announces itself as the experience of a non-negative im-possible.[118]

Derrida thematizes the 'impossible' and the 'non-symbolizable', which
are revealed 'from many figures of the impossible unconditional': for
example, 'hospitality, gift, forgiveness', 'unforeseeability', 'event'. It is
appropriate here to recall his critique of Lacanian theory: in Lacan, the
impossible was singular (letter = phallus as a singular signifier) and
negative (lack); this singular negativity affirms the stability of the
subject's transcendental system (the symbolic). On the other hand, in

---

117 Ibid., 14.
118 Ibid., 82–3.

Derrida, it is the multiple irruptions of the 'impossible' which can disturb and 'rout' the sovereign or symbolic order. The 'many figures of the impossible unconditional' threaten, as *Unheimliches*, 'chance' or 'disseminal remaining [*restance disséminale*]',[119] the stability of the sovereign order. They are the ones who can disrupt and alter the 'cruelty' from the interior of the state order itself. Regarding the 'gift', for example, Derrida emphasizes:

> There is gift, if there is any, only in what interrupts the system as well as the symbol, in a partition without return and without division [*repartition*], without being-with-self of the gift-counter-gift.[120]

The gift 'interrupts' the economic system, even the capitalist system as a system of exchange, to the extent that there is neither reciprocity nor return (the 'general economy' of the gift in the sense of Bataille). The expression 'a partition without returns and without division' obviously alludes to the Lacanian theory of the indivisible signifier (singularity of the signifier), which returns (return of the repressed). The singular signifier is the real as phallus and which constitutes and maintains the symbolic. On the other hand, the Derridian practice, as that of the gift, 'interrupts' and alters the symbolic and capitalist system. If the Lacanian impossible is the constituent element that forms and maintains the symbolic, the Derridian impossible is that which affects and alters it. This new theoretical development is therefore based on psychoanalytic theory but nonetheless radically alters and deconstructs it.[121]

---

119 « Résistances », in *Résistances — de la psychanalyse*, 49; 'Resistances' in *Resistances of Psychoanalysis*, 34.

120 Jacques Derrida, *Donner le temps, 1 : La fausse monnaie*, Galilée, 1991, 25–6; *Given Time, I: Counterfeit Money*, University of Chicago Press, 1992, 13. This text is taken from the seminar given at the École normale supérieure in 1977–78, two years after the seminar on *La vie la mort (Séminaire 1975-1976*, Seuil, 2019), the prototype of 'Speculate — on Freud'.

121 For example, Derrida begins *Given Time* by quoting a Lacanian thesis: 'Love is to give what one does not have' (*Donner le temps, 1: La fausse monnaie*, 12, note 1; *Given Time, I: Counterfeit Money*, 2, note 2). In the sense given to it by this thesis, the gift is 'impossible' in Lacan, in particular between the two partners in love by the effect of sexual difference: 'the woman *quoad matrem* and the man *quoad castrationem* (*Le séminaire*, Livre XX, « Encore », 36; *The Seminar*, Book XX, 'Encore', 35)' (quoted by Derrida in *Donner le temps, 1 : La fausse monnaie*, 13, note 1; *Given Time, I: Counterfeit Money*, 2, note 2). But, ultimately, what makes the gift impossible in Derrida is the moment when the other perceives and retains the intentional meaning of the gift, since

Derrida conceptualizes here the 'beyond' of the death drive or sovereign mastery, hence a position beyond cruelty. Let us specify the elaboration of this 'beyond'. First, the drive for sovereign mastery is, as a 'transcendental drive', the 'principle of principle' that all drives possess.
According to our reading, it functions under the title of 'self-mastery',
which controls the lethality of the death drive and which prevents the
irruption of excessive violence. In a political context, it corresponds to
the state monopoly on violence, which controls the explosion of extreme
violence and which establishes and maintains sovereign order. In this
sense, it is the controlled or 'deferred' violence that affirms the stability
of the symbolic system: 'Force against force, deferred economy of force,
that is the law'.[122] Second, the death drive threatens, as *Unheimliches* or
disseminal remaining, this symbolic order and disturbs it from the interior: the *Unheimliche* is a multiplicity insofar as it is 'disseminal' (unlike
the Lacanian theory). The death drive thus exists, according to the
nature of its destruction drive, 'beyond' symbolic economy. Third, in
order to resist the cruelty of the death drive or the drive for sovereign
mastery, Derrida proposes 'the beyond of the beyond' or the beyond of
cruelty — these correspond to hospitality, unconditional gift and

---

at that moment the counter-gift and the system of circulation take place; therefore
'There is no more gift as soon as the other *receives* — and even if he or she refuses the gift
that he or she has perceived or recognized as gift (ibid., 27; 14, translation modified). It
is thus that the 'impossible' condition of the gift is 'absolute forgetting' which prevents a
return (dissemination as 'that which does not *return* in general' [ibid., 68; 47]): 'So we
are speaking here', writes Derrida, 'of an absolute forgetting — a forgetting that also
absolves, that unbinds absolutely and infinitely more, therefore, than excuse, forgiveness,
or acquittal. As condition of a gift event, condition for the advent of a gift, absolute
forgetting should no longer have any relation with either the psycho-philosophical
category of forgetting or even with the psychoanalytic category that links forgetting to
meaning or to the logic of the signifier, to the economy of repression, and to the symbolic
order. The thought of this radical forgetting as thought of the gift should accord with a
certain experience of the trace as *cinder* or *ashes*' (ibid., 30; 16–17). The cinder as an
absolute forgetting breaks the psychoanalytic and capitalist system of return that ensures
the symbolic. Note that the thesis 'to give what one does not have' is also found in
Heidegger. The Heidegger-Lacan line, the most rigorous 'negative' theory, is always a
starting point for Derrida and the object that he deconstructs and ultimately transforms
into a non-negative theory, namely the affirmative theory of dissemination. On Derrida's
(ambivalent) relationship with Lacanian theory, see in particular, « Pour l'amour de
Lacan », in *Résistances — de la psychanalyse*; 'For the Love of Lacan', in *Resistances of
Psychoanalysis*. On the 'negative' theory of Heidegger-Lacan, see Philippe Lacoue-
Labarthe/Jean-Luc Nancy, *Le titre de la lettre*, Galilée, 1973; *The Title of the Letter*, State
University of New York Press, 1992, Chs. 2 and 3 of Part II.

122 *États d'âme de la psychanalyse*, 71.

forgiveness. These practices threaten, in the form of multiple 'irrup-tions', the cruelty of the sovereign order. To the extent that the 'irrup-tions' are unconditional (impossible), they exist 'beyond' the sovereign economy ('beyond the appropriable and the possible').[123]

To formalize the Derridean theory: 'the beyond of the beyond' has the same structure as the death drive in its mechanism of disturbance of the symbolic economy (the unforeseeable irruptions beyond the sover-eign or psychic economy). In Derrida, despite this affirmation, 'the beyond of a cruelty, a beyond that has nothing to do with either drives or principles',[124] 'the beyond of the beyond' is conceptualized in the same form as the death drive — and it is, so to speak, the death drive *without cruelty*. From this, we can say that what resists the death drive as cruelty is the death drive *without cruelty* which has the same form as the former.

In 'Resistances' (1995), Derrida deals with the relationship between the compulsion to repeat and the resistance. Reading Freud's 'Inhibitions, Symptoms and Anxiety', he draws attention to the 'resistance of the unconscious' which persists even after the resolution of the resistance brought by the 'counter-investments [*Gegenbesetzungen*]' of the ego:[125] it is the 'irreducible resistance' of the compulsion to repeat.[126] He notices this resistance for two reasons: first, 'it has no meaning (death drive)' and then, 'it resists analysis in the form of non-resistance' 'without saying yes or no, without accepting or opposing, speaking however but without saying anything, neither *yes* nor *no*, like *Bartleby The Scrivener*'.[127] The compulsion to repeat 'combines the two essential motifs of all *anal-ysis*, the regressive or archeotropic movement and the movement of dissolution that urges toward destruction, that loves to destroy by dissociation'.[128] In other words, it has the same form as psychoanalysis which it resists 'in the form of non-resistance', namely the structure of *analysis* (the movement of regression and dissolution).[129] This allows

---

123 Ibid.
124 Ibid., 14.
125 Sigmund Freud, 'Hemmung, Symptom und Angst', in *Gesammelte Werke*, Bd. XIV, 191–2; 'Inhibitions, Symptoms and Anxiety', in *Standard Edition*, Vol. XX, 159–60. Translation modified.
126 Jacques Derrida, « Résistances », in *Résistances — de la psychanalyse*, 37; 'Resistances' in *Resistances of Psychoanalysis*, 23.
127 Ibid., 38; 24. Translation modified.
128 Ibid., 37; 23.
129 Ibid., 33; 19–20. Derrida defines the 'analysis' of psychoanalysis as a combination of these two motifs: 'The concurrence of these two motifs figures in the figure from the

Derrida to conclude that 'it is that whose resistance psychoanalysis today represents, in the surest form of its ruse: disguised as non-resistance'.[130]

Here, we are again confronted with the paradoxical structure of the compulsion to repeat and the death drive: the death drive resists 'in the form of non-resistance', and it has the same form as what it resists. We can interpret this aspect of the death drive as a death drive *without cruelty*. In other words, it is the 'beyond of a cruelty' which resists cruelty 'in the form of non-resistance'. We have previously reflected on the mechanism by which the compulsion to repeat protects the subject by repeating traumatic impressions. Insofar as it does not give death to the subject and therefore protects the subject, it resists 'in the form of non-resistance' the cruelty of the trauma by repeating these traumatic impressions. And, to the extent that it resists the lethal cruelty of trauma, it even resists the lethal cruelty of the death drive. In the compulsion to repeat, the subject 'passively' repeats the trauma. This passivity is not, however, a simple passivity, since it resists death by repeating the trauma 'passively' — as Blanchot says, it is 'the beyond of all passiveness'.[131] The compulsion to repeat resists the lethal cruelty of the death drive in the form of non-resistance (repetition beyond all passiveness). We must

---

Greek language, namely, *analuein*. There is, *on the one hand*, what could be called the *archeological* or *anagogical* motif, which is marked in the movement of *ana* (recurrent return toward the principial, the most originary, the simplest, the elementary, or the detail that cannot be broken down); and, *on the other hand*, a motif that could be nicknamed *lytic, lytological*, or *philolytic*, marked in the *lysis* (breaking down, untying, unknotting, deliverance, solution, dissolution or absolution, and, by the same token, final completion)'. Recall that Freud defined the death drive as a 'return to the inorganic', on the one hand, and as a 'destruction drive', on the other.

130 Ibid., 38; 24.

131 Maurice Blanchot, *L'écriture du désastre*, Gallimard, 1980, 219; *The Writing of the Disaster*, University of Nebraska Press, 1995, 145. What Blanchot called 'the beyond of all passiveness' is again a figure of *Bartleby The Scrivener* by Melville: 'In *Bartleby*, the enigma comes from "pure" writing, which can only be that of a copyist (rewriting). The enigma comes from the passivity into which this activity (writing) disappears, and which *passes* imperceptibly and suddenly from ordinary passivity (reproduction), to the beyond of all passiveness: to a life so passive — for it has the hidden decency of dying — that it does not have death for an ultimate escape, nor does it make death an escape. Bartleby copies; he writes incessantly, and cannot stop long enough to submit to anything resembling control. *I would prefer not to*. This sentence speaks in the intimacy of our rights: negative preference, the negation that effaces preference and as effaced therein: the neutrality of that which is not among the things there are to do — the restraint, the gentleness that cannot be called obstinate, and that outdoes obstinacy with those few words; language perpetuating itself, keeps still'.

find this resistance of non-resistance 'beyond all passiveness' in Derrida's unconditional hospitality, gift and forgiveness.

Let us consider the notion of 'hospitality'. In *De l'hospitalité* (2001), Derrida raises a fundamental question about its use: 'the use of this word immediately raises the question of whether it can be translated by other words such as those of immigration or integration of foreigners. Are they homogeneous concepts? Are they the same things?'[132] In fact, 'hospitality' goes far beyond the mere notions of accepting or integrating immigrants: 'Pure hospitality, welcoming others unconditionally and without question, carries an *intrinsic threat of perversion*'.[133] For example, 'the one I welcome can be a rapist, a murderer, he can make a mess in the house: so many possibilities that cannot be ruled out. However, in pure hospitality, without guarantee, this possibility that the other will come to make the revolution or even a worse form of the unforeseeable and that one will be overwhelmed, must be accepted'.[134] Thus, unconditional hospitality is a crucial concept that includes even the acceptance of a 'worse form of the unforeseeable'; in this sense, it implies a 'perversion', even the death drive — insofar as it is the death drive *without cruelty*. For 'pure hospitality' resists, as 'the beyond of all passiveness', the cruelty of sovereign order in the form of non-resistance. Derrida defines it as follows: 'There is pure hospitality only when I welcome, not the guest, but the unexpected visitor, the one who invades me, in a certain way, who comes to my home while I was not prepared for it. And I have to do whatever it is necessary to adapt myself to him, transform my home, let my home transform so that this unexpected visitor can settle, even if he may seem threatening'.[135] To welcome the other as 'the one who invades me' and, thus, to let myself and my home 'transform' is a case of 'the beyond of all passiveness' as the death drive without cruelty; it is, furthermore, this 'beyond of all passiveness' that opens up the field for the unforeseeable irruptions of the other, which will transform me and rout the current order of sovereignty ('my home'). This 'beyond', in other words, the resistance of non-resistance, corresponds exactly to the death drive without cruelty.

Following   Derrida's   translation   of   the   Freudian   term

---

132 Jacques Derrida, « Une hospitalité à l'infini », in *De l'hospitalité*, La passe du vent, 2001, 117.
133 Ibid., 118. Our emphasis.
134 Ibid., 119.
135 Ibid., 123–4.

Bemächtigungstrieb, we called the cruelty of state sovereignty the 'drive for sovereign mastery'. This drive corresponds to the monopolization of violence by the state in order to control irruptions of excessive violence. It is the 'death drive without cruelty' — in other words, resistance as gift, forgiveness, hospitality — that resists the cruelty of state sovereignty. We could even call this Derridean resistance 'sovereignty without sovereignty', since Derridian strategies, notably forgiveness and hospitality, are in fact very close to strategies of state sovereignty. But we must immediately note that gift, forgiveness and hospitality are 'unconditional' in Derrida. For example, as we noticed, hospitality does not mean simply accepting immigration. When the sovereign order welcomes immigrants, the logic of selection (economic, intellectual, political conditions, etc.) necessarily intervenes. In contrast, Derridian strategy is defined as 'pure and unconditional' hospitality in which such selective logic never intervenes.

The same thing could be said about 'forgiveness'. This does not simply signify the abolition of the death penalty. Regarding the principle of forgiveness, Derrida explains: 'in the analysis of pure forgiveness, as in that of pure hospitality, I maintain that pure forgiveness must forgive the one who or which remains unforgivable. If I forgive something or someone that remains forgivable, I don't forgive, it's too easy. If I forgive the fault (the "what") of the one who has repented, or the one who has repented himself (the "who"), I forgive something or someone other than the crime or the criminal. The true "meaning" of forgiveness, therefore, is to forgive even the unforgivable and even someone who does not ask for forgiveness'.[136] Pure forgiveness forgives 'even the unforgivable and even someone who does not ask forgiveness'; in other words, pure forgiveness is 'unconditional'. The Derridian resistances thus radicalize strategies of sovereignty — eventually becoming 'unconditional' — and try to disrupt and alter the cruelty of state sovereignty through these 'unconditional' practices.

On Derrida's notion of 'sovereignty', let us refer to 'From Restricted to General Economy' (1967), where he discusses the difference between

136 Jacques Derrida, Elisabeth Roudinesco, *De quoi demain . . .*, Fayard/Galilée, 2001, 260; *For What Tomorrow . . .*, Stanford University Press, 2004, 161. Derrida deals with the thematic of 'forgiveness' in his seminar at EHESS (1999–2001) devoted to reflecting on the abolition of the death penalty. The question then was to think about 'forgiving the unforgivable'. See Jacques Derrida, *Séminaire La peine de mort*, Vol. I (1999–2000), II (2000–2001), Galilée, 2012, 2015; *The Death Penalty: The Seminars of Jacques Derrida*, Vol. I, II, University of Chicago Press, 2013, 2017.

'*Herrschaft*' in Hegel and 'sovereignty' in Bataille. Hegelian *Herrschaft* is first defined as follows:

> Lordship has a meaning. The putting at stake of life is a moment in the constitution of meaning, in the presentation of essence and truth. It is an obligatory stage in the history of self-consciousness and phenomenality, that is to say, in the presentation of meaning. For history — that is, meaning — to form a continuous chain, to be woven, the master must *experience his truth*. This is possible only under two conditions which cannot be separated: the master must stay alive in order to enjoy what he has won by risking his life; and, at the end of this progression so admirably described by Hegel, the 'truth of the independent consciousness is accordingly the consciousness of the bondsman'. And when servility becomes lordship, it keeps within it the trace of its repressed origin, 'being a consciousness within itself (*zurückgedrängtes Bewusstsein*), it will enter into itself, and change round into real and true independence'.[137]

A contradictory process is revealed here: what lordship means is first of all 'the putting at stake of life'; however, passing through the dialectic of lordship and bondage, the meaning of mastery is strangely altered: 'the master must stay alive in order to enjoy what he has won by risking his life'. At the end of this dialectical process, the master is forced to assume a position of self-conservation. This corresponds, in the context of empirical politics, to the monopolization of violence by the state in order to maintain control. To use Benjamin's expression, the founding violence of law is 'represented [*repäsentiert*]' in the conservative violence of law.[138] On the other hand, Bataillean 'sovereignty' is defined by Derrida as follows:

---

137 « De l'économique restreinte à l'économie générale », in *L'écriture et la différence*, 374–5; 'From Restricted to General Economy', in *Writing and Difference*, 321–2.

138 Walter Benjamin, 'Zur Kritik der Gewalt', in *Gesammelte Schriften*, Bd. II-1, Suhrkamp, 1977, 202; 'Critique of Violence' in *Selected Writings*, Vol. 1, Belknap Press of Harvard University Press, 1996, 243–4. See also Jacques Derrida, *Force de loi*, Galilée, 1994, 129; 'Force of Law: The "Mystical Foundation of Authority"', in Drucilla Cornel *et al.* eds., *Deconstruction and the Possibility of Justice*, Routledge, 1992, 55.

But, differing from Hegelian lordship, it [sovereignty] does not even want to maintain itself, collect itself, or collect the profits from itself or from its own risk.[139]

Bataillean sovereignty, in 'not even want[ing] to maintain itself, collect itself, or collect the profits from itself or from its own risk', is not self-conservative, but exposes itself to 'its own risk' in an extreme way. We find here the same strategy as that of Derrida to resist the cruelty of state sovereignty. The Derridian strategy involves transforming the 'self-conservative' policies of sovereignty (*Herrschaft*) into 'unconditional' practices of resistance ('unconditional hospitality', 'forgiving the unforgivable') by exposing oneself to 'one's own risk'. So, if we can call this strategy of resistance 'sovereignty without sovereignty', it is only to the extent that the first 'sovereignty' is understood in the Bataillean sense. Then hospitality and forgiveness, taking their own risk, become pure and unconditional, threatening and attempting to alter the cruelty of state sovereignty. It is precisely in this sense that we identified Derridean resistance as 'the death drive without cruelty'.

We have proposed an antinomic thesis on the death drive: on the one hand, the death drive is necessary for the survival of the subject; on the other hand, it can give death to the subject.[140] Referring to Derrida, we resolved this antinomy by the *différance* of the drive. However, if we go further, we are led to recognize two different modalities of the death drive: the *cruel* death drive that can give death to the subject and the death drive *without cruelty* that resists the excessive cruelty of the death drive itself.[141] Derrida called 'resistance of non-resistance' the death drive *without cruelty* which, in the form of non-resistance, resists the *cruel* death drive (failure of the drive's domination over oneself) as well as the cruelty of the 'drive for sovereign mastery [*Bemächtigungstrieb*]'. It is this resistance of non-resistance, the resistance beyond all passiveness, which exposes oneself to the irruptions of the other and thereby

---

139 « De l'économique restreinte à l'économie générale », in *L'écriture et la différence*, 388; 'From Restricted to General Economy', in *Writing and Difference*, 334.

140 What Derrida calls 'autoimmunity' designates exactly this antinomy of the death drive. See Jacques Derrida, *Voyous : Deux essais sur la raison*, Galilée, 2003, 83; *Rogues: Two Essays on Reason*, Stanford University Press, 2005, 55.

141 For example, the following study develops these two modalities of masochism: Benno Rosenberg, *Masochisme mortifère et masochisme gardien de la vie*, PUF, 1995, in particular Ch. II.

opens up the unforeseeable field of the event, the possibility of an alteration of the present sovereign order. It introduces auto-affection into
social formation through irruptions of the other, which Derrida defines
as 'auto-hetero-affection'.[142] Derridian resistance is therefore not *invol-
untary*, in the sense that one passively awaits the occurrence of the event.
It is located beyond all passiveness. Unconditional and impossible practices thus open up the field for the other's irruptions, namely the possibility of 'rupture'.

4.6 Derridian rupture

We have used the term 'rupture', which has a more or less Althusserian
tone. If we can use it, it is because 'rupture' and 'contingency' are, in our
view, key notions for linking Derrida to Althusser. For Althusser, the
rupture signifies the revolution in the Marxian sense, which is, however,
radically different from the traditional Marxist theory insofar as the
Althusserian rupture is 'overdetermined' by the causal multiplicity. It is
apparently difficult to find this 'structuralist' problematic in the
Derridian 'deconstructionist' theory. However, when he evokes, in
Specters of Marx (1993), 'the messianic without messianism' — which is
'a structural messianism, a messianism without religion' and therefore 'a
certain experience of the *emancipatory promise*'[143] — what is at stake is
exactly the problem of rupture.[144] The messianic without messianism is

---

142 See, for example, Jacques Derrida, *Le toucher, Jean-Luc Nancy*, Galilée, 1998,
328.

143 Jacques Derrida, *Spectres de Marx*, Galilée, 1993, 102; *Specters of Marx*,
Routledge, 2006, 74. Our emphasis. Fredric Jameson interprets the notion of 'messianic
without messianism' in the Benjaminian context: the messianic as a weak hope of
emancipation, a 'weak messianic power' in a time of absolute hopelessness ('Marx's
Purloined Letter', in Michael Sprinker, ed., *Ghostly Demarcations*, Verso, 1999). However,
even if this interpretation is quite persuasive, we put this Benjaminian interpretation
aside in order to understand 'the messianic' in its relation to the concept of rupture.
Derrida himself underlines that 'the messianic without messianism' should not be
reduced to the Benjaminian context, nor to the historical figures of messianism, since
'they are only possible on the universal and quasi-transcendental foundation of this
structure of '*without* messianism'' (Jacques Derrida, *Marx & Sons*, PUF/Galilée, 2002,
73).

144 Derrida uses the term 'rupture' to qualify social alteration or revolution. See
Spectres de Marx, 60; *Specters of Marx*, 36–7: 'the originary performativity [of the
political appeal or injunction, the pledge or the promise] that does not conform to

the injunction, the promise to introduce 'the democracy to come', namely 'justice'. To achieve this democracy to come, a rupture with the current social formation is necessary:

> This is where deconstruction would always begin to take shape as the thinking of the gift and of undeconstructible justice, the undeconstructible condition of any deconstruction, to be sure, but a condition that is itself *in deconstruction* and remains, and must remain (that is the injunction) in the disjointure of the *Un-Fug* [i.e., 'out of joint']. Otherwise it rests on the good conscience of having done one's duty, it loses the chance of the future, of the promise or the appeal, of the desire also (that is its 'own' possibility), of this desert messianism (without content and without identifiable messiah), of this also *abyssal* desert, 'desert in the desert'.[145]

This passage summarizes the main theses of *Specters of Marx*. But before discussing it, we must refer to an affirmation by Derrida in 'Force of Law': 'Deconstruction is justice'.[146] Deconstruction, once a purely and properly theoretical instrument, is reformulated there as an instrument for practice. It is 'justice' as 'an experience of the impossible'.[147] In this quote, he uses the term 'disjointure', which is, according to him, the condition of deconstruction: 'Otherwise, [. . .] it loses the chance of the future, of the promise or of the appeal' of the Messianic. This 'disjointure' ('Time is out of joint') refers to the 'non-knowledge' of the future, the 'opening' and 'spacing [*espacement*]' of time. The opening of time 'must have nothing to do with knowing. Nor therefore with ignorance. The opening must preserve this heterogeneity as the only chance of an affirmed or rather reaffirmed future'.[148] In other words, it is lack of knowledge or the unforeseeability of the future that opens up a space, the field of the irruption of the other:

---

preexisting conventions, unlike all the performatives analysed by the theoreticians of speech acts, but whose force of rupture produces the institution or the constitution, the law itself, which is to say also the meaning that appears to, that ought to, or that appears to have to guarantee it in return'.

145 Ibid., 56; 33.
146 *Force de loi*, 35; 'Force of Law', in *Deconstruction and the Possibility of Justice*, 15.
147 Ibid.
148 *Spectres de Marx*, 68; *Specters of Marx*, 45.

The messianic [is] the coming of the other, the absolute and unpredictable singularity of the *arrivant as justice*. We believe that this messianic
remains an *ineffaceable* mark — a mark one neither can nor should
efface — of Marx's legacy, and doubtless of *inheriting*, of the experience
of inheritance in general. Otherwise, one would reduce the event-ness
of the event, the singularity and the alterity of the other.[149]

For Derrida, the event signifies the alteration of the current sovereign
order, brought about by the irruption of radical otherness. Through
this irruption of the other, the 'synchronic reproduction' of the sovereign order will necessarily be ruptured. In other words, the introduction of the *Unheimliche* will alter the fixed order of social formation.
The otherness of the *Unheimliche* — that *inquiétante étrangeté* which is
closest to the ego and which threatens the ego with this very similarity
— disrupts and subverts the fixed modality of sovereign order. In this
sense, the messianic is one of the names of the revolutionary: 'The
messianic, including its revolutionary forms (and the messianic is
always revolutionary, it has to be), would be urgency, imminence but,
irreducible paradox, a waiting without horizon of expectation'.[150] The
messianic is therefore an appeal to rupture with the current sovereign
order.

The practice of non-resistance opens up the space for the irruption of
irreducible otherness. This spacing is the field of contingency which
resists the fixed reproduction of social formation. In other words, the
'Time is out of joint' (*Hamlet*/Derrida) means a void, a space that is the
field of contingency, in which one is surprised by radical otherness. Of
course, we cannot predict how this contingent element will alter the
sovereign order. But at the same time, the established order will never be
altered without this 'incalculable' or 'unforeseeable' element, and it is
exactly in this sense that 'menace and chance are inseparable'.[151] Derrida
continues in 'Force of Law':

---

149 Ibid., 56; 33.

150 Ibid., 267; 211. See also, *Force de loi*, 46; 'Force of Law', in *Deconstruction and the
Possibility of Justice*, 20: 'this anxiety-ridden moment of suspense — which is also the interval
of spacing in which transformations, indeed juridico-political revolutions take place'.

151 Expression by Jacques Derrida in his seminar at the EHESS: 'La bête et le
souverain' (2002–2003), 22 January 2003. This phrase is not reproduced in his Seminar
(*Séminaire La bête et le souverain*, Vol. II [2002–2003], Galilée, 2010; *The Beast and the
Sovereign*, Vol. II, University of Chicago Press, 2011) because it was improvised without
manuscript.

Law [*droit*] is not justice. Law is the element of calculation, and it is just that there be law, but justice is incalculable, it requires us to calculate with the incalculable; and aporetic experiences are the experiences, as improbable as they are necessary, of justice, that is to say of moments in which the decision between just and unjust is never insured by a rule.[152]

Justice is the experience of 'the incalculable', but 'it requires us to calculate with the incalculable'. In other words, we are necessarily and imperatively summoned to decide while facing the spacing of the incalculable. The 'messianic without messianism' orders decision making and appeals, as a 'promise' or an 'injunction', to practice resistance, resistance of non-resistance. The Derridian spacing or 'out of joint' then signifies a field of contingency to introduce the democracy to come.

---

152 *Force de loi*, 38; 'Force of Law', in *Deconstruction and the Possibility of Justice*, 16.

5

Ideology (Althusser)

5.1 A 'rupture' with regard to Lacanian theory

Having dealt with the problem of contingency and structural alteration in Derrida from his interpretation of the Freudian notion of 'death drive', we address, in the fifth and sixth chapters, the problem of the causality of structural becoming in Althusser. In this problematic, we will rely on a notion of contingency ('a letter can always not arrive at its destination') that is opposed to the Lacanian dialectic ('a letter always arrives at its destination'). Althusser discusses it from the perspective of the social and scientific revolution, but what matters to us here is the problem of the social revolution in its relation to the eventual 'rupture'. In order to clarify this question, we can rephrase the question as follows: according to what causality can a static social structure that reproduces itself 'synchronously' and incessantly be altered?

From our point of view, the logic of structural change has constituted a central subject in Althusser since the 1960s. Two hypotheses will allow us to discuss this. The first hypothesis asserts that the question of structural becoming cannot be separated from that of contingency. Althusser proposed 'aleatory materialism' in the 1980s and attempted to reconstruct the entire history of philosophy with the concept of contingency.[1]

---

1 See Louis Althusser, *Sur la philosophie*, Gallimard, 1994; « Le courant souterrain du matérialisme de la rencontre », in *Écrits philosophiques et politiques*, T. 1, Stock/ IMEC, 1994; 'The Underground Current of the Materialism of the Encounter', in *Philosophy of the Encounter, Later Writings, 1978-1987*, Verso, 2006. In 'The Underground

However, if we read his texts carefully, we can see that this problematic has already existed since the 1960s, in particular inseparably from that of the *irruption* [surgissement] of the new structure.

The second hypothesis concerns the question of the relationship between Lacanian psychoanalytic theory and Althusserian theory. The fact that Althusserian theory, especially that of ideology, relates closely to Lacanian theory has already been pointed out by many authors. This theory was judged as 'thinking with the borrowed concepts', because of its similarity to Lacanian theory (or the influence which the latter exerted on the former).[2] However, our thinking proceeds in a different way. Even if Althusser relies on Lacanian psychoanalytic concepts, he ends up modifying Lacan's theoretical dispositives in a *critical* manner (in the Kantian sense of the term); this *critical* modification of Lacanian theory progressively deepened throughout the 1960s and 1970s. In this regard, Étienne Balibar expresses his astonishment in a 1988 article concerning the text entitled 'The Discovery of Dr. Freud' (1976), which Althusser wrote for a colloquium on the unconscious in Tbilisi (USSR). According to Balibar, 'entire argumentative passages were indeed analogous, identical formulations' to those in the article on 'Freud and Lacan' (1964), except that 'the conclusions he drew from it were diametrically opposed'.[3] Here is the 'conclusion' in 1976: 'instead of offering a scientific theory of the unconscious, he [Lacan] gave an astonished world a philosophy of psychoanalysis. I say *a philosophy of psychoanalysis* in the sense in which Engels, speaking about the philosophy of Nature, the Philosophy of history, and so on, said that those disciplines have no right to exist because they have no object'.[4] In our view, it is *the critical modification of the dispositives of Lacanian theory in Althusserian theory* that leads to the assertion that Lacanian theory is 'a philosophy of

---

Current . . .', Althusser repeatedly evokes the Derridian philosophy of contingency, which is, he writes, 'the thesis of the primacy of "dissemination" over the postulate that every signifier has a meaning' (562; 189).

2 See David Macey, 'Thinking with Borrowed Concepts: Althusser and Lacan', in Gregory Elliott, ed., *Althusser: A Critical Reader*, Blackwell, 1994; Michèle Barrett, 'Althusser's Marx, Althusser's Lacan', in Michael Sprinker *et al.*, eds., *The Althusserian Legacy*, Verso, 1993.

3 Étienne Balibar, « Tais-toi encore, Althusser ! », in *Écrits pour Althusser*, Découverte, 1991, 63.

4 Louis Althusser, « La découverte du Docteur Freud », in *Écrits sur la psychanalyse*, Stock/IMEC, 1993, 203; 'The Discovery of Dr. Freud', in *Writings on Psychoanalysis: Freud and Lacan*, Columbia University Press, 1999, 91. Translation modified.

psychoanalysis' and has 'no object'. We call it, provisionally, the 'rupture' with regard to Lacanian psychoanalytic theory. In fact, Althusser himself reflected on the 'rupture' of Freudian theory with regard to previous disciplines, but on which Freud had to rely in order to create this totally new science, psychoanalysis:

We're dealing with the irruption [*surgissement*] of a scientific discipline that presents itself as totally new with regard to a field that was constituted earlier. We're dealing with the irruption of a new truth, of a new knowledge, thus with the definition of a new object that breaks with the field constituted earlier: breaks with a field against the background of which this new discipline stands out. A field that is already occupied, that is an ideological field in which it has no place. [. . .] To the extent to which we're dealing with an epistemological break, with a rupture in the continuity with the earlier field, we're dealing with a phenomenon of rupture that contains in itself, like a real virtuality, a capacity to upset the field into which it irrupts. [. . .] But, at the same time, this irruption into the background of a field in which all the places are taken occurs under conditions such that the irruption has a tendency to be contested and revoked by the field into the background of which it irrupts. The rupture that a new scientific discipline introduces into a field in which all the places are taken, in fact, poses problems for the thinker or scientist who tries to define his new object, problems that are at first practically insoluble. This rupture has to be carried out within the field itself where it is supposed to intervene, practically in the language itself with which this new discipline has to break. [. . .] And all the Freudian terminology itself relates to the concepts on the basis of which Freud conceives his discovery and with which he has to break. It's no accident that the psychology of the unconscious is defined as the negation of a psychology of consciousness. This legacy and this condition Freud cannot avoid weigh very heavily on the destiny of his thought.[5]

Freud established a science 'that presents itself as totally new with regard to a field that was constituted earlier'. But to create this new science,

---

5 Louis Althusser, *Psychanalyse et sciences humaines*, Le livre de poche, 1996, 78–9; *Psychoanalysis and the Human Sciences*, Columbia University Press, 2016, 48–9. Translation modified.

namely psychoanalysis, he was obliged to develop his thought in the terms of 'a field that was constituted earlier'— terms of the psychology of consciousness, neurology, biology, philosophy and so on. In other words, the creation of a new theory based on a 'rupture' necessarily develops while being 'haunted' by the terms of the 'field that was constituted earlier'. If we interpret the relationship between Althusserian theory and Lacanian theory from such a point of view, we could say that Althusser constructed, while being 'haunted' by Lacanian terms, a totally new theory that is quite distinct from Lacanian psychoanalytic theory. It is, moreover, this *critical* modification of the dispositives of Lacanian theory that allows the problem of the causality of structural becoming and that of resistance to emerge.

This perspective is indispensable for reflecting on the relationship between psychoanalytic theory and social theory. For example, Slavoj Žižek develops a theory of leftist politics by applying the Lacanian theory of the 'real' to social theory, but is it possible to theorize the problem of resistance and structural change in this context? In a book written in collaboration with Žižek and Laclau, Judith Butler wonders if 'the Lacanian view on the constitution of the subject is finally compatible with the notion of hegemony'[6] and continues as follows: 'If the subject always meets its limit in the selfsame place, then the subject is fundamentally exterior to the history in which it finds itself: there is no historicity to the subject, its limits, its articulability. Moreover, if we accept the notion that all historical struggle is nothing other than a vain effort to displace a founding limit that is structural in status, do we then commit ourselves to a distinction between the historical and the structural domains that subsequently excludes the historical domain from the understanding of opposition?'.[7] If 'the real' always determines the subject and the structure *in the same way*, the field of historicity is completely eliminated: this means that we cannot treat the *diachronic* problem as structural change. If Althusser developed a theory of subject formation by ideology and, at the same time, reflected on the causality of structural change, it is because, in a certain way, his attempt responds to the aporia produced by the application of psychoanalytic theory to social theory. It is therefore with this perspective that we offer a

6 Judith Butler, 'Restating the Universal', in Judith Butler, Ernesto Laclau, Slavoj Žižek, *Contingency, Hegemony, Universality*, Verso, 2000, 12.

7 Ibid., 13.

reinterpretation of Althusser's theory of ideology in this fifth chapter. This reinterpretation will require, in the sixth chapter, the examination of the Althusserian theory of structural becoming.

5.2 Regional theory and general theory

In 'Three Notes on the Theory of Discourse' (1966),[8] Althusser aims to construct a 'theory of discourse' based on psychoanalytic theory. The question for him was to evaluate a relation of identity and difference between four types of discourse (scientific, aesthetic, ideological, and unconscious discourses). What theory did he ultimately establish from this argument? We can immediately respond schematically by saying that he posits a theory of discourse as a 'general theory', pointing out, for example, that psychoanalysis is limited to a 'regional theory':

> [W]e can observe, within the regional theory itself, the absence of the general theory (the effects of this absence) at the theoretical level: for as long as the general theory is lacking, the regional theory strives to 'achieve closure', but fails to; or, to put it in other terms, it tries to define its own object *differentially* (in contradistinction to other theoretical objects: in the present case, those of biology, psychology, sociology, etc.), but *fails to*. This attempt and failure are the presence of this *de facto absence* of a general theory, the existence of which is nevertheless called for, *de jure*, in order to found these attempts.[9]

The 'theory of discourse' is therefore conceptualized, without being limited to psychoanalytic theory, as a 'general theory' of social formation. Concerning the Lacanian theory that uses linguistic notions as general principles, Althusser considers that it is aware 'of the need to elaborate a general theory', that it has 'a correct conception of the nature

---

8 This posthumous text was written in 1966 for the *Groupe de travail théorique* which was preparing a collective work on 'elements of dialectical materialism', and then only circulated among the members of this group (Alain Badiou, Étienne Balibar, Yves Duroux, Pierre Macherey and Michel Tort). See the presentation of this text by François Matheron and Olivier Corpet: Louis Althusser, *Écrits sur la psychanalyse*, 111–16; *The Humanist Controversies and Other Writings, 1966–67*, Verso, 2003, 33–7.

9 Louis Althusser, « Trois notes sur la théorie des discours », in *Écrits sur la psychanalyse*, 121; 'Three Notes on the Theory of Discourses', in *The Humanist Controversies and Other Writings*, 40.

of a general theory' and that it is at the 'beginnings of an elaboration of this general theory'.[10] We can thus understand why he aims to construct a general theory that installs 'discourse' as its core.

However, to those acquainted with psychoanalytic theory, the 'general theory' that Althusser proposes must seem strange. For if Lacanian theory is an attempt at a 'general theory' that uses the notion of *signifier* as a general principle,[11] Althusserian general theory, for its part, chooses the notion of *discourse*. In this same text, he even claims, 'I am beginning to be suspicious of this term ['signifier'], which is too deeply involved in the idealism of the connotations of Saussure's signifier-signified'.[12] Thus, the construction of the theory of discourse also implies a critique of the Lacanian theory of the signifier. However, why does Althusser establish the discourse, instead of the signifier, as the core of his general theory? He writes:

> If we compare the different existing *forms* of discourse — that is, the forms of unconscious discourse, ideological discourse, aesthetic discourse and scientific discourse — we can demonstrate the existence of *a common effect: every discourse produces a subjectivity-effect.* Every discourse has, as its necessary correlate, a *subject*, which is *one* of the effects, if not the major effect, of its functioning. Ideological discourse 'produces' or 'induces' a subject-effect, a subject; so do the discourse of science, the discourse of the unconscious, etc.[13]

The four types of discourse (unconscious, ideological, aesthetic and scientific) have, writes Althusser, 'a common effect': they all produce 'a subjectivity-effect'. On the other hand, Lacan defines the effect of the

10 Ibid., 125; 43.

11 This character of Lacanian theory does not change even after his theory of 'four discourses', which is presented for the first time in his seminar on 'The Other Side of Psychoanalysis' (1969–70). Lacan defines the signifying chain and the four discourses (discourse of the master, the university, the hysteric and the psychoanalyst) by relying on the relationship between 'the master signifier' (S_1) and all the other signifiers (S_2). In this sense, this theory is essentially constituted by the general principle of Lacanian theory: that of the signifier. On the other hand, Althusser seeks to establish a theory of discourse in which the signifying chain is not a privileged component.

12 « Trois notes sur la théorie des discours », in *Écrits sur la psychanalyse*, 168; 'Three Notes on the Theory of Discourses', in *The Humanist Controversies and Other Writings*, 81.

13 Ibid., 130–1; 48.

signifier as follows: 'a signifier is what represents the subject to another signifier'.[14] In Lacan, 'a signifier' designates the phallus, namely the lack of the subject brought about by the lack of the Other. The phallus is therefore a 'signifier of lack', repressed and veiled, and which appears in the signifying chain as an absence ('empty place', according to a sophisticated schematization by Deleuze[15]). If the subject is produced by this effect of the repression of the phallus, or of the absence of the signifier, it is represented in the signifying chain by the 'signifier of lack'. In other words, the subject is 'represented' by the Other, since a repressed 'signifier' (phallus) is found in the unconscious (instance of the Other). Althusser emphasizes that 'it is absent from the discourse of the unconscious by "delegation [*lieu-tenance*]"'.[16]

The subject is produced as an effect of the discourse (Althusser). The subject is produced as an effect of the signifier (Lacan). The difference between these two formulations seems extremely slight. Nevertheless, there is a radical difference between them. What does it consist in? To answer this question, it is necessary to introduce the perspective of social theory. Let us refer to *On the Reproduction of Capitalism* (1969), a manuscript on 'the reproduction of the relations of production', from which Althusser drew his famous article on 'Ideology and Ideological State Apparatuses'.[17] He writes:

---

14 « Subversion du sujet et dialectique du désir dans l'inconscient freudien », in *Écrits*, 819; 'The Subversion of the Subject and the Dialectic of Desire in the Freudian Unconscious', in *Écrits: The Complete Edition*, 694.

15 See Gilles Deleuze, « À quoi reconnaît-on le structuralisme ? », in *L'île déserte et autres textes*; 'How Do We Recognize Structuralism?', in *Desert Islands and Other Texts*.

16 « Trois notes sur la théorie des discours », in *Écrits sur la psychanalyse*, 131; 'Three Notes on the Theory of Discourses', in *The Humanist Controversies and Other Writings*, 49. Althusser repeats exactly the Lacanian definition of the signifier: 'it [the subject of unconscious discourse] is "represented" in the chain of signifiers by *one* signifier which "stands in" for it [*qui en « tient lieu »*], which is its "lieu-tenant" [*son « lieu-tenant »*]. Thus it is absent from the discourse of the unconscious by "delegation" [*par « lieu-tenance »*]'.

17 See Jacques Bidet, « En guise d'introduction : une invitation à relire Althusser », in Louis Althusser, *Sur la reproduction*, PUF, 1995; 'An Invitation to Reread Althusser', in Louis Althusser, *On the Reproduction of Capitalism*, Verso, 2014. See also Étienne Balibar, « Althusser et les 'Appareils Idéologiques d'État' », in *Sur la reproduction*, second edition, PUF, 2011; 'Althusser and the "Ideological State Apparatuses"', in *On the Reproduction of Capitalism*. The theory of the 'school apparatus' as the state apparatus, which subjects the subject by inculcating the dominant ideology and reproducing capitalist production relations, was already developed, before Althusser, by the *Groupe de travail sur l'École* (1968–69), whose members were Étienne Balibar, Christian Baudelot, Roger Establet,

Ideology can exist in the form of written discourses (books) or oral discourses (sermons, courses, speeches, and so on) that are supposed to be vehicles for 'ideas'. But, precisely, one's 'idea' of 'ideas' governs what occurs in these discourses. [...] let us say that *'ideas'* by no means have, as the ideology of ideas tends to suggest, an *ideal, idea-dependent* [idéal, idéelle], *or spiritual* existence; they have a *material existence.*[18]

The 'idea', the content of ideology, can exist in the form of 'discourse'. In other words, discourse is a *Träger* [carrier] of ideology, and in this sense, it has a 'material existence' that embodies ideology. However, this materiality is not exclusively reserved for ideological discourse: all types of discourse (unconscious, ideological, aesthetic and scientific) assume, as discourse, this material character and can take on the role of carrier of ideology. On the other hand, the signifier carries only the 'desire of the Other'; the Lacanian theory of the signifier therefore exists only in relation to the 'discourse of the Other', namely to the unconscious. This is how Lacanian theory aims to construct a 'general theory' (theory of

---

Pierre Macherey, and Michel Tort. See a series of documents entitled '*Travail collectif sur l'École*' deposited in IMEC (*Institut mémoire de l'édition contemporaine*). We cite here only two documents: 'In fact, between the school apparatus and the state apparatus, in the capitalist mode of production, there is more than a simple analogy. [...] the school apparatus ensures the *reproduction* of the division of labour, therefore the reproduction of the conditions of capitalist exploitation [*En fait, il y a entre les appareils scolaires et l'appareil d'État, dans le mode de production capitaliste, plus qu'une simple analogie.* [...] *les appareils scolaires assurent la* reproduction *de la* division *du* travail *donc la* reproduction des conditions de l'exploitation capitaliste*]' (Étienne Balibar, « Les appareils scolaires et l'appareil d'État », 9 septembre 1968, 20ALT14/7). 'The function of the school apparatus is to inculcate ALL aspects of the dominant ideology. Note: the school is not limited to inculcating the cultural ideology [...]. Inculcation always takes place at two levels: practical subjection, ideologico-theoretical subjection [*Les appareils scolaires ont pour fonction d'inculquer TOUS les aspects de l'idéologie dominante. Remarque : l'école ne se borne pas à inculquer l'idéologie culturelle* [...]. *L'inculcation se fait toujours à deux niveaux : assujettissement pratique, assujettissement idéologico-théorique*]' (Christian Baudelot, Roger Establet, « Sur l'école bourgeoise, la culture bourgeoise », 3 March 1968, 814ALT/14/3). About the history of this working group, see the following interview: Jun Fujita Hirose and Yoshiyuki Sato, « Critique de l'école dans la pensée française post-68 (1) : Entretien avec Étienne Balibar », Laboratoire d'analyse critique des modernités, 13 Septembre 2021, Laboratoiredanalysecritiquedesmodernites.wordpress.com; 'The Critique of the School in Post-'68 French Thought (1): Interview with Étienne Balibar', Verso blog, 21 March 2022.

18 *Sur la reproduction*, 187; *On the Reproduction of Capitalism*, 156.

the signifier) but always remains at a 'regional theory' which cannot go beyond the framework of psychoanalysis. This limit of Lacanian theory obliges Althusser to move towards the construction of a theory of discourse as a general theory.

5.3 Theory of ideology as a theory of discourse

Althusserian discourse theory critically modifies the concepts of Lacanian psychoanalysis, even though it often uses Lacanian terms. The passage from psychoanalytic theory to social theory as a 'general theory' forms exactly what we have called the 'rupture' with regard to Lacanian psychoanalytic theory. So, what psychoanalytic concept did Althusser modify? The following quote holds a key to answering this question:

> Increasingly, the notion of subject seems to me to pertain to *ideologi-cal* discourse alone, of which it is constitutive. I don't believe that one can talk about a 'subject of Science' or a 'subject of the unconscious' without playing on words and opening the door to serious theoretical ambiguities. For example, the way Lacan talks about the subject of science in his lecture (*Cahiers pour l'Analyse*) [. . .] seems to me highly questionable.[19]

In this quote, Althusser criticizes the Lacanian notion of the 'subject of the unconscious' by insisting on the idea that the notion of subject 'pertains to *ideological* discourse alone'. But what exactly is the issue? He continues:

> Similarly, it seems to me unwarranted to talk about the 'subject of the unconscious' in connection with the *Ich-Spaltung*. There is no

---

19 « Trois notes sur la théorie des discours », in *Écrits sur la psychanalyse*, 164–5; 'Three Notes on the Theory of Discourses', in *The Humanist Controversies and Other Writings*, 77. On the 'subject of science' in Lacan, see « La science et la vérité », in *Écrits*, in particular 857–9; 'Science and Truth', in *Écrits: The Complete Edition*, in particular 728–30. This Lacan text is a transcription of the opening session of the seminar on 'The Object of Psychoanalysis' (1965–66) held at the École normale supérieure. The text first appeared in *Cahiers pour l'Analyse* 1 (1966), published by the *Cercle d'épistémologie* of the École normale supérieure, whose members were more or less close to Althusser.

divided or *split* subject, but something else entirely; alongside the *Ich*, there is a *Spaltung*, that is, literally, an abyss, a precipice, an absence, a lack. This abyss is not a subject, but that which opens up *alongside a subject*, alongside the *Ich*, which is well and truly a subject (and falls within the province of the *ideological*. Freud, it seems to me, gives us the necessary grounds for thinking this on a number of different occasions). This *Spaltung* is the type on specific differential relation or articulation that binds (in the form of an abyss, a lack) unconscious discourse to the element or, rather, structural category of ideological discourse called the *Ich*. In a word, Lacan would appear to *establish the abyss or lack as a subject*, by way of the concept of the division of the subject. There is no 'subject of the unconscious', although the unconscious can exist only thanks to this abyssal relation with an *Ich* (the subject of the ideological). The lack of the subject cannot be called a subject, although the (ideological) subject is implied or reflected in Freud's second topic, in an original way, *through* this lack, which is not a subject, but something *altogether different*.[20]

Althusser's argument can be summarized in two points: first, the subject, belonging to the 'structural category of ideological discourse', is identified with the *Ich* (the preconscious–conscious system) and is distinguished from the unconscious system; second, since the 'divided or split' subject does not exist, and there is a '*Spaltung*' or a lack 'alongside' the subject (the preconscious–conscious system), the subject is always already *(ideologically) sutured*.[21] From this Althusserian definition of the subject, according to which the subject is always already sutured and that the repressed and divided instance of the unconscious is 'alongside' the sutured subject, the Lacanian term of the 'subject of the unconscious' becomes contradictory,

---

20 « Trois notes sur la théorie des discours », in *Écrits sur la psychanalyse*, 165; 'Three Notes on the Theory of Discourses', in *The Humanist Controversies and Other Writings*, 77–8.

21 Alain Badiou shares these two points in a 1969 article. See Alain Badiou, « Marque et manque : À propos du zéro », *Cahiers pour l'analyse* 10, 1969, in particular 156; 'Mark and Lack', in *Concept and Form: Key Texts from the* Cahiers pour l'Analyse, Vol. 1, Verso, 2012, 165: 'The signifier in general is not articulated to lack through the concept of suture, whose purchase demands that the signifier satisfy a certain condition. And the construction of that condition is not the task of psychoanalysis but of historical materialism: only the *ideological* signifier is sutured'.

because it confuses the ego (the preconscious–conscious system) with the unconscious.[22]

Why does Althusser identify the ego (*Ich*) with the subject that only relates to ideological discourse? To answer this question, we must consult the definition of the ideological subject:

> [I]deological discourse, in which the subject-effect is present in person and is thus a signifier of this discourse, the main signifier of this discourse, possesses a structure of *specular centration*; the subject induced is duplicated by a producing subject (the empirical subject is duplicated by the transcendental subject, the man-subject by God, etc.).[23]

Althusser defines the effect of ideological discourse as 'a structure of *specular centration*' — that is, as empirico-transcendental reduplication. This definition of the subject formation will later be shared by Foucault and Deleuze/Guattari. 'Specular centration' means, a 'specular' duplication of the empirical subject by the transcendental subject (ideological instance), and it is by this operation that the subject is formed, sutured and subjected to ideological discourse. We cannot use the notion of 'the *subject* of the unconscious' here, because the unconscious is always split, barred, and divided, and the subject always already exists as an effect of the ideological suture.

Here we must reflect on the mechanism of the subject's ideological suture. Let us refer to the famous article 'Ideology and Ideological State Apparatuses' (1969–70). In this text that completely renewed the theory of ideology, Althusser puts forward this proposition: 'Ideology

---

22 In his book on ideology, Terry Eagleton asserts that since the Lacanian 'subject' is divided and crossed by unstable desire, Althusser misreads Lacanian theory by confusing the symbolic 'subject' (barred and unstable) with the imaginary 'ego' (unified). From where he judges, Althusserian 'political pessimism' on the theory of ideology derives from this misunderstanding of Lacanian theory (Terry Eagleton, *Ideology: An Introduction*, Verso, 1991, 144). However, from our point of view, Althusser does not misread Lacanian theory — he tries to modify Lacanian theoretical dispositives in a materialist way. And it is exactly this process of theoretical modification that makes possible the Althusserian problematic of resistance that is not based on the Lacanian dialectic of the subject and the Other. We will discuss this later in this chapter.

23 « Trois notes sur la théorie des discours », in *Écrits sur la psychanalyse*, 132; 'Three Notes on the Theory of Discourses', in *The Humanist Controversies and Other Writings*, 49–50. Translation modified.

interpellates individuals as subjects'.[24] The interpellation is carried out by the ideological state apparatuses — note the plural: the apparatuses correspond to the various instruments that reproduce the relations of production (family, school, Church, etc.) — which makes the subject obey the dominant ideology. The ideological suture of the subject is thus ensured by this incessant interpellation of the ideological state apparatuses. At the same time, this interpellation rests on a material basis, as it ensures subjection to the dominant ideology by determining the *practical acts* of the subject:

> This ideology talks of actions: we shall talk of actions inserted into practices. And we shall point out that these *practices* are regulated by the *rituals* in which these practices are inscribed, within the *material existence of an ideological apparatus*, be it only a small part of that apparatus: a small mass in a small church, a funeral, a minor match at a sports' club, a school day, a political party meeting, etc.[25]

Ideological discourse sutures the subject through 'rituals' in which the practices are inscribed. In other words, it 'regulates' subjection to the dominant ideology by inculcating the subject with practical norms. To explain this main thesis about ideology, Althusser cites as an example Pascal's phrase: 'Kneel down, move your lips in prayer, and you will believe'.[26] Hence, the problem is not an ideal level in belief: it is the *actions* themselves (kneeling down, moving lips in prayer) that inculcate the *idea* of 'belief'. The primacy of practice over idea constitutes the core of his theory of ideology. And what 'regulates' actions and ensures subjection to the dominant ideology is precisely the interpellation of ideological discourse.

Here, we are led to clarify another point: if the interpellation of ideological discourse sutures the subject in practice, what role does the 'unconscious discourse' assume? If we neglect this question, we cannot understand what the Althusserian 'rupture' with regard to Lacanian theory means. Let us refer to 'Three Notes on the Theory of Discourse':

---

24 Louis Althusser, « Idéologie et appareils idéologiques d'État », in *Sur la reproduction*, 302; 'Ideology and Ideological State Apparatuses', in *On the Reproduction of Capitalism*, 261.

25 Ibid., 300–1; 260. Translation modified.

26 Ibid., 301; 260.

To say that the unconscious produces its formations, or some of them, in concrete 'situations' (of everyday life, family relations, workplace relations, chance relations, etc.) thus literally means that it produces them in formations of ideological discourse, in formations of the ideological. It is in this sense that we can say that the unconscious reveals the principle of its *articulation* with the ideological. It is in this sense that we can say that the unconscious 'functions' on ideology.[27]

Here Althusser explores the principle of the 'articulation' of the unconscious onto the ideological, whereby ideological formations are produced, by passing through the unconscious, in concrete 'situations'. In other words, ideological discourse sutures the subject only by passing through the unconscious discourse that assumes the role of the carrier [*Träger*] of the former discourse. But by what unconscious mechanism does ideological discourse suture the subject?

To use an extremely approximate language, we can suggest that the ideological formations in which the formations of a particular unconscious 'take hold' constitute the 'material' (informed in its turn) in which certain typical formations of this unconscious 'take hold'. Thus it would be by way of these ideological formations *among others* that, in the phenomenon described by Freud, unconsciouses 'communicate'; the situation of the transference would come about in this way as well.[28]

Here Althusser tries to elucidate the mechanism of the ideological suture. Ideological formations realize the 'situation of the transference' to the dominant ideology. If the subject is sutured by the ideological interpellation, this ideological suture is realized exactly by means of this transference to the dominant ideology.

The ideological suture is defined, in Althusser, as 'centration'. How can we interpret this definition in relation to the mechanism of transference? To understand this, we must return to Lacan's seminar on 'The Four Fundamental Concepts of Psychoanalysis' (1964), where he deals with the transfer from the analysand to the analyst:

---

27 « Trois notes sur la théorie des discours », in *Écrits sur la psychanalyse*, 142; 'Three Notes on the Theory of Discourses', in *The Humanist Controversies and Other Writings*, 58–9.

28 Ibid., 143–4; 59. Translation modified.

There is another use of the term transference that is worth pointing out, as when one says that it structures all the particular relations with that other who is the analyst, and that the value of all the thoughts that gravitate around this relation must be connoted by a sign of particular reserve. Hence the expression — which is always added as a kind of after-thought or parenthesis, as if to convey some kind of suspicion, when used about the behaviour of a subject — *he is in full transference*. This presupposes that his entire mode of apperception has been restructured on the dominant centre of the transference.[29]

In transference, the entire mode of apperception of the analysand is 'restructured on the prevailing centre of the transference': in other words, in the transference situation, the analysand's ego is *metonymically* 'restructured' on the ego of the analyst; this situation is realized only through the unconscious. We could say that 'centration' designates this mechanism of transference by which the ego is restructured on the Other. In psychoanalytic theory, the dissymmetry of knowledge between the analysand and the analyst, and the latter's speech, ensures transference from the analysand to the analyst. Lacan positioned the analyst as the 'subject supposed to know [*sujet supposé de savoir*]'.[30] In contrast, when Althusser defines the ideological suture of the subject as 'centration', the 'dominant centre' corresponds to the dominant ideology inculcated by the ideological state apparatuses. By 'restructuring' the ego onto the dominant ideology through the mechanism of the unconscious (transference), the subject is ideologically sutured. And it is exactly the materiality of the discourse inculcated in the practices ('rituals'), that ensures this 'restructuring', the transference to the dominant ideology. What allows transference to the dominant ideology in the ideological suture is therefore the *ritual practice* or the *materiality* of the discourse. Althusser carefully manipulates the theoretical dispositives of psychoanalysis and fundamentally transforms their general framework from a materialist perspective. What we have called a 'rupture' with regard to Lacanian theory designates exactly this process of *materialist*

---

29 *Le séminaire*, Livre XI, « Les quatre concepts fondamentaux de la psychanalyse », 114; *The Seminar*, Book XI, 'The Four Fundamental Concepts of Psychoanalysis', 124. Translation modified.

30 See, for example, Jacques Lacan, « Fonction et champ de la parole et du langage en psychanalyse », in *Écrits*, 308, note 2; 'The Function and Field of Speech and Language in Psychoanalysis', in *Écrits: The Complete Edition*, 267, note 41.

transformation of psychoanalytic theory. And it is this *materialization* of Lacanian psychoanalytic theory that establishes a theoretical basis for resisting the dominant ideology.[31]

5.4 From psychoanalytic theory to the theory of structural becoming

In *The Sublime Object of Ideology*, Slavoj Žižek criticizes the Althusserian theory of ideology and proposes a modification. He chooses the law as an example of ideological state apparatuses to develop his argument. The fundamental characteristic of the Law as an ideological state apparatus is its 'incomprehensibility', 'exteriority' to the subject it interpellates: the subject does not obey the Law because it is just, but because it is the Law, writes Žižek, quoting Pascal. In other words, the subject obeys the interpellation of the Law only because of the lack of metalanguage that founds the Law, or because of the incomprehensibility of the foundation of the Law.[32] Žižek explains that it is this mechanism of transference that ensures such obedience to 'authority without truth':

> The necessary structural illusion which drives people to believe that truth can be found in laws describes precisely the mechanism of transference: transference is this supposition of a Truth, of a Meaning behind the stupid, traumatic, inconsistent fact of the Law.[33]

According to Žižek, the interpellation of the Law is always 'traumatic' and 'inconsistent', because the Law does not possess a metalanguage that founds it. The interpellation cannot therefore be completely internalized by the subject: 'there is always a residue, a leftover'. To repress this non-symbolizable 'residue', the subject transfers the Law and attempts to identify with it. He concludes that Althusser misses, in his theory of ideology, this mechanism of the subject's identification with the ideological interpellation in order to repress the non-symbolizable residue.[34]

---

31 We will discuss this point in section 5.5.
32 Slavoj Žižek, *The Sublime Object of Ideology*, Verso, 1989, 36–7.
33 Ibid., 38.
34 Ibid., 43.

The problem of this criticism is that it is constituted by an 'extrapola-tion' (Deleuze/Guattari) of psychoanalytic theory to social theory and also that it reduces the Althusserian attempt at constructing a general theory to psychoanalytic theory. In fact, we could easily formalize Žižek's argument within the framework of psychoanalysis. The Law as an ideological state apparatus in Žižek corresponds to the Other of Lacanian theory: the Other is incomprehensible and 'inconsistent' for the subject. In other words, there is no metalanguage that founds the Other ('there is no Other of the Other').[35] Lacan expressed this character of the Other by a matheme $\cancel{A}$: the barred Other. At the same time, the subject is also barred ($\cancel{S}$, which means the lack of the subject) by this 'traumatic' and 'inconsistent' character of the Other. To repress this lack, the subject tries to suture his *Spaltung* by 'fantasy' ($\cancel{S} \lozenge a$).[36] In Žižek, it is this mechanism of (ideological) fantasy that allows the subject to iden-tify with the dominant ideology.

Althusser explained the mechanism of transference to the domi-nant ideology through 'rituals' that inculcate ideology and that exist everywhere in daily life (in family, school, etc.). In the ideological transference, the practice or the materiality of the discourse takes precedence over the idea. On the other hand, Žižek's critique of Althusser completely avoids explaining this materiality. Moreover, Žižek reduces the multiplicity of ideological state apparatuses to law alone. The multiple interpellations of the ideological apparatuses are then reduced to the 'traumatic, senseless injunction'[37] of the Law. In other words, his critique of Althusserian theory reduces the plurality of ideological state apparatuses to 'juridico-discursive' power, to use Foucault's expression (the law imposes the *prohibition* on the subject).[38] In fact, Žižek accounts for the Althusserian notion of 'ideological state apparatuses' in the singular form ('the Ideological State Apparatus' as Law),[39] while Althusser defines the ideological state apparatuses in their multiplicity:

---

35 « Subversion du sujet et dialectique du désir dans l'inconscient freudien », in *Écrits*, 813; 'The Subversion of the Subject and the Dialectic of Desire in the Freudian Unconscious', in *Écrits: The Complete Edition*, 688.
36 Ibid., 816; 691.
37 *The Sublime Object of Ideology*, 43.
38 See *La volonté de savoir*, 107–20; *The History of Sexuality, Vol. 1*, 81–91.
39 See, for example, *The Sublime Object of Ideology*, 43.

[T]he Ideological State Apparatuses are multiple, distinct, relatively autonomous, and prone to providing an objective field to contradictions which express, in forms that are as a rule limited, but in some cases extreme, the effects of the clashes between the capitalist class struggle and the proletarian class struggle.[40]

Ideological state apparatuses are 'multiple' and 'prone to providing an objective field to contradictions'. In other words, they contain, in their multiplicity, *contradictions* that constitute the effects of resistance ('class struggle'). When Althusser defines ideological state apparatuses as a multiplicity, what is therefore at stake is to expose the 'contradictions' as the effects of resistance ('class struggle') and the possibility of structural change. The *materialization* of Lacanian theory in Althusser is totally repressed in Žižek; this means that there is not any possibility of structural change in Žižek.

It is from this point of view that, for our part, we will approach the central problem of Lacanian theory. In his seminar, Lacan uses the word 'extimacy [*extimité*]' at least three times. This term, introduced to elucidate the character of the field of the Other,[41] is a portmanteau of the words 'intimacy [*intimité*]' and 'exteriority [*exteriorité*]'. Lacan explains this in the seminar '*D'un Autre à l'autre*' (1968–69):

It [the object *a*] is here in a place that we can designate with the term extimate [*extime*], conjoining the intimate [*intime*] with the radical exteriority [*extériorité*]. It is insofar as the object *a* is extimate, and purely in the relation established by the institution of the subject as an effect of signifier, and as determining by itself an edge structure in the field of the Other.[42]

According to Lacan, 'the object *a* is extimate' insofar as it is 'in the relation established by the institution of the subject as an effect of

---

40 *Sur la reproduction*, 170; *On the Reproduction of Capitalism*, 140.

41 See Jacques-Alain Miller, « Extimité », in *Lacanian Theory of Discourse*, New York University Press, 1994.

42 Jacques Lacan, *Le séminaire*, Livre XVI, « D'un Autre à l'autre », Seuil, 2006, 249: « *Il [l'objet* a*] est ici à une place que nous pouvons désigner du terme d'extime, conjoignant l'intime à la radicale extériorité. C'est à savoir que c'est en tant que l'objet* a *est extime, et purement dans le rapport instauré de l'institution du sujet comme effet de signifiant, et comme par lui-même déterminant dans le champ de l'Autre une structure de bord* ».

signifier'. The object *a* is the 'object cause of desire [*objet cause de désir*]'[43] which motivates desire and is found as an unrepresentable object in the field of the Other (the unconscious). If the field of the Other is 'extimate', it constitutes the most intimate field of the subject (as an object cause of desire) and, at the same time, it forms the most radical exteriority (as the non-symbolizable). It is by the effect of this extimacy of the Other that the subject sutures the gap with his fantasy. We can recognize here a typically Lacanian schematization of the Other: the field of the Other is the *transcendent* instance which determines the subject as radical exteriority (Other as the non-symbolizable) and, at the same time, it is the *transcendental* instance (the unconscious) in which the Other is internalized as the non-symbolizable. In this sense, we can say that the field of the Other is *transcendent(al)*.

Žižek formulated his critique of Althusser from this Lacanian schema. In his theorization, in fact, the transcendent(al) instance of the Other is replaced by the Law as the only Ideological State Apparatus. This 'extrapolation' of psychoanalytic theory to social theory poses a problem: in Žižek, the Law as the Ideological State Apparatus forms the transcendent instance that determines the subject by its radical exteriority; the subject who internalizes the ideological interpellation cannot resist this transcendence of the Ideological State Apparatus. Thus, we cannot conceive, within this theorization, of resistance and structural change. The subject will constantly internalize this 'traumatic' and 'inconsistent' exteriority called the Law. By definition, resistance to ideological state apparatuses and structural change cannot arise.[44]

---

43 See Jacques Lacan, *Le séminaire*, Livre X, « L'angoisse », Seuil, 2004, 120, 221; *The Seminar*, Book X, 'Anxiety', Polity Press, 2014, 101, 189.

44 In *Contingency, Hegemony, Universality*, Žižek attempts to suggest a possibility of resistance, using the Lacanian concept of 'separation': 'This dimension of the "big Other" is that of the constitutive alienation of the subject in the symbolic order: the Big Other pulls the strings; the subject does not speak, he "is spoken" by the symbolic structure. In short, this "big Other" is the name for the social Substance, for all that on account of which the subject never fully dominates the effects of his acts — on account of which the final outcome of his activity is always something other than what he aimed at or anticipated. It is crucial here, however, to note that in the key chapters of *Seminar XI*, Lacan struggles to delineate the operation that follows alienation and is in a sense its counterpoint, that of separation: alienation in the big Other is followed by the separation from the big Other. Separation takes place when the subject realizes how the big Other is in itself inconsistent, purely virtual, barred, deprived of the Thing [. . .] — to experience his subjective position as correlative to the big Other's inconsistency/impotence/lack: in separation, the subject experiences how his own lack with regard to the big Other is

5.5 Structural causality and contingency

Faced with this psychoanalytic concept of the Other, what attitude does Althusser take? To reflect on 'the determination of the elements of a structure [. . .] by the effectivity of this structure'[45] in Marxian theory, he proposes, in *Reading Capital* (1965), two kinds of causality: 'structural causality' and 'metonymic causality'. Their difference is very slight, but to us, it seems distinct. In explaining this difference, Althusser compares two terms used by Marx: *Darstellung* and *Vorstellung*, which both mean 'representation'. In *Vorstellung*, 'we do have a position, but which presents itself *in front*, which therefore supposes something held *behind* this preposition, something represented by what is held in front'. However, in *Darstellung*, '*there is nothing behind*: the very thing is there, "*da*", offered in the position of presence'. After this comparison, he continues:

> This is why, *according to the level at which one places oneself*, we can say that the '*Darstellung*' is the concept of the *presence of the structure in its effects*, that of the modification of the effects by the effectivity of the structure present in its effects, — or on the contrary that the '*Darstellung*' is the concept of the *effectivity of an absence*. It is in this second sense that Rancière used the *decisive* concept of '*metonymic causality*', elaborated in depth by Miller last year during our seminar on Lacan. I believe that, understood as the concept of the *effectivity of an absent cause*, this concept is admirably suited to denote the very absence of the structure in the effects viewed from the grazing perspective of their existence. But we must insist on the other aspect of the phenomenon, that of the *presence*, the immanence of the cause in its effects, in other words, that of the *existence of the structure* in its effects.[46]

---

already the lack that affects the big Other itself' (Slavoj Žižek, 'Da Capo senza Fine', in *Contingency, Hegemony, Universality*, 253–4). But he does not clearly explain how this 'separation' can occur in social formation, although this explanation is quite persuasive within the framework of psychoanalytic theory. In other words, how can 'separation' take place if transference to the dominant ideology is maintained in the ideologically constituted social formation? It is this question that we address in this chapter.

45 Louis Althusser, « L'objet du 'Capital' », in *Lire le Capital* (1965/68), nouvelle edition revue, coll. « Quadrige », PUF, 1996, 401; 'The Object of *Capital*', in *Reading Capital: The Complete Edition*, Verso, 2016, 341.

46 « L'objet du 'Capital' », in *Lire le Capital*, 646, variant [66] (first edition, T. II, Maspero, 1965, 170–1). This paragraph exists in the first edition (1965), but it is entirely deleted in the second edition (1968).

Althusser defines 'structural causality' as the *presence or immanence* of the structure in its effects, and 'metonymic causality' as the *absence* of the structure in its effects (or the effectivity of an *absent* cause). We first emphasize that, in these two causalities, the cause is not supposed to be located behind the phenomenon, because it is, as presence or absence, always in the *effects* of the structure.

Let us recall the Freudian concept of the unconscious. Freud noticed the formations of the unconscious, such as the symptom, the missed act, the dream, etc., according to which he assumed the existence of the unconscious. Thus, the unconscious does not exist as substance: it exists only in the *formations* of the unconscious as the *effects* of the unconscious. Althusser deduces from Freud's discovery a causality in which the cause appears only as the effects in the phenomenon; structural causality and metonymic causality share this character. On the other hand, their difference lies in the fact that, in structural causality, the cause is *present* in the effects of the structure, while in metonymic causality, the cause exists as an *absence* in the effects of the structure. What does this mean?

We will start with metonymic causality. This notion refers to Jacques-Alain Miller's formalization of Lacanian theory, where the question is exactly the absence of a cause in the structure. In 'Suture' (1966), Miller formalizes the Lacanian theory by referring to Frege's *Grundlagen der Arithmetik*.[47] Frege defines natural numbers in terms of sets: 0 is identified with the empty set $\emptyset$ (the set having no elements); 1 is identified with the set $\{\emptyset\}$ (the set having $\emptyset$ as its sole element); 2 is identified with the set $\{\emptyset, \{\emptyset\}\}$ (the set having the two elements $\emptyset$

---

47 Jacques-Alain Miller, « La suture : Élément de la logique du signifiant », in *Cahiers pour l'analyse* 1, 1966; 'Suture: Elements of the Logic of the Signifier', in *Concept and Form: Key Texts from the* Cahiers pour l'Analyse, Vol. 1, Verso, 2012. This text was read on 24 February 1965 in Lacan's seminar. Miller's formalization of Lacanian theory would later be introduced inversely to Lacanian theory. Lacan's argument on 'extimacy' is therefore based on Miller's formalization. In fact, in the session of 12 March 1969 of the seminar 'D'un Autre à l'autre', Lacan himself invokes 'Freudian logic' and the position of 'one or zero in logic' (*Le séminaire*, Livre XVI, « D'un Autre à l'autre », 224). On this point, see the critical and meticulous analysis by Koji Togawa, *Seishinbunseki heno teikô* [*Resistance to Psychoanalysis*], Seido-sha, 2000, Ch. 7. With regard to Frege's theory, see also the analysis by Yves Duroux: « Psychologie et logique », in *Cahiers pour l'analyse* 1; 'Psychology and Logic', in *Concept and Form: Key Texts from the* Cahiers pour l'Analyse, Vol. 1. This text is a reading of the *Grundlagen der Arithmetik*, which was read on 27 January 1965 in Lacan's seminar and which laid the foundations for the formalization of Lacanian theory by Miller.

and {∅}); and so forth[48]. Miller emphasizes that this system defines 1 by the set {∅} which has the empty set ∅ as its element. According to him, this manipulation consists of displacing 0 to 1: 'This system is thus so constituted *with the 0 counting as 1*. The counting of the 0 as 1 (whereas the concept of the zero subsumes nothing in the real but a blank) is the general support of the series of numbers.'[49] To define natural numbers, we must thus displace 0 to 1 and metonymically suture a lack.[50]

Miller then applies this logic to the relationship between the subject and the Other. The subject is divided, barred by the inconsistency of the Other; at the same time, it 'sutures' its lack in the form of a fantasy by internalizing the non-symbolizable Other:

> In effect, what in Lacanian algebra is called the relation of the subject to the field of the Other (as the locus of truth) can be identified with the relation which the zero entertains with the identity of the unique as the support of truth. This relation, insofar as it is matrical [*matriciel*], cannot be integrated into a definition of objectivity [. . .]. The engendering of the zero, from this non-identical with itself under which no thing of the world falls, illustrates this to you.[51]

Just as the zero is metonymically sutured by the one, the subject is sutured by the Other. As we have seen, the 'phallus' is *a* repressed signifier which appears, literally, as an *absence* (an empty place) in the signifying chain; it is through this *effect of the absence of a signifier* that the subject sutures its gap. The 'effectivity of an absent cause' (Althusser) designates this mechanism in which the 'phallus', an *absent* signifier in the signifying chain, sutures the subject in its *effect*.

---

48 This explanation of Frege's mathematical logic is entirely due to the work of Alain Sokal and Jean Bricmont: *Impostures intellectuelles*, Le livre de poche, 1999, 67, note 33; *Intellectual Impostures: Postmodern Philosophers' Abuse of Science*, Profile Books, 2003, 27, note 29.

49 « La suture », in *Cahiers pour l'analyse*, no. 1, 45; 'Suture', in *Concept and Form: Key Texts from the* Cahiers pour l'Analyse, Vol. 1, 97.

50 Recall that, in Lacan, metonymy means 'displacement', 'transfer of signification'. See « L'instance de la lettre dans l'inconscient freudien ou la raison depuis Freud », in *Écrits*, 511; 'The Instance of the Letter in the Unconscious or Reason since Freud', in *Écrits: The Complete Edition*, 425.

51 « La suture », in *Cahiers pour l'analyse*, no. 1, 47; 'Suture', in *Concept and Form: Key Texts from the* Cahiers pour l'Analyse, Vol. 1, 100.

In the previous quote from *Reading Capital*, Althusser wrote: 'we must insist on the other aspect of the phenomenon [the effectivity of an absent cause], that of the *presence*, the immanence of the cause in its effects, in other words, that of the *existence of the structure* in its effects'. We can elucidate the reason he adopted structural causality and not metonymic causality, which relies on the Lacanian concept of the Other as 'extimacy'. If one extrapolates, as Žižek does, the psychoanalytic concept of the Other to social theory, this can only induce the transcendence of power dispositives. Althusser carefully avoids this pitfall by choosing structural causality, which means 'the existence of the structure in its effects'. In other words, structural causality refers to the determination of one structure (for example, the subject) by another structure (for example, the ideological state apparatuses); the cause (= another structure) determining the structure is then present there. In this sense, it is a '*cause immanent* in its effects in the Spinozist sense of the term'.[52] In this causality, the transcendent instance does not exist by definition. From this, we can affirm: *the possibility of resistance to the dominant ideology exists within the very process of the interpellation of the ideological state apparatuses*, or *the possibility of structural becoming exists within the social formation itself, which continuously reproduces itself*.[53]

Where, then, does Althusser locate the possibility of resistance to the dominant ideology? In *On the Reproduction of Capitalism*, he distinguishes two modalities of ideology:

We shall therefore say that a distinction must be made here. We must distinguish between, on the one hand, the determinate elements of the State Ideology that are realized in, and exist in, a determinate Apparatus and its practices, and, on the other, the ideology that is 'produced' in this Apparatus by its practices. To mark this distinction terminologically, we shall call the former ideology the 'Primary

---

52 « L'objet du 'Capital' », in *Lire le Capital*, 405; 'The Object of *Capital*', in *Reading Capital: The Complete Edition*, 344. Our emphasis.

53 On the relationship between structural causality and structural change, See « Lettre à D . . . », in *Écrits sur la psychanalyse*, Stock/IMEC, 1993, 106–7; 'Letter to D . .', in *Writing on Psychoanalysis: Freud and Lacan*, Columbia University Press, 1999, 73–4. Althusser reflects on the relationship between the internalization of the language structure by the small child and the 'irruption [*surgissement*]' of the unconscious structure ('The unconscious is structured like a language').

Ideology', and the latter — a by-product of the practice in which the Primary Ideology is realized — the 'secondary, subordinate ideology'.[54]

The Primary Ideology is realized and exists in a determinate Apparatus; in contrast, the secondary ideology is *produced*, as a by-product of the Primary Ideology, within this apparatus. What is the difference between these two modalities?

> We shall say that this secondary ideology is 'produced' by the practice of the apparatus that realizes the Primary Ideology. But that is just a convenient way of putting it: for *no practice in the world produces 'its' ideology all by itself*. There is no 'spontaneous' ideology, although it can be useful, in other words, terminologically convenient when making a specific point, to use the expression 'spontaneous' ideology. In the case to hand, these secondary ideologies are produced by a conjunction of complex causes. Among them are, alongside the practice in question, the effect of other, external ideologies, other external practices and, in the final instance, the effects — however veiled — of the *class struggle*, even its remote effects, which are in fact very close.[55]

Primary Ideology is realized, as the dominant ideology, in ideological state apparatuses and is embodied in ideological interpellation (or in 'rituals'). However, when this Primary Ideology is inculcated in the subject as its 'destination',[56] it is transformed 'by a conjunction of complex causes', by a *conjuncture*. In other words, the dominant ideology is not internalized in the subject in its pure form: in the process of ideological interpellation, it is transformed by a social conjuncture. *The subject is therefore not perfectly sutured by the dominant ideology*. It is exactly in this sense that the de-subjection of the subjected subjects (Althusser calls it the production of 'bad subjects'[57]) is always possible. And this is where the effect of the 'class struggle' or resistance appears.[58]

---

54 *Sur la reproduction*, 114; *On the Reproduction of Capitalism*, 83.

55 Ibid., 115; 83.

56 « Idéologie et appareils idéologiques d'État », in *Sur la reproduction*, 302; 'Ideology and Ideological State Apparatuses', in *On the Reproduction of Capitalism*, 261.

57 Ibid., 310; 269.

58 In *On the Reproduction of Capitalism*, Althusser considers the class struggle as the proletarian struggle. However, from our perspective, we can redefine this notion as

Note that the effect of the class struggle appears in the secondary ideology. Ideological apparatuses aim to inculcate the dominant ideology (Primary Ideology) through ritualistic practices; in other words, the dominant ideology tries to suppress other ideologies and the class struggle. However, the latter is always found in 'another reality [*une autre réalité*]'.[59] This expression reminds us of the Freudian term 'another scene [*ein anderer Schauplatz*]', which designates the unconscious.[60] Just as the unconscious appears as an effect in the formations of the unconscious, the class struggle appears as an effect in the secondary ideology.[61] And this effect denotes the existence of the class struggle or resistance:

> That is why we can derive from this thesis *of the primacy of the class struggle over the dominant ideology and the Ideological State Apparatuses* another thesis, its direct consequence: the Ideological State Apparatuses are necessarily both the site and the stake of a class struggle that extends the general class struggle dominating a social formation into the apparatuses of the dominant ideology. If the function of the ISAs [Ideological State Apparatuses] is to inculcate the dominant ideology, the reason is that there is *resistance*; if there is

---

that which includes minority struggles: struggles of women, colonized people, LGBTQ people, victims of pollution, etc. As one of these attempts, see Éric Alliez/Maurizio Lazzarato, *Guerre et capital*, Éditions Amsterdam, 2016; *Wars and Capital*, Semiotext(e), 2018. In a 1978 text — the period of the 'crisis of Marxism' — Althusser himself tries to broaden the notion of class struggle. See « Le marxisme comme théorie 'finie' », in *Solitude de Machiavel*, 289; 'Marxism as Finite Theory', *Viewpoint Magazine*, 14 December 2017, viewpointmag.com (this English edition is a translation of an article published in *Il Manifesto* and is shorter than the original French text): 'An important tendency is actually taking shape, to take politics out of its bourgeois juridical status. The old party/union distinction is put to a harsh test, totally unforeseen political initiatives emerge outside the parties, and even outside the workers' movement (ecology, women's struggles, youth struggles, etc.), in a great confusion certainly, but which can be productive'. Translation modified. We will discuss the carriers of resistance in our Conclusion.

59 *Sur la reproduction*, 116; *On the Reproduction of Capitalism*, 85.

60 *Die Traumdeutung*, in *Gesammelte Werke*, Bd. II/III, 541: 'der Schauplatz der Träume ein anderer sei als der des wachen Vorstellungslebens'.

61 But we cannot reduce the class struggle to the 'unconscious' of social formation. The unconscious only exists as the formations of the unconscious, and its existence is only assumed; on the other hand, the class struggle or the resistance always exists, as a political reality, in social formation. Althusser therefore replaces the psychoanalytic term 'another scene' with 'another reality'.

resistance, the reason is that there is struggle. In the final analysis, this struggle is a direct or indirect echo of the class struggle, sometimes a close echo, more often a distant one. The May 1968 events brought this fact into the broad light of day, revealing a struggle that had until then been mute and suppressed.[62]

Even if the ideological state apparatuses function 'to inculcate the dominant ideology', this ideology is transformed by the conjuncture, namely the class struggle; resistance to the dominant ideology (de-subjection of the subjected subjects) emerges in this transformation. Using a 1980s Althusserian term, we call this process of ideological transformation a 'deviation' of ideology.[63]

In Lacanian psychoanalytic theory, this deviation does not exist. Althusser raises this question in 'The Discovery of Dr. Freud' (1976):

In his famous seminar on the purloined letter, after a meticulous and intriguing analysis of Poe's text, Lacan concludes, 'according to which a letter always arrives at its destination'. It is a line excessively encumbered with meanings and echoes in a philosophy of the signifier, the letter, the unconscious as signifier. To that declaration, which is supported by a whole philosophy not of the addressee [*destinataire*] but of destiny [*destin*], and thus of the most classical finality, I will simply oppose the materialist thesis: *it happens that a letter does not arrive at its destination* [il arrive qu'une lettre n'arrive pas à destination].[64]

---

62 Louis Althusser, « Note sur les AIE », in *Sur la reproduction*, 255; 'Note on the ISAs', in *On the Reproduction of Capitalism*, 220.

63 « Le courant souterrain du matérialisme de la rencontre », in *Écrits philosophiques et politiques*, T. I, 541; 'The Underground Current of the Materialism of the Encounter', in *Philosophy of the Encounter*, 169. In this 1982 text, Althusser describes a scene of the creation of the world theorized by Epicurus and Lucretius: 'The clinamen is an infinitesimal *swerve*, "as small as possible"; "no one knows where, or when, or how" it occurs, or what causes an atom to "swerve" from its vertical fall in the void, and, breaking the parallelism in an almost negligible way at one point, induce *an encounter* with the atom next to it, and, from encounter to encounter, a pile-up and the birth of a world — that is to say, of the agglomeration of atoms induced, in a chain reaction, by the initial swerve and encounter'.

64 « La découverte du Docteur Freud », in *Écrits sur la psychanalyse*, 203–4; 'The Discovery of Dr. Freud', in *Writings on Psychoanalysis*, 91–2. Translation modified. See also, Louis Althusser, *L'avenir dure longtemps*, Le livre de poche, 1994, 210–11; *The Future Lasts Forever*, New Press, 1993, 187–8. In this autobiographical text, Althusser explains what is at stake in his materialist thesis ('it happens that a letter does not reach

Althusser opposes his 'materialist thesis' ('it happens that a letter does not arrive at its destination') to the Lacanian thesis ('a letter always arrives at its destination'). What is at stake in these two completely opposite theses? What Lacan tried to show in 'The Seminar on "The Purloined Letter"' is that the law proper to the signifying chain relates the subject to the symbolic order; in other words, the subject is sutured (i.e., related to the symbolic order) by the signifier of the lack ('the *purloined* letter') in the signifying chain. 'A letter' then designates the signifier of a lack, and 'destination' signifies the subject. But why does a letter *always* arrive at its destination for Lacan? It is exactly at this point that the 'intersubjective'[65] relationship between the subject and the Other emerges. Let us refer again to 'Suture':

> If now we were to try and develop in time the relation which engenders and supports the signifying chain, we would have to take into account the fact that temporal succession is under the dependency of the linearity of the chain. The time of engendering can only be circular — which is why both these propositions are true at one and the same time, that subject is anterior to signifier and that signifier is anterior to subject — but only appears as such after the introduction of the signifier. The retroaction consists essentially of this: the birth of linear time. We must hold together the definitions which make the subject *the effect of the signifier* and the signifier *the representative of the subject*: it is a circular, though non-reciprocal, relation.[66]

Miller asserts that 'we must hold together the definitions which make the subject *the effect of the signifier* and the signifier *the representative of the subject*'. According to the first definition, the signifier of lack, which

---

its destination'): 'I was to remain true to my critique of classic dialectical materialism'. The philosophy of 'destiny, and thus of the most classical finality' designates the teleological dialectic represented by the Hegelian dialectic. This makes it possible to understand the Althusserian thesis as a theory of deviation, totally distinct from Hegelian teleology shared by classical Marxism and Lacanian theory. In Chapter 4, we reflected on this Derridean thesis: 'a letter can always not arrive at its destination'. The Derridian thesis and the Althusserian 'materialist' thesis respond to each other, as we shall see, through the notions of contingency and resistance.

65 « Le séminaire sur 'La lettre volée' », in *Écrits*, 41; 'Seminar on "The Purloined Letter"', in *Écrits: The Complete Edition*, 30.

66 « La suture », in *Cahiers pour l'analyse*, no. 1, 48–9; 'Suture', in *Concept and Form: Key Texts from the* Cahiers pour l'Analyse, Vol. 1, 101.

is located in the transcendent(al) instance of the Other, produces the subject as an effect; in contrast, as per the second definition, the signifier of lack as an instance of the Other represents the subject. If we notice this 'circularity', the subject is represented by the signifier (subject → Other); but at the same time, it is sutured by this representation (Other → subject). This is how the signifier *always* arrives at its destination (subject) via *the Other*, and it is how the subject is *always already* sutured by the instance of *the Other*. The 'intersubjective' relationship between the subject and the Other is therefore only asymmetrical; likewise, the instance of the Other is only transcendent(al).

Althusser proposed a 'materialist thesis' to criticize this transcendent(al) instance of the Other, as the basis of Lacanian psychoanalytic theory. In Althusserian theory, interpellation by ideological state apparatuses entails a *deviation* in the process of ideological interpellation/introjection: in other words, the dominant ideology is forced to undergo an alteration during this deviation, which demonstrates the social existence of resistance. The intervention of *contingency* ('conjuncture') appears here in differentiating itself from the philosophy of *destiny*, namely from Lacanian theory. In this sense, 'metonymic causality' corresponds to the 'destinal' character of the Lacanian theory of the signifier, and 'structural causality' corresponds to the Althusserian theory of contingency and resistance. The 'materialist thesis' which Althusser opposes to Lacanian theory designates the unstable field of power relations (class struggle) — in other words, *the field of contingency*. And *what produces this contingency, the deviation from the reproductive law of capitalist society, is the collective class struggle, which de-subjects the subjects.* This problematic of contingency allows Althusser to theorize resistance and structural change. From this perspective, in the next chapter, we will approach the problem of the relationship between the causality of structural change and contingency.

5.6 On 'specular centration'

We have shown that the possibility of resistance to the dominant ideology and structural change exists in the Althusserian theory of ideology. However, there is a seemingly contradictory element within his theory itself: at the end of 'Ideology and Ideological State Apparatuses', Althusser cites an example of Christian religious ideology to explain the 'formal'

structure of all ideology based on the relationship between God (Unique
and Absolute Subject) and the subjects He addresses:

> We observe that the structure of all ideology, interpellating individu-
> als as subjects in the name of a Unique and Absolute Subject, is *specu-
> lar*, i.e. a mirror-structure, and *doubly* specular: this mirror duplica-
> tion is constitutive of ideology and ensures its functioning. This
> means that all ideology is *centred*, that the Absolute Subject occupies
> the unique place of the Centre, and interpellates around it the infinity
> of individuals into subjects in a double mirror–connexion such that it
> *subjects* the subjects to the Subject, while giving them in the Subject in
> which each subject can contemplate its own image (present and
> future) the *guarantee* that this really concerns them and Him, and
> that since everything takes place in the Family (the Holy Family: the
> Family is in essence Holy), 'God will *recognize* His own in it', i.e. those
> who have recognized God, and have recognized themselves in Him,
> will be saved.[67]

Althusser shows that the relationship between God as an Absolute
Subject and the subjects He interpellates (Unique Subject interpellates individuals as subjects) is *specular*. The problem is that this
'abstract' schematization of the *specular* relation misses the problem
of resistance, especially that of the *deviation* of ideology. In *On the
reproduction of Capitalism*, he develops the question of the multiplicity of ideological state apparatuses and of the ideological deviation in
capitalist production relations. However, relying on Marx and Engels'
thesis in *The German Ideology* ('ideology has no history'),[68] he asserts
that 'the formal structure of all ideology is always the same' and
restricts his analysis 'to a single example': that of Christian religious
ideology.[69] It is from there that he deduces the transcendence of the
ideological state apparatus as an Absolute and Unique Subject.[70] How

---

67 « Idéologie et appareils idéologiques d'État », in *Sur la reproduction*, 310; 'Ideology
and Ideological State Apparatuses', in *On the Reproduction of Capitalism*, 268. Translation
modified.

68 Ibid., 294; 254. See also, Karl Marx/Friedrich Engels, *Die deutsche Ideologie*, in
Marx-Engels Werke, Bd. 3, Dietz,1969, 26–7; *The German Ideology*, in *Collected Works*,
Lawrence & Wishart, 2010, 36–7.

69 « Idéologie et appareils idéologiques d'État », in *Sur la reproduction*, 307; 'Ideology
and Ideological State Apparatuses', in *On the Reproduction of Capitalism*, 266.

70 Akira Asada criticized this point in an article on the Althusserian theory of

can we think of this *décalage* [discrepancy] in Althusserian theory itself?[71]

In the same text, Althusser himself criticizes the *formal* and *abstract* character of the Marxian schema of superstructure and base:

> The greatest disadvantage of this representation of the structure of every society by the spatial metaphor of an edifice is obviously the fact that it is metaphorical: i.e., it remains descriptive. [. . .] We do not mean by this that we want to reject the classical metaphor, for that metaphor itself requires that we go beyond it. And we are not going beyond it in order to reject it as outworn. We simply want to attempt to think what it gives us in the form of a description.[72]

The 'descriptive' theory is, so to speak, a schematic abstract which obliges to be overtaken by a 'concrete-of-thought', to use Althusser's term.[73] At this point, we can understand why Althusser could not go beyond his own 'descriptive' theory and what was precisely the 'obstacle' (in the Bachelardian sense of the term) for him.

In his lecture 'On Feuerbach' (1967), Althusser defines the structure of 'specular reflection' in Feuerbach's philosophy by an equation: 'a subject's essential object = that subject's objectified essence'. He continues as follows:

> This equation expresses an — in principle — *perfect correspondence* between, on the one hand, the essence of a being or subject, and, on the other, his *proper* object, called his essential object. It is peculiar to him in the narrow, positive sense of the term, because it is nothing other than this being's or subject's *objectification*, externalization, or adequate manifestation. This immediately brings to mind a structure

ideology: '*Arutyusêruha ideorogîron no saikentô* [Reexamination of the Althusserian theory of ideology]', *Shisô* [*Thought*] 707, 1983.

71 On the Althusserian notion of *décalage* [discrepancy], see Louis Althusser, « Sur le contrat social : Les décalages », in *Cahiers pour l'analyse* 8, 1967; 'Rousseau: The Social Contract', in *Politics and History: Montesquieu, Rousseau, Hegel and Marx*, NLB, 1972.

72 « Idéologie et appareils idéologiques d'État », in *Sur la reproduction*, 276; 'Ideology and Ideological State Apparatuses', in *On the Reproduction of Capitalism*, 238. Translation modified.

73 See, for example, Louis Althusser, « Soutenance d'Amiens », in *Solitude de Machiavel*, 221; 'Is it Simple to be a Marxist in Philosophy?', in *Essays in Self-Criticism*, NLB, 1976, 190.

that is typical of the relationship between these concepts: a relation of subject to object (objects) or essence to phenomenon, a relation in which the centre is constituted by the constitutive subject, from which there emanates a space of objects concentric to this centre, objects objectifying the essence of this subject or being, who is thus the subject that constitutes them.[74]

In Feuerbach's philosophy, the subject (the essence of being) and the object (its alienated form) are 'concentric' and reflect each other in a 'specular' manner. If we recall that Althusser defined the structure of the ideological subject as 'specular centration', we can see that common elements exist between his analysis of the structure of Feuerbachian philosophy and this definition of the structure of ideology. Moreover, this interpretation of Feuerbachian philosophy is largely inspired by Lacanian theory. In Lacan's essay on 'The Mirror Stage', the subject acquires its body image through the specular image: the subject's own image is alienated as if it were the image of the other, and it is this 'alienating identity' that gives the subject its own form.[75] We could therefore say that the Feuerbachian theory is analysed here by means of Lacan's theory.

Althusser then aims to connect Feuerbach's philosophy to the theory of ideology. He first recognizes the structure of 'specular centration' and 'reduplication' in Feuerbachian theory, and he adds the following point that does not exist there:

> This effect of the specular relation with reduplication [*effet de relation spéculaire à redoublement*] leads to *a displacement, from the original centration to a centration that reduplicates the first*. There results a specific, *supplementary* effect whose functioning we saw when we discussed the ontological significance of the relation between subject and object, the centre and its horizon. This effect is now displaced on to the reduplicated Subject, here God. The relation subject = object, once it is caught up in the reduplication of this decentration, takes on a new form, becoming a relation of the *absolute subordination of the*

---

74 Louis Althusser, « Sur Feuerbach », in *Écrits philosophique et politique*, T. II, 181; 'On Feuerbach', in *The Humanist Controversy and Other Texts*, 95. Translation modified.

75 Jacques Lacan, « Le stade du miroir comme formateur de la fonction du Je », in *Écrits*, 97; 'The Mirror Stage as Formative of the *I* Function', in *Écrits: The Complete Edition*, 78.

first subject to the Second Subject. The first subject becomes *accountable* to the Second Subject; the first subject is a subject subjected to the Second Subject, who is Sovereign and Judge. The specular relation becomes a relation of moral accountability, that is, responsibility. On the other hand, the Second Subject serves the first as a guarantee. The couple submission/guarantee (a highly provisional formulation) thus reveals itself to be basic to the structure of any ideology.[76]

This quote includes everything that Althusser presented in the structure of Christian religious ideology: the subjection of the subjects to the Absolute Subject, the recognition of the subjects by the Subject and the specular relation between Subject and subjects. This 'specular' relation between Subject and subjects is reproduced identically as the structure of Christian ideology developed in the article on Ideological State Apparatuses. However, in this 'abstract' explanation, the problem of the materiality of the ideological interpellation and the problem of ideological deviation do not intervene. This 'descriptive' schematization therefore does not contain the class struggle in capitalist production relations. In this sense, doesn't it miss the materialist side of the ideology? Even if the mechanism of recognition/denial [*reconnaissance/méconnaissance*] between the Absolute Subject and the subjects is relevant to explain the structure of religious ideology in pre-modern society (God exists there exactly as transcendence), it cannot explain the problem of resistance, of the class struggle in capitalist production relations.

In this sense, Althusser rejects the problem of ideological deviation and formulates the timeless structure of ideology (because 'ideology has no history') as 'specular centration'. But in their relationship with the mutation of the social structure, *ideologies have a history of their own*.[77] This history is that of practices and resistances (class struggle). But why does Althusser finally reject this problem of resistance that he himself initiated? We can answer this question provisionally as follows: by formulating the diachronic structure of ideology as 'specular centration', he made this very formulation an 'obstacle' to theorizing the problem of resistance.

76 « Sur Feuerbach », in *Écrits philosophique et politique*, T. II, 220; 'On Feuerbach', in *The Humanist Controversy and Other Texts*, 129–30. Translation modified.

77 « Idéologie et appareils idéologiques d'État », in *Sur la reproduction*, 295; 'Ideology and Ideological State Apparatuses', in *On the Reproduction of Capitalism*, 255.

The class struggle in capitalist production relations causes the interpellation of the dominant ideology to deviate, and the schema of Christian religious ideology ('specular centration' between the Absolute Subject and the subjects) cannot explain this deviation. According to the theory of ideological deviation, there is a *discrepancy* between the interpellation and the introjection of ideology, and this discrepancy cannot be reduced to a 'specular' relation. It is for this reason that we define the mechanism of the ideological suture as a *transference* to the dominant ideology, and not as a '*specular* centration'. This ideological transference means the restructuring of the ego on the dominant ideology, in which the unconscious 'selects', by responding to the ideological interpellation, the forms, elements or relations 'suitable' to it.[78]

The ideological state apparatuses, which form contradictions among themselves, are 'vulnerable' in their multiplicity[79] and, in this sense, are never transcendent. On the other hand, the theory of 'specular centration' is based on the transcendence of the Unique and Absolute Subject in relation to the subjects; it therefore excludes the problem of contingency and resistance. It is exactly at this point that we find an unsolved problem in Althusser.

---

78 « Lettre à D . . . », in *Écrits sur la psychanalyse*, 108–9; 'Letter to D . . ', in *Writings on Psychoanalysis*, 75: 'Now I wonder whether one can't say that the unconscious also needs "something" to function, and this "something" is, it seems to me, in the last analysis, the ideological. [. . .] To say that the unconscious "functions with ideological imaginary" is thus to say that it "selects" in the ideological imaginary the forms, elements, or relations "suitable" to it'.

79 *Sur la reproduction*, 184; *On the Reproduction of Capitalism*, 153.

6

Structure (Althusser)

6.1 Decentration of social formation

In his theory of ideology, Althusser sought to transform and materialize Lacanian psychoanalytic theory. In other words, he tried to introduce contingent elements into the Lacanian 'philosophy of destiny'. This materialist transformation of Lacanian theory allows him to reflect on the mechanism of the becoming of social formation. But in order to think about this mechanism, we must first examine the specificity of the Althusserian definition of social formation. The notion of 'decentration', used by Althusser in his famous article 'Freud and Lacan' (1964), which first introduced Lacanian theory into the philosophical field, will serve us as a guiding thread:

> Since Marx, we have known that the human subject, the economic, political, or philosophical ego, is not the 'centre' of history we have even known, against the philosophers of the Enlightenment and against Hegel, that history has no 'centre' but possesses a structure that has a necessary 'centre' solely in ideological denial [*méconnaissance idéologique*]. Freud in turn reveals to us that the real subject, the individual in his singular essence, does not have the form of a self, centred in an 'ego', 'consciousness', or 'existence', be it the existence of the for-itself, the body proper, or 'behaviour' that the human subject is decentred, constituted by a structure that, too, has a 'centre' solely in the imaginary denial of

the 'ego', that is, in the ideological formations in which it 'recognizes' itself.[1]

In the same way that history has no 'centre', the subject does not have the
form of a self, centred in an 'ego', a consciousness, or an existence: the
subject is 'decentred'. But in what sense does Althusser use this notion of
decentration?

As mentioned in the previous chapter, in 'Three Notes on the Theory
of Discourse', he distinguishes four types of discourse: scientific,
aesthetic, ideological, and unconscious. The ideological discourse has a
structure of 'centration': the subject recognizes itself in the dominant
ideology by the effects of the ideological interpellation. The subject is
then sutured by the ideological centration. On the other hand, scientific
discourse takes a completely different form, that of decentration:

> [S]cientific discourse, in which the subject-effect is absent in person
> and thus is not a signifier of this discourse, possesses a *structure of
> decentration* (that of a *system of* abstract *relations*, whose elements are
> concepts, none of which is 'constituent': as soon as a concept becomes
> 'constituent', we move from scientific discourse to ideological
> discourse).[2]

Scientific discourse has a 'structure of decentration', in other words, 'a
system of relations' in which no element is constituent. From this, we
can understand that Althusser's 'structure of decentration' has no
constituent or privileged element. Various instances and elements coexist in the structure, but no instance, no element is constituent of it, nor
transcendent (the structure 'has no centre'). The structure exists purely
as a system of 'disjunctive' relations (Deleuze/Guattari).

As we have seen, Lacan uses the term 'excentric [*excentrique*]' almost
in the same sense as the term 'decentred [*décentré*]'.[3] But why does

---

1 Louis Althusser, « Freud et Lacan », in *Écrits sur la psychanalyse*, 47; 'Freud and
Lacan', in *Writings on Psychoanalysis*, 31. Translation modified.

2 « Trois notes sur la théorie des discours », in *Écrits sur la psychanalyse*, 132; 'Three
Notes on the Theory of Discourses', in *The Humanist Controversies and Other Writings*,
50. Translation modified.

3 We discussed this in section 2.2. See *Le séminaire*, Livre II, « Le moi dans la théorie
de Freud et dans la technique de la psychanalyse », 17; *The Seminar*, Book II, 'The ego in
Freud's Theory and in the Technique of Psychoanalysis', 9.

Lacan use these two terms in the same context? For Althusser, the term 'decentred' means that 'there is no centre', so it is not compatible with 'excentric' that retains the notion of centre. Althusser defines unconscious discourse as follows:

> [T]he discourse of the unconscious, in which the subject-effect is absent by 'delegation [*lieu-tenance*]', we are dealing with a pseudo structure of centration, subtended by a structure of flight or 'lack [*béance*]' (a metonymic structure?).[4]

The discourse of the unconscious possesses, writes Althusser, 'a pseudo structure of centration', not the structure of 'decentration', because 'the "subject" of the unconscious does not appear in person in the discourse of the unconscious, but by "delegation [*lieu-tenance*]"'.[5] The 'delegation [*lieu-tenance*]' designates the lack in the signifying chain, namely the repressed phallus that represents the renunciation of the satisfaction of desire. According to Althusser, 'the subject of the unconscious' is certainly excentric but is not 'decentred', because it has 'a pseudo structure of centration'. What does this affirmation mean?

Let us recall the Lacanian notion of 'extimacy'. The instance of the Other (the unconscious) is the most intimate and at the same time the most external for the subject. The 'subject of the unconscious' is metonymically displaced to this instance of the 'excentric' Other in relation to the ego. What we have called the transcendent(al) instance corresponds to this structure of displacement of the ego onto the Other in the Lacanian notion of the unconscious. In other words, the Lacanian 'subject of the unconscious' is 'excentric' but always retains a displaced 'centre', namely the Other: the subject is not 'decentred' in the strict sense of the term. In Lacan, the subject is determined by the 'phallus', the negative signifier repressed in the transcendent(al) instance of the Other. In this process, the barred subject still has an extimate 'centre'. For example, Lacan qualifies the Freudian 'Copernican revolution' as follows:

---

4 « Trois notes sur la théorie des discours », in *Écrits sur la psychanalyse*, 132; 'Three Notes on the Theory of Discourses', in *The Humanist Controversies and Other Writings*, 50. Translation modified.

5 Ibid., 145; 60.

For such a step [Freudian 'Copernican step'] to be constituted, is it enough that a privilege should be revoked — in this case, the one that put the earth in the central place? Man's subsequent destitution from an analogous place due to the triumph of the idea of evolution gives one the sense that such revocation implies an advantage that is confirmed by its constancy.

But can we be so sure this is an advantage or real progress? Does anything make it seem that the other truth, if we may so term revealed truth, has seriously suffered as a result? Don't we realize that, by exalting the centre, heliocentrism is no less of a lure than seeing the earth as the centre, and that the existence of the ecliptic probably provided a more stimulating model of our relations with truth, before it lost much of its interest when it was reduced to being no more than the earth bowing assent?[6]

What matters to Lacan is not the 'destitution' of the centre, but the 'ecliptic' position of the subject (barred subject) achieved by the *extimacy* of the Other. We can now understand why Lacan uses the term 'decentred' in the same sense as 'excentric'. If the subject is 'excentric' in relation to the instance of the Other (extimate instance), then this instance takes hold of the 'centre' of the subject. It is this subject *barred* (*eclipsed*) by the incidence of the Other that Lacan qualified as 'decentred'.

For Althusser, the concept of decentration refers only to a structure that has no centre. He therefore carefully avoids the term 'excentric', which retains the notion of centre:

> For Marxist philosophy there can be no Subject as an Absolute Centre, as a Radical Origin, as a Unique Cause. Nor can one, in order to get out of the problem, rely on a category like that of the '*ex*-Centration of the Essence' (Lucien Sève), since it is an illusory compromise which — using a fraudulently 'radical' *term*, one whose root is perfectly conformist (ex-*centration*) — safeguards the umbilical cord between Essence and Centre and therefore remains a prisoner of idealist philosophy: since there is no Centre, every *ex*-centration is superfluous or a sham. In reality Marxist philosophy thinks in and according

---

6 « Subversion du sujet et dialectique du désir dans l'inconscient freudien », in *Écrits*, 796–7; 'The Subversion of the Subject and the Dialectic of Desire in the Freudian Unconscious', in *Écrits: The Complete Edition*, 674.

to quite different categories: determination in the last instance — which is quite different from the Origin, Essence or Cause *unes* — determination by Relations (*idem*), contradiction, process, 'nodal points' (Lenin), etc.[7]

Althusser rejects the notion of 'centre', thus excluding the existence of a single constituent element in the structure. For example, the Lacanian 'phallus' occupies a privileged position in structuring the subject: the 'phallus' is a 'privileged' signifier that determines all the other signifiers through the effect of repression; it is thus a transcendent(al) signifier belonging to the instance of the Other. On the other hand, in the Althusserian theory, any privileged instance or element is strictly forbidden.

Let us refer to the article 'Contradiction and Overdetermination' (1962), where Althusser reflects on the 'inversion of the dialectic' in Marx. Following the classical interpretation, Marx inverted Hegel's 'idealistic' dialectic in which the Spirit [*Geist*] determines reality. By this inversion, he established the 'materialist' dialectic in which reality determines the Spirit. However, for Althusser, the problem is not an inversion of the 'sense' of the dialectic, but of the 'transformation of its structures'.[8] If the Hegelian dialectic defines history as a phenomenon [*Erscheinung*] of Spirit, and if the Marxist dialectic defines the superstructure as a reflection of the economic base, then these two dialectics take the same form at the level of the logical structure: that of a virtual identity between an Essence and its phenomenon. Althusser, for his part, defines the specificity of Marx's thought in a different way:

> For Marx, this tacit identity (phenomenon-essence-truth-of . . .) of the economic and the political disappears in favour of a *new conception* of the relation between *determinant instances* in the structure-superstructure complex which constitutes the essence of any social formation. Of course, these specific *relations* between structure and superstructure still deserve theoretical elaboration and investigation. However, Marx has at least given us the 'two ends of the chain', and

7 Louis Althusser, *Réponse à John Lewis*, Maspero, 1973, 94; 'Reply to John Lewis', in *Essays in Self-Criticism*, NLB, 1976, 96.

8 Louis Althusser, « Contradiction et surdétermination », in *Pour Marx* (1965), Découverte, 1996, 91; 'Contradiction and Overdetermination', in *For Marx*, Verso, 2005, 93.

has told us to find out what goes on between them: on the one hand, *determination in the last instance by the* (economic) *mode of production*; on the other, *the relative autonomy of the superstructures and their specific effectivity.*[9]

The Marxian notion of social formation rejects the Hegelian couple of 'essence-phenomenon'. According to Althusser's interpretation, social formation is a 'system of relations' made up of various instances in which there is no 'centre'. In other words, there is no privileged element in this social formation. Therefore, the thesis of 'relative autonomy of superstructures' only means that of each instance in relation to the others. For example, in a 1976 text, Althusser compares Marx to Freud and states:

> At this point, if from a distance, we cannot help but think of the revolution introduced by Marx when he renounced the ideological bourgeois myth that thought the nature of society as a *unified and centred whole* and began to think any social formation as a system of instances *without a centre*. Freud, who did not know Marx, thought his object (which had nothing in common with that of Marx) in the spatial figure of a 'topic' (we are reminded of the 1859 preface to the *Contribution*) and a *topic without a centre*, the diverse instances of which have no other unity than the *unity of their conflictual functioning* in what Freud called the 'psychic apparatus', a term (apparatus) that cannot but make us think, if discretely, of Marx.[10]

Social formation is 'a system of instances without a centre', and, in this sense, radically decentred. No instance is transcendent in relation to the others; the economic instance is not 'constituent' — in the strong sense of the term — in social formation. Thus, the political is not the 'phenomenon' of the economic, and the economic is not the 'essence' of the political. The 'structured whole' equals this 'system of instances without a centre'. He conceptualized it by analogy with the Freudian topic. Let us recall the second Freudian topic, which is made up of the id, the ego,

9 Ibid., 111; 111. Translation modified.
10 Louis Althusser, « Sur Marx et Freud », in *Écrits sur la psychanalyse*, 241; 'On Marx and Freud', in *Rethinking Marxism: A Journal of Economics, Culture & Society* 4: 1, 1991, 28.

and the superego. The ego is derived from the id under the influence of the external world through the intermediary of the perception-consciousness system, it is 'essentially representative of the external world', while 'the superego stands in contrast to it as the representative of the internal world, of the id'.[11] The Freudian topic is this 'conflictual'[12] system 'of instances without a centre' where each instance has a 'relative autonomy' with regard to the others. It has the same structure as the Marxian social formation. Althusser avoids being Lacanian in order to exclude the 'pseudo structure of centration'. In other words, *he thinks of the political and the economic as a Freudian.*

Social formation is 'a system of instances without a centre' where the economic instance is not transcendent, and the contradictions are therefore not determined by a single instance:

[T]he 'contradiction' is inseparable from the total structure of the social body in which it is found, inseparable from its formal *conditions* of existence, and even from the *instances* it governs; it is radically *affected by them*, determining, but also determined in one and the same movement, and determined by the various levels and instances of the social formation it animates; it might be called *overdetermined in its principle*.[13]

The contradiction is 'overdetermined', writes Althusser. It is not determined by a single element, but by 'the various levels and instances of the social formation'. The term 'overdetermination' is borrowed from Freudian theory. According to Freud, the manifest content of the dream, which is a formation of the unconscious, cannot be reduced to a single

---

11 *Das Ich und das Es*, in *Gesammelte Werke*, Bd. XIII, 264; 'The Ego and the Id', in *Standard Edition* 19, 36.

12 Ibid: 'Conflicts between the ego and the ideal will, as we are now prepared to find, ultimately reflect the contrast between what is real and what is psychical, between the external world and the internal world'. Étienne Balibar and Pierre Macherey suggest the importance of the analogy between the class struggle (power relations) and psychic apparatus (conflictual relations of instances) in the Althusserian 'topic'. See Étienne Balibar, « L'objet d'Althusser », in Sylvain Lazarus, dir., *Politique et philosophie dans l'œuvre de Louis Althusser*, PUF, 1993, 113–14; 'Althusser's Object', in *Social Text* 39, 1994, 179–80; Pierre Macherey, « Althusser : Lénine et la philosophie », in *Histoires de dinosaure*, PUF, 1999, 276–8.

13 « Contradiction et surdétermination », in *Pour Marx*, 99–100; 'Contradiction and Overdetermination', in *For Marx*, 101.

element, for it is made up of the *condensation* of various unconscious elements; in other words, it is 'overdetermined'. In the same sense, the contradiction is 'overdetermined' by various instances in social formation — it is not determined by a single economic instance (for example, a contradiction between the force of production and the relation of production), but overdetermined by multiple instances (the political, ideological, economic instances, etc.).[14]

We must stop here and ask a crucial question: if social formation is 'a system of instances without a centre' in which no instance is 'constituent', and if each instance remains disjunctively autonomous in relation to the others, how is the thesis of 'determination in the last instance' compatible with this decentred structure of social formation? How does 'determination in the last instance' intervene in the development of a social formation in which no instance is either transcendent or constituent?

6.2 The economic and the political

To reflect on the notion of 'determination in the last instance', let us consult two texts written at different times: 'Contradiction and Overdetermination' (1962) and 'Elements of Self-Criticism' (1972).

We will start with 'Contradiction and Overdetermination', where the 'determination in the last instance' is cited from Engels:

> Listen to the old Engels in 1890, taking the young 'economists' to task for not having understood that this was a *new relationship*. Production is the determinant factor, but only 'in the last instance': 'More than this neither Marx nor I have ever asserted'. Anyone who 'twists this' so that it says that the economic factor is *the only* determinant factor, 'transforms that proposition into a meaningless, abstract, empty phrase'. And as explanation: 'The economic situation is the basis, but the various elements of the superstructure — the political forms of the class struggle and its results: to wit

---

14 If Althusser so persisted in rejecting the economic determinism of Hegelo-Marxism, it is first of all to reflect on the question of 'the revolution against *Capital*' (Gramsci) — all the revolutions realized in history took place in underdeveloped countries like Russia, China and Cuba — and then to ask why the revolution is not realized in highly developed capitalist countries. See ibid., 92–7; 94–9.

constitutions established by the victorious class after a successful battle, etc., juridical forms, and then even the reflexes of all these actual struggles in the brains of the participants, political, juristic, philosophical theories, religious views and their further development into systems of dogmas — also exercise their influence upon the course of the historical struggles, and in many cases preponderate in determining their form'.[15]

The 'determination in the last instance' by the economic instance means that the economic factor is not '*the only* determinant factor'. Social formation is thus 'a system of instances without a centre' in which each instance has relative autonomy with regard to the others — it has a 'disjunctive' relationship to the others. The economic instance assumes literally the role of the base [*Basis*] on which the other instances are inscribed, in a disjunctive way.[16] However, it is never the transcendent or privileged instance, because the instances of the superstructure remain decisive with the economic base, and they often 'preponderate' in determining contradictions. Althusser continues:

This *overdetermination* is inevitable and thinkable as soon as the real existence of the forms of the superstructure and of the national and international conjuncture has been recognized — an existence largely specific and autonomous, and therefore irreducible to a pure *phenomenon*. We must carry this through to its conclusion and say that this overdetermination does not just refer to apparently unique and aberrant historical situations (Germany, for example), but is *universal*; the economic dialectic is never active *in the pure state*; in

15 Ibid., 111–12; 111–12.
16 See Louis Althusser, « Soutenance d'Amiens », in *Solitude de Machiavel*, PUF, 1998, 209–10; 'Is it Simple to be a Marxist in Philosophy?', in *Essays in Self-Criticism*, 176–7: 'In the determination of the topic, the last *instance* really is the *last* instance. If it is *the last one*, as in the legal image which it invokes (court of the last instance), that is because there are others, those which figure in the legal-political and ideological superstructure. The mention of the last instance in determination thus plays a double role: it divides Marx sharply off from all mechanistic explanations, and opens up within determination the functioning of different instances, the functioning of a real difference in which the dialectic is inscribed. The topic thus signifies that the determination in the last instance by the economic base can only be grasped within a differentiated, therefore complex and articulated whole (the "*Gliederung*"), in which the determination in the last instance fixes the real difference of the other instances, their relative autonomy and their own mode of effectivity on the base itself'. Translation modified.

History, these instances, the superstructures, etc. — are never seen to step respectfully aside when their work is done or, when the Time comes, as his pure phenomena, to scatter before His Majesty the Economy as he strides along the royal road of the Dialectic. From the first moment to the last, the lonely hour of the 'last instance' never strikes [*l'heure solitaire de la « dernière instance » ne sonne jamais*].[17]

Althusser proposes a famous thesis here: 'the lonely hour of the "last instance" never strikes'. What does it mean?

We can answer briefly that 'the economic dialectic is never active *in the pure state*'. In other words, there is no 'pure' contradiction determined by '*the only* determinant factor' (economic base). The contradiction can always be 'overdetermined' by multiple determinants such as the political, the ideological, the legal, the economic, etc. In this sense, the emphasis of this thesis is on the term 'lonely [*solitaire*]'. If the contradiction is overdetermined by multiple instances, the last instance (the economic instance) alone could never determine the contradiction. The contradiction or the structural becoming that it brings about is always overdetermined by multiple instances in a social formation *without a centre*.

In 'Elements of Self-Criticism' (1972), in which Althusser makes a self-criticism on his 'theoreticist deviation' of the 1960s, he cites his own thesis on determination in the last instance, *this time evoking the notion of 'absent cause'*:

[I]t is also not possible to 'put your finger' on this contradiction, determinant 'in the last instance', as *the* cause. One can only grasp it and understand it within the forms of the class struggle which constitutes, in the strict sense, its *historical* existence. To say that 'the cause is absent' thus means, in Historical Materialism, that the 'contradiction determinant in the last instance' is *never present in person* on the scene of history ('the hour of the determination in the last instance never strikes [*l'heure de la détermination en dernière instance ne sonne jamais*]') and that one can never grasp it directly, as one can a 'person who is present'. It is a 'cause', but in the dialectical sense, in the sense

---

17 « Contradiction et surdétermination », in *Pour Marx*, 113; 'Contradiction and Overdetermination', in *For Marx*, 113. Translation modified.

that it determines *what*, on the scene of the class struggle, is the 'decisive link' which must be grasped.[18]

Let us notice a curious detail: in the 1962 text, Althusser, asserting that 'the *lonely* hour of the "last instance" never strikes', insists that the structural becoming is not determined by the economic instance *alone*; however, this self-quote inserted in the 1972 text does not include the word 'lonely' ('the hour of the determination in the last instance never strikes'). Note this little *lapsus*. How can we understand this thesis in 'Elements of Self-Criticism'?

We should first note that the 'contradiction in the last instance' is defined here in its relation to the 'absent cause', which is extracted from the formalization of Lacanian theory. In Lacan, the 'phallus' is *a* signifier of the lack that exists as an absence or an empty place in the signifying chain; through this absence, it gives meaning to all the other signifiers. It is therefore a 'privileged signifier' (Lacan). In other words, it determines, as a transcendent(al) signifier, the subject by its 'absent cause'.

In the 1972 text, the economic instance assumes exactly the same role as an absent signifier: it determines the contradiction in the last instance, but it 'is *never present in person* on the scene of history' ('the hour of the determination in the last instance never strikes'). It is therefore a 'non-presence'[19] on the scene of history insofar as it determines the contradiction *in its effects of absence*. Thus, determination by the economic instance is never present in history; at the same time, though, it appears, as a series of absent effects, in all the realized determinations. The economic instance thus occupies the position of the transcendent(al) signifier which is never present as such, but which determines all present reality through its effects. In 'Elements of Self-Criticism', we must then understand the expression 'determination in the last instance' in a totally different context from that of the 1962 text. The fact that Althusser, who had avoided this theoretical negativity, ends up choosing it is *symptomatic* and prefigures a theoretical shift: from this moment, it is the 'class struggle', as an *unstable field of power relations*, instead of the economic instance, that occupies the scene of history.

18 Louis Althusser, « Éléments d'autocritique », in *Solitude de Machiavel*, 178, note 31; 'Elements of Self-Criticism', in *Essays in Self-Criticism*, 126, note 20. Translation modified.

19 Expression by Jacques Derrida: *Politique et amitié*, Galilée, 2011, 71; 'Politics and Friendship', in Michael Sprinker *et al.*, eds., *The Althusserian Legacy*, Verso, 1993, 208.

In 'Elements of Self-Criticism', the economic instance moves away from the scene of history and the class struggle, contingency in the political field, then assumes a decisive role in his theory (primacy of the political contingency over the economic). In this sense, the shift towards 'aleatory materialism' already began in 1972.[20]

The thought on political contingency corresponds to reflections on the singular conjuncture, the 'singularity of the case' that irrupts in history. In *Machiavelli and Us* (1972–86),[21] Althusser defines the specificity of Machiavellian thought by comparing it to Montesquieu:

We then appreciate that Machiavelli is a different thinker from Montesquieu. What interests him is not 'the nature of things' in general (Montesquieu), but (to give the expression all its force) '*la verità effectuale* della *cosa*', of *the* thing in the singular — the singularity of its 'case'. And *the* thing is also *the* cause, *the* task, the singular problem to be posed and resolved. In this minor difference we can discern what shifts and separates the whole discourse. Yes, Machiavelli's object is knowledge of the laws of history or politics; but at the same time, this is not the case. For his object, which is not an object in this sense, is the formulation of a concrete political problem. Formulation of the problem of political practice is at the heart of everything: all the theoretical elements (as many 'laws' as you like) are arranged as a function of this central political problematic. We can now understand why Machiavelli does not have all the 'laws' intervene, and why he does not offer a general and systematic exposition, but deploys only the theoretical fragments conducive to clarification of the formulation and understanding of this singular concrete case. So much for the fragments (and hence the contradictions as well).

---

20 Antonio Negri deals with the problem of the Althusserian *Kehre* towards 'aleatory materialism' and identifies the year 1977, the time of his reflection on the 'crisis of Marxism', as the period in which the turn takes place. He finds this turn in 'the accentuation of the consideration of the aleatory of the event' (Antonio Negri, « Pour Althusser : Notes sur l'évolution de la pensée du dernier Althusser », in *Futur antérieur*, « Sur Althusser. Passages », L'Harmattan, 1993). But from our point of view, it had already started silently in 1972, the period of his self-criticism.

21 According to the presentation of the text by François Matheron, the first version of this text was written in 1971–72, but around 1975–76 and 1986, the text was largely modified to introduce the notion of the aleatory. See *Écrits philosophiques et politiques*, T. II, 39–41; *Machiavelli and Us*, vii–ix.

Above all, however, a *theoretical dispositive* is here brought to light that breaks with the habits of classical rhetoric, where the universal governs the singular.[22]

In Machiavelli, political practice is, as a 'thing in the singular' or 'singularity of its "case", placed at the heart of all theoretical investigation; and 'all the theoretical elements (as many "laws" as you like) are arranged as a function of this central political problematic'. In other words, the 'laws' or the 'theoretical elements' are provided by this 'singularity' of political practice. Let us compare this with the 1972 text. In 'Elements of Self-Criticism', the non-present economic instance ultimately determined the present political conjuncture (the class struggle); on the other hand, in *Machiavelli and Us*, it is the singularity of the conjuncture that determines the constellation of 'laws', of theoretical fragments. The singular conjuncture then dominates, as the political contingency, the 'law' or 'the universal'.

Machiavelli's 'thought under the conjuncture'[23] refers to the singularity of actuality, of case, of conjuncture, which allows Althusser to qualify Machiavellian thought — which deals with this singularity — as a 'form of exceptional thought':

[W]e are then in the presence of an exceptional form of thought. On the one hand, we have conditions specified with the utmost precision, from the general state of the Italian conjuncture to the forms of the encounter between *fortuna* and *virtù*, and the exigencies of the process of political practice. On the other, we have a total lack of specification as to the site and subject of political

---

22 Louis Althusser, « Machiavel et nous », in *Écrits philosophiques et politiques*, T. II, 57–8; *Machiavelli and Us*, Verso, 1999, 16.

23 Ibid., 60; 18. 'To think under the conjuncture [*Penser sous la conjoncture*] is quite literally to submit to the problem induced and imposed by its case: the political problem of national unity and the constitution of Italy into a national state. Here the terms must be inverted: Machiavelli does not think the problem of national unity in terms of the conjuncture; it is the conjuncture itself that negatively, yet objectively, poses the problem of Italian national unity. Machiavelli merely registers in his theoretical position a problem that is objectively, historically posed by the case of the conjuncture: not by simple intellectual comparisons, but by the confrontation of existing class forces and their relationship of uneven development — in fact, by their aleatory future'. See also François Matheron, « La récurrence du vide chez Louis Althusser », in *Future antérieur*, « Lire Althusser aujourd'hui », L'Harmattan, 1997.

practice. The striking thing is that Machiavelli firmly grasps the two ends of the chain — in short, thinks and formulates this theoretical disjuncture, this 'contradiction', without wishing to propose any kind of theoretical reduction or resolution of it, whether notional or oneiric. This thinking of the disjuncture stems from the fact that Machiavelli not only formulates, but thinks, his problem *politically* — that is to say, as a contradiction in reality that cannot be removed by thought, but only by reality. It can be removed only by the sudden appearance — necessary, but unforeseeable and inascribable as regards place, time and person — of the concrete forms of the political encounter whose general conditions alone are defined. In this theory that ponders and preserves the disjuncture, room is thereby made for political practice. Room is made for it through this organization of disjoined theoretical notions, by the discrepancy [*décalage*] between the definite and indefinite, the necessary and the unforeseeable. This discrepancy, thought and unresolved by thought, is the presence of history and political practice in theory itself.[24]

If Machiavellian thought is 'exceptional', it is because it comprises two totally contradictory poles: 'the definite and the indefinite', or 'the necessary and the unforeseeable'. Machiavellian thought is inscribed in this *irreducible discrepancy* [décalage] between the necessity of the law and the singularity of the conjuncture. 'thought under the conjuncture' is therefore to remain in this discrepancy between the necessary-*to-actualize* and the *inconceivable* contingency.[25] What Althusser will call 'aleatory materialism' is a theory capable of assuming this discrepancy in which the singularity of the conjuncture surpasses the generality of the law.

To remain in this discrepancy between the necessary law and the

---

24 Ibid., 133–4; 80. Translation modified.

25 Ibid., 100; 51–2: 'So Machiavelli's utopianism does not consist in resort to Rome as the prop for a moral ideology that is required in the present. It consists in recourse to Rome as *guarantee* or *rehearsal* for a *necessary* task, whose concrete conditions of possibility are, however, *impossible* to define. Rome ensures and guarantees the link between this necessity and this impossibility. Accordingly, the discrepancy that makes it a utopia is a discrepancy not between the narrowness of the actual sociopolitical content and the necessary universal illusion of moral ideology, but between a *necessary* political task and its conditions of realization, which are possible and conceivable, and yet at the same time *impossible* and *inconceivable*, because aleatory'. Translation modified.

unforeseeable irruption, the theory must be inscribed in actuality or the present moment. In a 1978 text, Althusser discusses this problem of temporality:

> I believe that *Marxist theory is 'finite'* and limited: that it is limited to the analysis of the capitalist mode of production, and of its contradictory tendency, which opens up the possibility of the transition to the abolition of capitalism and its replacement by 'something else' which already appears implicitly in capitalist society. I believe that *Marxist theory is entirely the opposite of a philosophy of history* which 'encompasses' the whole future of humanity, and which would thus be capable of defining the end [*terme*]: communism, in a *positive* manner. Marxist theory [. . .] is inscribed within and limited to the *actual phase*: that of capitalist exploitation.[26]

The Hegelian philosophy of history positively preserves the end and understands history in retrospect to that end. In contrast, Marxist theory is 'inscribed within and limited to the actual phase', writes Althusser. It does not understand history as a teleological self-development of the end [*terme*], determined in advance, but as the infinite possibility of an unforeseeable becoming. To say that it is 'finite' means that it is limited to the actuality which is always a singular, not by the 'end' of a teleological philosophy of history. Thus, 'thought under the conjuncture' means that it is inscribed in the power of becoming (the class struggle) that the present moment possesses.

6.3 Contingency and structural becoming

During the 1970s, in shifting to the primacy of political contingency, Althusser attempted to understand the political through the thought that remains in the discrepancy between 'the definite and the indefinite', between the necessity of the law and the singularity of the irruption. However, does this constitute his particularity from that moment?

---

26 « Le marxisme comme théorie 'finie' », in *Solitude de Machiavel*, 285; 'Marxism as Finite Theory', *Viewpoint Magazine*, 14 December 2017, viewpointmag.com. Translation modified.

Rather, doesn't he always remain in this discrepancy when he reflects on structural becoming?

In Althusser, the problem of structural becoming is deeply concerned with the problem of 'irruption [*surgissement*]'. In a 1966 letter addressed to his psychoanalyst, René Diatkine, he addresses the question of the irruption of the unconscious in the small child:

> [U]ltimately, 'to undertake the genesis' of a phenomenon means to explain how it was born *from what is not it*. To undertake the genesis of A is to explain through what mechanism non-A (what is *other than* A) produces A. To assume or take on that contradiction is to accept that what one is seeking in order to explain the mechanism through which A irrupts [*surgit*] *is not A*, nor is it its prefiguration, germ, draft, promise, etc.[27]

It is generally considered that the phenomenon A comes from what contains the cause of this phenomenon (e.g., the germ). However, if we take the example of the 'irruption' of the unconscious in the child, we find another causality. In 'The Function and Field of Speech and Language in Psychoanalysis', Lacan emphasizes that the small child [*infans*] becomes a subject by appropriating the structure of language (i.e., the original repression, or 'the killing of the thing').[28] In the little child who will become a subject, the 'cause' of the irruption of the unconscious does not exist. The structure of the unconscious arises, so to speak, 'from nothing'.[29] The irruption is a mechanism by which the non-A produces A and which is therefore totally different from 'the mechanisms induced by the ideology of genesis, namely, the

---

27 « Lettre à D . . . », in *Écrits sur la psychanalyse*, 89; 'Letter to D . .', in *Writings on Psychoanalysis*, 58. Translation modified.

28 Jacques Lacan, « Fonction et champ de la parole et du langage en psychanalyse », in *Écrits*, 319; 'The Function and Field of Speech and Language in Psychoanalysis', in *Écrits: The Complete Edition*, 262.

29 Expression by Althusser in his letter to Franca Madonia dated 29 September 1962: 'Machiavelli's central problem from a *theoretical* viewpoint could be summed up in the question of the beginning, starting from nothing [*commencement à partir de rien*], of an absolutely indispensable and necessary new state' (Louis Althusser, *Lettre à Franca 1961–1973*, Stock/IMEC, 1998, 224. Quoted in *Écrits philosophiques et politiques*, T. II, 12; *Machiavelli and Us*, XV). See also François Matheron, « La récurrence du vide chez Louis Althusser », in *Future antérieur*, « Lire Althusser aujourd'hui ».

mechanisms of procreation, development, *filiation*, etc.'[30] To deal with this problem, Althusser avoids the term 'genesis', which over-supports evolutionary ideology, and replaces it with 'irruption'. What he sees there is a *radical break* between A and non-A.

From there, Althusser tries to find this question of the 'irruption' in Marx's text. In his letter to Diatkine, he interprets the passage of the mode of production as an 'irruption':

> It concerns the problem of the irruption mechanism of *one* deter-
> mined mode of production, the capitalist mode of production. When
> one reads *Capital* rather closely, it appears that contrary to the genetic
> ideology currently applied to Marx (or the evolutionist ideology,
> which is the same thing), the capitalist mode of production was not
> 'engendered' by the feudal mode of production as its own *son*. There
> is no *filiation* properly (precisely) speaking between the feudal mode
> of production and the capitalist mode of production. The capitalist
> mode of production irrupts from the *encounter* [rencontre] [. . .] of a
> certain number of very precise elements and from the specific combi-
> nation of those elements ('combination' translates the Marxist concept
> of *Verbindung*: your concept of *organization* would fit quite well, or
> the concept of *arrangement*). The feudal mode of production *engen-
> ders* [. . .] only those *elements*, of which certain ones, moreover (the
> accumulation of money in the form of capital), go back to before the
> feudal mode of production or can be produced by other modes of
> production.[31]

The capitalist mode of production was not 'engendered' by the feudal mode of production: there is no 'filiation', but a break between them. Certainly, the feudal mode of production contains elements for the

---

30   « Lettre à D . . . », in *Écrits sur la psychanalyse*, 90; 'Letter to D . . .', in *Writings on Psychoanalysis*, 59. Althusser poses these two premises to develop the notion of 'irrption': '(a) renouncing the search for whatever, before the "birth" of A, "resembles" (germ, prefiguration, draft, promise, presentiment, etc.) A but searching instead for what effectively *intervenes* in the production of the "A effect" (in this case, the unconscious) and that in all likelihood does not "resemble" A [. . .]; (b) searching for the *specific mechanism* that produces the irruption of the "A effect", beginning by giving up the belief that this mechanism can have something in common with the mechanisms induced by the ideology of genesis, namely, the mechanisms of procreation, development, *filiation*, etc.'

31   Ibid., 91–2; 61.

'irruption' of the new mode of production (accumulation of capital, workers deprived of their means of production, and development of techniques). However, we should not consider that these elements operate as 'germs' to explain the 'genesis' of the capitalist mode of production. It is not structural elements that realize the new mode of production: it is a *specific, singular combination* of these elements ('*Verbindung*') that produces it.

But why does Althusser insist so much on the problem of 'irruption'? What is at stake here is the rejection of Hegelo-Marxist teleology. Marx writes in the preface to *A Contribution to the Critique of Political Economy*:

> The material productive forces of society, at a certain degree of their development, enter into contradiction with the existing relations of production, or — this is merely a legal term designating them — with the property relations within which they had hitherto operated. From forms of development of the productive forces, these relations are transformed into fetters on the productive forces. There then begins a period of social revolution. With the changes in the economic base, the whole immense superstructure is overturned, more or less slowly or rapidly.[32]

Marx uses here the famous concept of contradiction between productive forces and relations of production: if the development of the productive forces exceeds a certain limit, it produces a contradiction with the existing relations of production, which causes the social revolution. In *On the Reproduction of Capitalism*, Althusser comments on and criticizes this passage:

> This conception [of the contradiction between productive forces and relations of production] is that of alienation, which finds expression in the dialectic of correspondence and non-correspondence (or 'contradiction', 'antagonism') between *Form* and *Content*. The dialectic of non-contradiction ('correspondence') and contradiction

---

32 Karl Marx, *Zur Kritik der Politischen Ökonomie*, *Marx-Engels Werke*, Bd. 13, Dietz, 1961, 9; translated and quoted by Althusser in « Du primat des rapports de production sur les forces productives », *Sur la reproduction*, 244–5; 'On the Primacy of the Relations of Production over the Productive Forces', *On the Reproduction of Capitalism*, 210–11.

('non-correspondence') between Form and Content as well as the dialectic of *degrees* of development of the productive forces (in Hegel, the *moments* of the development of the Idea) are 100 per cent Hegelian.[33]

Marx is here too Hegelian, writes Althusser. In the previous quote from Marx, the contradiction between the relations of production (Form) and the productive forces (Content) causes the revolution, and by that, it relieves [*aufhobt*] the mode of production (the negation of the negation). This logic is based on the 'filiation' between previous and new relations of production. In this sense, it takes the same form as the Hegelian self-development of the Idea. On the other hand, Althusser tried to conceive a logic of the irruption in which there is a radical break between previous and new relations of production. The logic of the irruption is totally opposed to the Hegelian logic of the self-development of the Idea. Althusser addresses this problem in *Reading Capital*:

We are beginning to suspect, and even to be able to prove in a number of already studied examples, that the history of reason is neither a linear history of continuous development, nor, in its continuity, a history of the progressive manifestation or emergence into consciousness of a Reason which is completely present in germ in its origins and which its history merely reveals to the light of day. We know that this type of history and rationality is merely the effect of the retrospective illusion of a given historical result which writes its history in the 'future anterior', and which therefore thinks its origin as the anticipation of its end. The rationality of the Philosophy of the Enlightenment to which Hegel gave the systematic form of the development of the concept is merely an ideological conception both of reason and of its history. The real history of the development of knowledge appears to us today to be subject to laws quite different from this teleological hope for the religious triumph of reason. We are beginning to conceive this history as a history punctuated by radical discontinuities (e.g., when a new science detaches itself from the background of earlier ideological formations), profound

---

33 « Du primat des rapports de production sur les forces productives », in *Sur la reproduction*, 246; 'On the Primacy of the Relations of Production over the Productive Forces', in *On the Reproduction of Capitalism*, 212.

reorganizations which, if they respect the continuity of the existence of regions of knowledge (and even this is not always the case), nevertheless inaugurate with their rupture the reign of a new logic, which, far from being a mere development, the 'truth' or 'inversion' of the old one, *literally takes its place*.

We are thereby obliged to renounce every teleology of reason, and to conceive the historical relation between a result and its conditions of existence as a relation of production, and not of expression, and therefore as what, in a phrase that clashes with the classical system of categories and demands the *replacement* of those categories themselves, we can call *the necessity of its contingency*.[34]

The Hegelian history of the self-development of the Idea 'thinks its origin as the anticipation of its end'. In the preface to *A Contribution*, Marx presupposes in the same way an end ('social revolution' or communism) in the self-development of social formation: this end is registered, as a 'germ in its origins', in linear history. In contrast, Althusser considers history as 'a history punctuated by radical discontinuities'. In other words, history is reflected in its relation to the 'necessity of contingency', namely the *singular* combination of structural elements capable of causing the irruption of a new structure.

We cannot envisage the structural irruption through the dialectical logic as a contradiction between relations of production and productive forces. With the structural elements (accumulation of capital, workers deprived of their means of production, and development of techniques), a singular *Verbindung* must intervene in order to achieve the irruption: 'History shows several situations in which only two of those elements are united, but not the third; in such cases no new mode of production irrupts, and the capitalist mode of production is not "born"'.[35] In this sense, 'the necessity of contingency' signifies the *actualisation* of the singular and contingent *Verbindung* — it is a thought that remains in the discrepancy between the contingency of the singular *Verbindung* and the necessity of its actualisation.

In Althusser, the problem of structural becoming is thus thought

---

34 « Du 'Capital' à la philosophie de Marx », in *Lire le Capital*, 45–6; 'From *Capital* to Marx's Philosophy', in *Reading Capital: The Complete Edition*, 45.

35 « Lettre à D . . . », in *Écrits sur la psychanalyse*, 93; 'Letter to D . .', in *Writings on Psychoanalysis*, 62.

within a discrepancy between the definite and indefinite, the necessary and the unforeseeable. His position on this problem has been constant since the 1960s. Let us refer to 'On the Materialist Dialectic' (1963), where Althusser proposes a reflection on 'the law of uneven development of contradictions'.[36] In social formation, each instance produces various contradictions from internal causes. There is a hierarchy between these contradictions (dominant contradiction: the economic; subordinated contradiction: the political). However, in order that the subordinated contradictions become revolutionary forces capable of provoking structural change, the 'displacement' of their role and 'condensation' must intervene:

If all contradictions are under the sway of the great law of unevenness, and to be a Marxist and to be able to act politically (and, I should add, to be able to produce theoretically), it is necessary at all costs to distinguish the principal from the secondary among contradictions and their aspects, and if this distinction is essential to Marxist theory and practice — this is, Mao comments, because we must face up to concrete reality, to the reality of the history that men are living, if we are to explain a reality in which *the identity of opposites* is supreme, that is (1) the passage in indeterminate conditions of one opposite into the place of another, the exchange of roles between contradictions and their aspects (I shall call this phenomenon of substitution *displacement*), (2) the 'identity' of opposites in a real unity (I shall call this phenomenon of 'fusion' *condensation*). Indeed, the great lesson of practice is that if the structure in dominance remains constant, the disposition of the roles within it changes: the principal contradiction becomes a secondary one, a secondary contradiction takes its place, the principal aspect becomes a secondary one, the secondary aspect becomes the principal one. There is always one principal contradiction and secondary ones, but they exchange their roles in the structure articulated in dominance while this latter remains stable. [. . .] But this principal contradiction produced by *displacement* only becomes 'decisive', explosive, by *condensation* (by 'fusion'). It is the latter that constitutes the 'weakest link' that, as Lenin said, must be grasped and pulled in political practice (or in theoretical practice . . .)

36 Louis Althusser, « Sur la dialectique matérialiste », in *Pour Marx*, 206; 'On the Materialist Dialectic', in *For Marx*, 200–1. Translation modified.

so that the whole chain will follow, or, to use a less linear image, it is the latter which occupies the strategic nodal position that must be attacked in order to produce '*the dissolution of* (the existing) *unity*'.[37]

Althusser introduces the notions of 'displacement' and 'condensation'. According to the principle of determination in the last instance, a form of hierarchy exists within the contradictions ('there is always one principal [economic] contradiction and secondary [political] ones'); But they exchange their roles in the political conjuncture, namely in the class struggle (the 'displacement' of contradictions: 'the principal [economic] contradiction becomes a secondary one, a secondary [political] contradiction takes its place'). It is the condensation of contradictions having exchanged their roles that causes structural change.

Here we find Althusserian thought inscribed in the discrepancy between the necessary and the unforeseeable. Between the contradictions produced by the structural elements, there is a hierarchy: determination in the last instance by the economic. But *in order that the structural becoming is realized, unforeseeable elements must intervene — displacement and condensation between the economic contradiction and the political contradiction must take place in the class struggle.* In other words, *it is the antagonistic collective struggle of the de-subjected subjects (the class struggle) that realizes the unforeseeable displacement and condensation of contradictions*:

[W]e can explain the crucial distinction for political practice between the distinct moments of a process: '*non-antagonism*', '*antagonism*' and '*explosion*'. Contradiction, says Lenin, is always at work, in every moment. So these three moments are merely three forms of its existence. I shall characterize the first as the moment when the overdetermination of a contradiction exists *in the dominant form of displacement* (the 'metonymic' form of what has been enshrined in the phrase: '*quantitative changes*' in history [...]); the second, as the moment when overdetermination exists *in the dominant form of condensation* (acute class conflict in the case of society [...]); and the last, the revolutionary explosion (in society [...]), as the moment of unstable global condensation inducing the dissolution and resolution of the

37 Ibid., 216–17; 210–11.

whole, that is, a global restructuring of the whole on a qualitatively new basis.[38]

Note that displacement and condensation are notions borrowed from Freud. In *The Interpretation of Dreams*, Freud uses these notions to explain the mechanism of dream formation: the difference between the manifest content and the latent thoughts of the dream is produced by the displacement [*Verschiebung*] and the condensation [*Verdichtung*] of the unconscious elements. What he called 'overdetermination [*Überderminierung*]' refers to this mechanism of dream formation.[39] The mechanism of displacement and condensation is realized by an energetic investment in the unconscious, where the energy is totally free and mobile: the energetic investments, writes Freud, 'can easily be completely transferred, displaced and condensed'.[40] In other words, displacement and condensation are the other names of contingency. In Althusser's theory, they disturb and deviate, as an irruption of contingency in the political conjuncture (the class struggle), the necessity of dialectic law. In 'On Marx and Freud', he explains:

> Concerning the dialectic, Freud furnished it with some surprising figures that he never treated as 'laws' (that questionable form of a certain Marxist tradition): for example, the categories of displacement, condensation, overdetermination, and so on as well as in the ultimate thesis, a meditation on which would take us a long way, that the 'unconscious does not know contradiction' and that the absence of contradiction is the condition of any contradiction. There is in this everything necessary to 'explode' the classical model of contradiction, a model too inspired by Hegel to serve the 'method' of Marxist analysis.[41]

Classical Marxist theory grasps contradiction as the motor of the 'negation of negation'. We can see in it a process of self-development of contradiction in which the end is inscribed in advance. In this sense, the

---

38 Ibid., 222; 216.

39 *Die Traumdeutung*, in *Gesammelte Werke* Bd. II/III, 313; *The Interpretation of Dreams*, in *Standard Edition*, Vol. IV, 307–8.

40 *Jenseits des Lustprinzips*, in *Gesammelte Werke*, Bd. XIII, 35; *Beyond the Pleasure Principle*, in *Standard Edition*, Vol. XVIII, 34.

41 « Sur Marx et Freud », in *Écrits sur la psychanalyse*, 224–5; 'On Marx and Freud', in *Rethinking Marxism* 4: 1, 19.

Hegelian dialectic is based on necessary 'laws' that eliminate contingency.[42] The Freudian 'dialectic',[43] for its part, grasps the movement of

42 See, for example, G.W.F. Hegel, *Phänomenologie des Geistes*, Werke, Bd. 3,
Suhrkamp, 1970, 37–8; *The Phenomenology of Spirit*, Cambridge University Press, 2018,
22: 'This movement of pure essentialities [autonomous movement of concepts]
constitutes the nature of scientific rigor per se. As the connectedness of its content, this
movement is both the necessity of that content and its growth into an organic whole. The
path along which the concept of knowing is reached likewise itself becomes a necessary
and complete coming-to-be, so that this preparation ceases to be a contingent
philosophizing which just happens to fasten onto this and those objects, relations, or
thoughts arising from an imperfect consciousness and having all the contingency such a
consciousness brings in its train; or, it ceases to be the type of philosophizing which
seeks to ground the truth in only clever argumentation about pros and cons or in
inferences based on fully determinate thoughts and the consequences following from
them. Instead, through the movement of the concept, this path will encompass the
complete worldliness of consciousness in its necessity'. Thus, contingency is not the
determining element in the movement of the self-development of the Idea in Hegel. In
this sense, contingency does not exist, at least positively, in Hegelian philosophy. On this
point, see the following Althusserian criticism of the Hegelian notion of contingency: 'Is
it necessary to return to Hegel once again to show that, for him, the "circumstances" or
"conditions" are ultimately no more than phenomena and therefore evanescent, since in
that form of "contingency" christened the "existence of Necessity", they can never
express more than a manifestation of the movement of the Idea; that is why "conditions"
do not really exist for Hegel since, under cover of simplicity developing into complexity,
he always deals with a pure interiority whose exteriority is no more than its phenomenon.
[. . .] the conditions of existence really are the very contingency that will be resorbed,
negated-superseded by the Spirit which is its free necessity and which already exists in
Nature even in the form of contingency (the contingency that makes a small island
produce a great man!). This is because natural or historical conditions of existence are
never more than *contingency* for Hegel, because in no respect do they determine the
spiritual totality of society; for Hegel, the absence of conditions (in the nonempirical,
non-contingent sense) is a necessary counter-part to the absence of any real structure in
the whole, and to the absence of a structure in dominance, the absence of any basic
determination and the absence of that reflection of the conditions in the contradiction
which its "*overdetermination*" represents' (« Sur la dialectique matérialiste », in *Pour
Marx*, 213–14; 'On the Materialist Dialectic', in *For Marx*, 208–9).

43 In the previous quote from 'On Marx and Freud', Althusser uses the term
'dialectic' to denote Freudian notions such as overdetermination, displacement and
condensation, which are totally different figures from the Hegelian dialectic. According
to Jacques Derrida, 'Althusser, in any case, remains a dialectician. Even if he complicates
things, even if he fought to complicate the dialectic by introducing a principle of
overdetermination, the dialectical motif remains dominant in his work' (*Politique et
amitié*, 67–8; 'Politics and friendship', in *The Althusserian Legacy*, 206). If Althusser did
not abandon, as Derrida says, the dialectical motif (recall the famous 'determination in
the last instance'), it is because he tried to transform the structures of the Hegelian
dialectic, which leads us to the Freudian 'dialectic': a dialectic suspended by the irruption
of contingency.

contradiction from the contingency that disturbs and deviates the necessary 'laws' ('the unconscious does not know contradiction'). The 'laws' designate the primacy of the economic over the political as well as the teleological self-development of social formation (the linear transition of the relations of production, which is caused by the accumulation of structural contradictions). In Althusser, on the other hand, contradiction signifies *overdetermination* of contradiction: the irruption of contingent elements (displacement and condensation, *Verbindung*) deviates dialectical 'laws' and irrupts the new structure, totally different from the old one. This contingency is precisely the other name of 'conjuncture' or 'conjunction of events'[44] which allows the 'becoming of things', or the becoming of social formation.

We nevertheless insist that it is not the simple contingency that determines the structural becoming. What we mean is that the accumulation of the internal contradictions of the structure (namely, the structural elements) is not enough to actualize the structural becoming. It is a singular *Verbindung* that disrupts and deviates the dialectical law and brings about the new structure. In this sense, overdetermination is the other name of structural causality, the '*original* combination' of structural elements.[45] In other words, as an immanent cause, a singular *Verbindung* disrupts *necessity* in the double sense of the term: the dialectical law as the primacy of the economic over the political (the Hegelian thesis), but also the atemporal, synchronic reproduction of social formation (the anti-Hegelian, anti-evolutionist thesis). If this is the case, we can argue that overdetermination, structural causality, is a mechanism in which the singular *Verbindung* of structural elements disrupts and deviates the necessary laws.[46] In Chapter 5, we reflected on the deviation

---

44 *Sur la reproduction*, 37; *On the Reproduction of Capitalism*, 15.

45 « Lettre à D . . . », in *Écrits sur la psychanalyse*, 106; 'Letter to D . . ', in *Writings on Psychoanalysis*, 72: 'The unconscious irrupts not as the effect of a series of linear causes but as the effect of a complex causality, which may be termed *structural* (without centre, without origin), made of the *original combination* of the structural forms presiding over the "birth" (the irruption) of the unconscious'. Translation modified.

46 Deleuze and Guattari, as well as Althusser, define the event as 'a deviation with respect to laws'. In this unexpected concordance between Deleuze/Guattari and Althusser, we are invited to see a common problematic. See Gilles Deleuze/Félix Guattari, « Mai 68 n'a pas eu lieu », in *Deux régimes de fou*, 215; 'May '68 Did Not Take Place', in *Two Regimes of Madness*, 233: 'the event is itself a splitting off from, or a breaking with causality; it is a bifurcation, a deviation with respect to laws, an unstable condition which opens up a new field of the possible'.

of ideology in its relation to structural causality. It is exactly this deviation that deviates, as an *immanent cause*, the law of dialectical determination and synchronic reproduction. We can find here the dominant motive of Althusserian theory: the irruption of contingency, or of the singular *Verbindung* that deviates the law in the political conjuncture (the class struggle). And this thought, which remains in the discrepancy between the necessary and the unforeseeable, authorizes the thought of structural becoming in Althusser.

Let us offer one more possibility on this question of structural becoming. In 1975, Althusser noticed the virtual power of contradictions that had not yet actualized the structural becoming. He calls it 'underdetermination',[47] the virtuality of the event that has not yet crossed the 'threshold of determination'.[48] In social formation, there always exist underdetermined events, which constitute the virtuality of structural becoming. Althusser designates it by the 'interstices of capitalist society': 'Marx thinks of communism as a *tendency* of capitalist society. This tendency is not an abstract result. There already exist concretely, in the "interstices of capitalist society" (like commercial exchanges existed "in the interstices" of slave or feudal society), virtual forms of communism'.[49] In this sense, the possibility of structural becoming is always already inscribed in social formation itself. The 'interstices of capitalist society' designate this possibility of the becoming of social formation.

---

47 The term 'underdetermination' is used only once in *Reading Capital* in 1965, but the definition of the term is not given (see *Lire le Capital*, 293; *Reading Capital: The Complete Edition*, 254). The period when Althusser begins to use this term, this time with an exact definition, is dated 1975–76 (« Soutenance d'Amiens » et « Histoire terminée, histoire interminable »), which corresponds to the period of the turn to the primacy of the political contingency. On the notion of 'underdetermination', see the analysis of Étienne Balibar: « Avant-propos pour la réédition de 1996 », in *Pour Marx*, XII–XIII.

48 « Soutenance d'Amiens », in *Solitude de Machiavel*, 217; 'Is it Simple to be a Marxist in Philosophy?', in *Essays in Self-Criticism*, 187.

49 « Le marxisme comme théorie 'finie' », in *Solitude de Machiavel*, 285.

Appendix 2
From State Apparatus to Power Dispositives: Foucault and Althusser

Penal Theories and Institutions and *The Punitive Society* by Michel Foucault, texts based on two lecture courses given at the Collège de France in 1971–72 and 1972–73, are his most Marxist works. Using the notion of 'civil war' that recalls the Marxist notion of 'class struggle', Foucault analyses, in the first lecture course, the popular seditions at the end of the absolutist regime and the formation of the police, namely the 'state apparatus [*appareil d'État*]' which has the function of preventing sedition.[1] In the second lecture course, he examines the formation of the proletariat and its moralization or normalization in the period of capitalist development. This notion of 'civil war' designates, in the first lecture course, the process in which the absolutist state oppresses popular sedition, and in the second lecture course, it is the process in which the bourgeois class conquers and proletarianizes the lower class through disciplinary power. What interests us here is this: Foucault clarifies in these lecture courses, notably in *The Punitive Society*, that the 'state apparatus' plays an important role in the formation of disciplinary power, even if it is not centred on the state.

In Foucault's notion of 'state apparatus', we can hear the resonance of

---

1 On the relationship between *Penal Theories and Institutions* and Althusserian 'repressive state apparatus', see the analysis by Étienne Balibar: « Lettre d'Étienne Balibar à l'éditeur du cours », in Michel Foucault, *Théories et institutions pénales, Cours au Collège de France, 1971–1972*, EHESS/Gallimard/Seuil, 2015, 286–7; 'Letter from Étienne Balibar to the Editor', in *Penal Theories and Institutions, Lectures at the Collège de France, 1971–1972*, Palgrave Macmillan, 2019, 279–83.

the notion of 'ideological state apparatus [*appareil idéologique d'État*]' that Althusser proposed in his article on 'Ideology and Ideological State Apparatuses' (1970). According to the prevailing interpretation, the Foucauldian notion of 'disciplinary power' is very close to the Althusserian notion of 'ideological state apparatuses' insofar as both modalities of power function to subject individuals at the level of daily practice. However, there is an important difference: for Althusser, these apparatuses are centred on the state insofar as they are the 'ideological state apparatuses', while, for Foucault, the 'disciplinary power' is not centred on the state. Such an interpretation, however, runs the risk of suggesting that Foucauldian theory deals only with micropower that is irreducible to the state apparatus and that it thus cannot reflect on state power. On the other hand, if we consider that the Foucauldian notion of 'disciplinary power' has a close relationship with the state apparatus, we can rely on Foucauldian theory in order to analyse the mechanism of state power. The resulting reflection also leads us to reconsider the theoretical distance between Foucault and Althusser. From this perspective, we can evaluate, through reading these two Foucauldian lecture courses, the relationship between disciplinary power and the state apparatus, as well as Althusser's influence on the formation of the theory of disciplinary power.

To start this reflection, we propose the following hypothesis: in *Penal Theories and Institutions*, Foucault begins by analysing the 'repressive state apparatus' in the Althusserian sense, but, in *The Punitive Society*, he shifts his analysis towards the relationship between capitalism and power and constructs a notion of disciplinary power which goes beyond the Althusserian notion of 'state apparatus' or 'ideological state apparatus'. Finally, in *Psychiatric Power* (1973–74), and *Discipline and Punish* (1975), this notion is reformulated as 'power dispositives [*dispositifs de pouvoir*]' made up of disciplinary power. To demonstrate this hypothesis, we read *Penal Theories and Institutions* and *The Punitive Society* to examine the relationship between disciplinary power and the state apparatus.

1 What is a 'dispositive'?

To consider the relationship between disciplinary power and state apparatus in Foucauldian thought, let us first refer to the definition of disciplinary power in *Discipline and Punish*:

[I]t [the political technology of the body, namely, the disciplinary power] cannot be localized in a particular type of institution or state apparatus. For they have recourse to it; they use, select or impose certain of its methods. But, in its mechanisms and its effects, it is situated at a quite different level. What the apparatuses and institutions operate is, in a sense, a microphysics of power, whose field of validity is situated in a sense between these great functionings and the bodies themselves with their materiality and their forces.

Now, the study of this microphysics presupposes that the power exercised on the body is conceived not as a property, but as a strategy, that its effects of domination are attributed not to 'appropriation', but to dispositions, manoeuvres, tactics, techniques, functionings.[2]

According to Foucault, disciplinary power is not reduced to the institution nor the state apparatus; rather, it is they that use the technology of disciplinary power. This is an implicit refutation of the Althusserian notion of the state apparatus. For Althusser, 'state apparatuses' are reduced to the institutions such as the repressive state apparatus (police, army, justice, etc.) and ideological state apparatuses (school, Church, etc.). In contrast, for Foucault, disciplinary power means the tactics of subjection that operate between institutions (state apparatuses) and bodies. Disciplinary dispositive thus means *the set of tactics (Foucault calls it 'strategy') that is not centred either on the state or the institutions.* It is defined, in the lecture course on *Psychiatric Power*, as the 'productive instance of discursive practice'[3] concerning the norm, namely as *the set of tactics of power-knowledge that disciplines and normalizes the subjects.*[4]

---

2 *Surveiller et punir*, 31; *Discipline and Punish*, 26.

3 Michel Foucault, *Le pouvoir psychiatrique, Cours au Collège de France, 1973–1974*, Gallimard/Seuil, 2003, 14; *Psychiatric Power, Lectures at the Collège de France, 1973–1974*, Palgrave Macmillan, 2006, 14.

4 The Foucauldian notion of 'power-knowledge' tacitly criticizes the Althusserian notion of 'ideology'. For Foucault, the problem was not the Althusserian opposition between science and ideology, but the science or knowledge produced in power relations. See, for example, the following quote from *Discipline and Punish*: 'One often speaks of the ideology that the human "sciences" bring with them, in either discreet or prolix manner. But does their very technology, this tiny operational schema that has become so widespread (from psychiatry to pedagogy, from the diagnosis of diseases to the hiring of labour), this familiar method of the examination, implement, within a single mechanism, power relations that make it possible to extract and constitute knowledge? It is not simply at the level of consciousness, of representations and in what one thinks

In *Psychiatric Power*, Foucault specifies that he 'cannot use the notion of "state apparatus" because it is much too broad, much too abstract to designate these immediate, tiny, capillary powers that are exerted on the body, behaviour, actions, and time of individuals. The state apparatus does not take this microphysics of power into account.'[5] For Foucault, the 'state apparatus' is a notion that designates the *institution* reproducing the state power, thus a concept too broad to designate the *tactics* of micropower exerted on individuals' bodies. Hence, Foucault will choose the notion of 'power dispositives' which allows him to analyse the tactics of subjection arranged by disciplinary power.

Regarding the Foucauldian notion of 'dispositives', let us refer to 'What Is a Dispositive?' by Gilles Deleuze. This text, read at the colloquium entitled 'Michel Foucault philosopher' (1988), sheds light on the position of 'disciplinary dispositives' that we have just discussed:

> Foucault's philosophy is often presented as an analysis of concrete 'dispositives'. But what is a dispositive? First of all, it is a skein, a multilinear whole. It is composed of lines of different natures. The lines in the dispositive do not encircle or surround systems that are each homogenous in themselves, the object, the subject, language, etc., but follow directions, trace processes that are always out of balance, that sometimes move closer together and sometimes farther away. Each line is broken, subject to *changes in direction*, bifurcating and forked, and subjected to deviations. Visible objects, articulable utterances, forces in use, subjects in position are like vectors or censors. Thus the three main instances, Foucault successively distinguishes — Knowledge, Power and Subjectivity — by no means have contours that are defined once and for all but are chains of variables that are torn from each other.[6]

According to Deleuze, Foucauldian 'dispositives' mean 'a multilinear whole' 'composed of lines of different natures'. In this sense, Foucauldian power dispositives are a multiplicity of different *forces* or *tactics*, which are not centred on the state. They are, therefore,

---

one knows, but at the level of what makes possible the knowledge that is transformed into political investment' (*Surveiller et punir*, 187; *Discipline and Punish*, 185).

5 *Le pouvoir psychiatrique*, 17, note*; *Psychiatric Power*, 16, note*.

6 Gilles Deleuze, « Qu'est-ce qu'un dispositif ? », in *Deux régimes de fous*, 316; 'What Is a *Dispositif*?', in *Two Regimes of Madness*, 338. Translation modified.

different from the Althusserian 'state apparatus', the *institution* centred on the state.

We then ask ourselves the following questions: If Foucauldian power dispositives are not centred on the state, what is the relationship between power dispositives and state apparatuses? What did Foucault learn about the notion of the Althusserian state apparatus? How did he differentiate his notion of power dispositives from the Althusserian notion of state apparatus? With these questions, we first examine *Penal Theories and Institutions* in its relation to the Althusserian notion of the state apparatus.

2 The 'repressive state apparatus' in *Penal Theories and Institutions*

In *Penal Theories and Institutions*, Foucault develops a careful analysis of the institutionalization of the police and the prison — two institutions of the 'repressive state apparatus [*appareil répressif d'État*]' in the Althusserian sense — under the absolutist regime. He examines the *Nu-pieds* [Barefeet] sedition in the seventeenth century and its repression by the absolutist state. The *Nu-pieds* sedition was a popular riot, but it escalated with the support of the Norman aristocracy. The absolutist state crushed it with difficulty; after that, to prevent the increasing revolts taking place in the seventeenth century, it founded two institutions of the repressive state apparatus other than the army: the police and the prison. Foucault here classifies the prison as a repressive state apparatus, since in the seventeenth century, it did not yet function to normalize subjects as disciplinary power would have. In this sense, *the absolutist power of this period is pure sovereign power that only holds the repressive state apparatus.*

According to Foucault, the absolutist state faced a sort of antinomy in this period: if it arms the aristocracy to repress popular sedition, and if the aristocracy supports this popular sedition, this measure risks overthrowing the absolutist regime itself; however, if the absolutist state has an army in every region, this measure requires a huge budgetary expenditure. To resolve this antinomy, the absolutist state invented the police and the prison, two institutions of the repressive state apparatus. Foucault sheds light on this point in *Penal Theories and Institutions*:

To escape this antinomy, in which Séguier's repression was still caught, the state put in place two institutions:

– A police: centralized (the lieutenant general of police in Paris had powers of intervention throughout the kingdom), and local (lieutenants of police in all towns from 1699). Police, that is to say:

  – an armed force, but one which does not have military tasks;

  – an armed force which, blended into the population, has capabilities of immediate intervention and especially of prevention that the army does not have;

  – an armed force whose presence does not have the disastrous economic consequences of an army in the field.

– The other, even newer institution is confinement or deportation, that is to say the *removal* [*soustraction*] of a fringe of population.

  – Hitherto punishment, the threat against sedition, was the army's presence, it was invasion.

  – Now it is removal [*prélèvement*] of the dangerous population.

To remove [*soustraire*] or threaten to remove a part of the population does not have the economic drawbacks of invasions.

  – It keeps wages low: people prefer low wages to being confined.

  – Stimulation of production at low cost (for export); stimulation of colonial trade.[7]

Foucault thus examines two institutionalizations of the repressive state apparatus that could resolve the antinomy in question. First, institutionalizing the police allows them to penetrate the population to give themselves the capacity for intervention and prevention in a more direct and flexible way than the army. Second, the institutionalization of the prison: confinement in the prison 'removes [*prélève/soustrait*]' 'the dangerous population' such as the unemployed and the lower class, to prevent popular sedition.

What is interesting here is that the repressive state apparatus, like the police and the prison, 'is linked to the development of capitalist production'.[8] The repressive state apparatus threatens the lower class with imprisonment to maintain low wages and to stimulate production at low prices. In this sense, the prison 'constitutes [. . .] a reserve of wages and prices regulation'. The prison and the army, as a 'centralized

---

7 *Théories et institutions pénales*, 95; *Penal Theories and Institutions*, 95.
8 Ibid., 96; 96.

repressive state apparatus', controlled the dangerous lower class and prevented popular sedition; at the same time, they developed capitalist production in seventeenth-century society. Foucault nevertheless asserts that the 'economic role [of the prison] is marginal',[9] since the seventeenth-century prison did not discipline or normalize subjects. It was a purely repressive state apparatus and was not yet a disciplinary dispositive.

The repressive state apparatus is neither the simple translation nor the expression of economic relations, contrary to the assertion of classical Marxism. Rather, it intervenes in economic relations and supports the development of capitalism. Regarding this point, Foucault proposes the following theses:

> – It may be true that juridical forms (both the principles of law and the procedural rules) reflect, express economic relations;
> – It may be true that the basic role of decisions of justice is to reproduce relations of production;
> – There is however another level where the functioning of the judicial apparatus comes to light. At this level, it is neither expression nor reproduction of economic relations. As power relation it operates within economic relations, and thereby modifies them: it transcribes economic relations within power relations and thereby modifies them.
> An apparatus like the judicial apparatus is not solely an expression or instrument of reproduction. It is one of the systems by which:
> – the investment of the political by the economic takes place,
> – the insertion of the political in the economic takes place.
> It assures at once
> – the omnipresence of the political to the economic
> – and the gap from one to the other.[10]

According to Foucault, economic relations determine power relations, and, at the same time, power relations determine economic relations. In other words, power relations are not the simple 'instrument of reproduction' of economic relations, but they determine economic relations essentially. We could also say that this quote follows the Althusserian thesis on 'the relative autonomy of the superstructure with relation to

---

9 Ibid.
10 Ibid., 171–2; 171–2.

the economic basis'. However, we interpret this quote in a strict way: *Foucault criticizes this Althusserian thesis by introducing the notion of 'power relations' in order to propose a new thesis on the 'autonomy and reciprocal intervention of economic relations and of power relations'.* He specifically criticizes these two Marxist theses: 1) The superstructure is an expression of the economic base (classical Marxist thesis); 2) The economic base is relatively or absolutely predominant with regard to the superstructure ('relative autonomy of the superstructure with regard to the economic base', 'the determination in the last instance by the economic base': Althusserian thesis).

To demonstrate this hypothesis, we cite the Foucauldian definition of the state apparatus.

> In studying a state apparatus, we should no doubt distinguish:
> – its structure: which does indeed have a repressive nature;
> – its strategy (the strategy of its decisions) which is indeed orientated towards reproduction,
> – and its functioning as an apparatus which manifests the interplay of relations of power and relations of production with regard to each other.[11]

In the first two distinguished points, Foucault asserts that the state apparatus is repressive and that its strategy is oriented towards reproduction. These two characteristics are very similar to the definition of the repressive state apparatus that Althusser proposed in his article on 'Ideology and Ideological State Apparatus'. According to Althusser, the repressive state apparatus 'functions by violence', such as the army, police, and justice;[12] it is oriented towards the reproduction of capitalist relations of production. On these two points, the notion of state apparatus is therefore used in the same sense as Althusser's 'repressive state apparatus'. However, with the third point, Foucault introduces a new concept, the 'power relations', in order to get out of the Althusserian problematic. By introducing this notion, Foucault proposes a thesis on 'reciprocal autonomy and intervention of economic relations and power relations':

---

11 Ibid., 172; 172.
12 « L'idéologie et les appareils idéologiques d'État », in *Sur la reproduction*, 281, 283; 'Ideology and Ideological State Apparatuses', in *On the Reproduction of Capitalism*, 243, 244.

economic relations then determine power relations, and, at the same time, power relations intervene in economic relations and support the development of capitalism. Foucault thus frees himself from both the classical Marxist framework and the Althusserian problematic.

3 State apparatus and disciplinary power in *The Punitive Society*: from the punitive society to the disciplinary society

Let us now turn to *The Punitive Society*, the lecture course that followed *Penal Theories and Institutions*, in order to reflect on the formation of the notion of 'disciplinary power' and the relationship between disciplinary power and the state apparatus.

In *The Punitive Society*, Foucault uses two similar notions: the 'punitive society' and the 'disciplinary society'. According to his explanation, the former was established in the eighteenth century and the latter in the nineteenth century in order to discipline and normalize subjects.

What is the difference between these two concepts? Disciplinary society is made up of power dispositives that are not centred on the state (disciplinary dispositives disposed in the school, hospital and factory), while punitive society is centred on the state apparatus (such as the prison). Foucault defines punitive society as follows:

I have tried to show the rise of a coercive system that in its nature and functioning was heterogeneous to the eighteenth-century penal system. [. . .] This coercive system was gradually shifted in its points of application and instruments, and was taken over by the state apparatus at the end of the eighteenth century, and we can say that at the end of the first twenty years of the nineteenth century the state apparatus had, for the most part, taken over responsibility for the coercive system, which was in turn grafted onto the penal system, so that for the first time we have a penal system that is a penitentiary system. In short, we are dealing with something that I call the punitive society, that is to say a society in which the judicial state apparatus makes additional use of corrective and penitentiary functions.[13]

---

13 Michel Foucault, *La société punitive, Cours au Collège de France, 1972–1973*, Gallimard/Seuil, 2013, 143; *The Punitive Society, Lectures at the Collège de France, 1972–1973*, Palgrave Macmillan, 2015, 139–40.

According to Foucault, punitive power, represented by the prison, disciplines subjects using coercion. Thus the punitive apparatus developed at the end of the eighteenth century is no longer a simple repressive apparatus; it has been transformed into a *punitive state apparatus to discipline subjects.*

What, then, is the relationship between punitive power and disciplinary power? We propose the following hypothesis: *disciplinary power was established on the basis of the punitive state apparatus; it is punitive power generalized in a capillary manner throughout the society.*

We will first reflect on the formation of the 'punitive society' in England. Since the end of the seventeenth century, the period of the emergence of capitalism, people began to spontaneously form the groups which 'explicitly adopted the aim of supervision, control, and punishment', namely 'maintaining order':[14] first, the organization of the police by the Quaker and Methodist communities; second, the emergence of related societies such as the 'Society for the Reformation of Manners', which aimed to moralize society; third, the spontaneous organization of self-defence groups of a paramilitary sort to maintain political and criminal order; fourth, the organization of private police by great companies and great commercial firms to defend their property, their stock and their merchandise against riot, banditry, everyday pillage and petty thievery.[15]

These private groups organized themselves as a result of the development of capitalism, namely the displacement of populations and the accumulation of capital. With the accumulation of capital and the development of the division of labour, expensive machinery and stocks become exposed to risks of robbery, plunder and daily depredation.[16] To reduce the risk of wealth loss for the bourgeoisie, the latter tries to moralize workers and simultaneously demands that the state take charge of such moralization:

> We have, then, a double movement: on the one hand, through these groups of control and superintendence, there is a junction of the moral and the penal. Now in the theory of criminal law that appears

---

14 Ibid., 105; 102.

15 Ibid., 105–7; 102–4. See also « La vérité et les formes juridiques », in *Dits et écrits*, T. II, 596–8; 'Truth and Juridical Forms', in *Essential Works*, Vol. 3, 60–2.

16 *La société punitive*, 108; *The Punitive Society*, 104.

at the end of the eighteenth century with Beccaria and Bentham, there is a break between moral wrongdoing and infraction. All the theorists of penal law separate the two: for them, laws do not have to punish the moral conduct of people; they are concerned only with the utility of society and not individual morality. Now, at the same time, we have all this practice of spontaneous superintendence organized by groups and, finally, by one class of another, a whole practice of superintendence that attempts to re-moralize penality and invest it in a kind of moral atmosphere, in short, that seeks to establish continuity between moral control and repression on the one hand, and the penal sanction on the other. So what we see is a moralization of the penal system, despite the practice and discourse of this system. All this movement allows penality to spread widely into everyday life. On the other hand, and at the same time, we have a second, very important movement by which the demand for moralization shifts towards the state: a movement of takeover by the state. The upper classes, insofar as they control power, are the bearers of this demand, whereas the labouring and lower classes become the point of application of the moralization of penality. The state sees itself called upon to become the instrument of the moralization of these classes.[17]

First, to moralize the workers, the principle of 'supervision and punishment' [*surveiller et punir*] was established by the bourgeoisie; this movement was then taken over by the state, so that the penal system moralized. Moralization here means the disciplinarization that produces disciplined workers, and the state then became the instrument for doing so. Thus, the 'civil war' between the bourgeois class and working class — namely the disciplinarization of the workers by the bourgeoisie — is institutionalized. It is state apparatuses like the police and the prison that would henceforth discipline workers.

What is important here is that this state movement produces not only 'an ethical-juridical control' and 'a state control to the advantage of a class', but also 'the coercive' and 'the penitentiary', which aim at correcting and normalizing individuals.[18] The coercive is 'a junction of the moral and the penal' insofar as it corrects individuals' nature and character. In this sense, it normalizes individuals by means of penalty; it

---

17 Ibid., 111; 107–8.
18 Ibid., 113–14; 110–11.

becomes the penitentiary insofar as the correction and disciplinarization of individuals is carried out in the form of prison confinement. The
penitentiary was established in England in the years from 1790 to 1800.
It was in 1793 that Bentham devised his Panopticon, which would
become the architectural matrix of prisons in Europe and around the
world.

We must now ask a more fundamental question: for what purpose do
the coercive and the penitentiary practice the correction of individuals?
Foucault answers: their aim is not to consolidate the state function, but
to develop the capitalist mode of production:

> The coercive is precisely the condition of the prison's acceptability. If
> the prison, with its geographical and religious features, was able to
> insert itself into the penal system, it is because capitalism utilized
> coercion in setting up its specific forms of political power. We have
> therefore two ensembles: *the penal ensemble, characterized by the
> prohibition and the sanction, the law*; and *the punitive ensemble, char-
> acterized by the coercive penitentiary system*. The first ensemble brings
> with it a certain theory of the infraction as an act of hostility towards
> society; the second brings with it the practice of confinement. The
> first is deduced, in an archeologically correct fashion, from the state
> institutionalization of justice, which means that, from the Middle
> Ages, we have a practice of justice organized by reference to the exer-
> cise of sovereign political power: this gives procedures of inquisition,
> the intervention of someone like the prosecutor, and so on. A theory
> of the infraction as act of hostility towards the sovereign was derived
> from this whole practical ensemble. The other ensemble is formed in
> a movement of development, not of the state itself, but of the capitalist
> mode of production; in this second system, we see this mode of
> production provide itself with the instruments of a political power,
> but also of a moral power.[19]

Foucault distinguishes two kinds of state apparatus: first, *the penal
system as a repressive state apparatus (the judiciary and the police)*
controls criminals, 'enemies of society'; second, *the coercive system as a
punitive state apparatus (the prison)* disciplines and corrects them. These
two systems are indeed state apparatuses, however, the first tries to

---

19 Ibid., 114–15; 111. Our emphasis.

guarantee the stable reproduction of society by repressing criminals, while *the second tries to form a proletarian class composed of docile worker-subjects by disciplining the lower class and thus tries to develop the capitalist mode of production.* It is in this sense that 'morality does not exist in people's heads; it is inscribed in power relations'.[20] In other words, what is at stake in the disciplinarization and normalization of the working class is the development of capitalism.

In the disciplinary society established in the nineteenth century, the judiciary, the police and the prison have functioned together: the judiciary and the police exclude the lumpenproletariat from society, and the prison confines and disciplines them. This perspective was gained through the struggle of the Prisons Information Group (*Groupe d'Information sur les Prisons*: GIP, 1971–72), in which Foucault engaged during the same period as his lecture course on *Penal Theories and Institutions.* Since the police and the judiciary threaten the lumpenproletariat with imprisonment, the latter is forced to work with unfairly low wages. And since the bourgeoisie opposes the lumpenproletariat against the proletariat, the latter is integrated into the process of disciplinarization. This is how the lumpenproletariat constitutes a 'relative surplus population' (Marx)[21] which functions to reduce wages.[22] For Foucault, the practice of the GIP involved not differentiating the lumpenproletariat from the proletariat in order to expose the 'intolerable'[23] of punitive and disciplinary power that these two classes both undergo.[24]

In the nineteenth century, disciplinary power was established on the basis of punitive power; henceforth it became generalized in a capillary

20 Ibid., 117; 113.
21 Karl Marx, *Das Kapital*, Bd. 1, *Marx-Engels Werke*, Bd. 23, 657–77; *Capital*, Vol. 1, 781–802.
22 Michel Foucault, « Sur la justice populaire : Débats avec les Maos » (1972), in *Dits et écrits*, T. II, 348–51.
23 About the 'intolerable' of prison power, see Groupe d'information sur les prisons, *Intolérable* 1-4, 1971-72; réédition présentée par Philippe Artières, Verticales, 2013.
24 The members of the *Gauche prolétarienne* belonging to the GIP demanded that the detained comrades should have the status of political prisoner, while Foucault gave priority to solidarity with the so-called ordinary prisoners in order to reveal the 'intolerable' of prison power. On this point, see Daniel Defert, « L'émergence d'un nouveau front : les prisons », in *Le groupe d'information sur les prisons : Archives d'une lutte 1970-1972*, documents réunis par Philippe Artières *et al.*, Éditions de l'IMEC, 2003; 'The Emergence of a New Front: The Prisons', in *Intolerable: Writing from Michel Foucault and the Prisons Information Group* (1970–1980), Kevin Thompson *et al.*, eds., University of Minnesota Press, 2021.

manner throughout society. The general principle of disciplinary power is to 'supervise and punish'. This functioning disciplines and normalizes the lower class and transforms it into labour power: 'The supervision-punishment couple [*Le couple surveiller-punir*] is imposed as an indispensable power relation for the fixation of individuals to the production apparatus, for the formation of productive forces, and characterizes the society that may be called disciplinary. We have here a means of ethical and political coercion that is necessary for the body, time, life, and men to be integrated, in the form of labour, in the interplay of productive forces'.[25] Disciplinary power acts on the individual's whole body, time and life, correcting and integrating them into productive forces and fixing individuals to apparatuses of production, education and repression. Foucault calls this functioning of disciplinary power 'sequestration', distinguishing it from the classical type of confinement:

> So what is involved is a confinement for fixing individuals to and distributing them across social apparatuses. These institutions of confinement function, so to speak, adjoined to the apparatuses of production, transmission of knowledge, and repression, and they assure the kind of supplement of power the latter need in order to function. They are no longer institutions of the classical type of confinement, but rather of what we may call sequestration, by reference to that kind of arbitral authority that seizes something, withdraws it from free circulation, and keeps it fixed at a certain point, for a certain time, until the court's decision.[26]

The power of 'sequestration' or disciplinary power is adjoined to apparatuses of production, education and repression, and it supplements the power these apparatuses require in order to function. How then does 'sequestration' transform individuals into labour power? According to Foucault, the first function of sequestration is 'to subject the time of life to the time of production':

> The first function appears quite clearly in the regulation of [a silk mill at] Jujurieux: the total acquisition of time by the employer. Actually, the latter not only acquires individuals, but also a mass of time that he

---

25 *La société punitive*, 201; *The Punitive Society*, 196. Translation modified.
26 Ibid., 214; 208–9.

controls from start to finish. This characterizes the policy of capitalism at the beginning of the nineteenth century: it does not need full employment [*plein emploi*] but a mass of unemployed workers in order to put pressure on wages; on the other hand, to ensure that some workers are not employed, it needs the full employment of time [*plein employ du temps*], and work of twelve or fifteen hours is not uncommon. [. . .] Such is the first function of sequestration: to subject the time of life to the time of production.[27]

Foucault refers here to the Marxian theory of 'relative surplus population': capital does not need 'full employment' to produce relative surplus population and thus to reduce the wage, but it needs the workers' 'full employment of time'. It is this total acquisition of time by the employer that Foucault calls 'to subject the time of life to the time of production'. He cites the example of the regulation of the silk mill at Jujurieux, established in 1840: 'rise at 5 o'clock, fifty minutes for washing, dressing, and breakfast; workshop from 6.10 until 20.15, with a one hour break for lunch; dinner, prayers, and bed at 21.00'.[28] The time of life is thus fully taken by the employer, and it is subjected to the temporal processes of production; individuals must be tied to a production apparatus according to a certain pre-established allocation of time.[29]

The second function of sequestration is to allow capital to control the very existence — the body, sexuality, and individual relationships — of workers. It thus prevents workers from using their force outside of production,[30] including for resistance to the production mechanism: 'a way has to be found, on the one hand, to attach somehow the sequestrated population to society's collective forms of existence, and, on the other, to have at one's disposal a means of supervision enabling one to prevent the formation within the sequestration itself of a kind of counter-force, a counter-collectivity that might threaten the institution itself'.[31] The aim of sequestration or disciplinary power is thus, on the one hand, to subject the workers to collective forms of production and, on the other hand, *to prevent the formation of their collective power of resistance*. In *Discipline and Punish*, Foucault theorizes, in exactly the

27 Ibid., 215–17; 210–11. Translation modified.
28 Ibid., 207; 201.
29 Ibid., 235; 231.
30 Ibid., 217; 212.
31 Ibid., 219; 213.

same way, the mechanism of the formation of 'docile bodies' by disciplinary power:

Thus discipline produces subjected and practised bodies, 'docile' bodies.
Discipline increases the forces of the body (in economic terms of utility) and diminishes these same forces (in political terms of obedience).
In short, it dissociates power from the body; on the one hand, it turns it
into an 'aptitude', a 'capacity', which it seeks to increase; on the other
hand, it reverses the course of the energy, the power that might result
from it, and turns it into a relation of strict subjection. If economic
exploitation separates the force and the product of labour, let us say that
disciplinary coercion establishes in the body the constricting link
between an increased aptitude and an increased domination.[32]

Disciplinary power increases the forces of the body in economic terms
of utility (capitalist subjection), and decreases the same forces in political terms of obedience (political subjection). In other words, it fully
employs the productive forces of workers while reducing their collective
power of resistance. In this sense, disciplinary power or sequestration is
'constitutive' of the capitalist mode of production:

The power [of sequestration] is, in fact, one of the constitutive
elements of the mode of production and functions at its heart. This is
what I wanted to show when I talked about all those apparatuses of
sequestration, which are not all linked to a state apparatus, far from it,
but which all, whether provident banks, factories-prisons, or reform-
atories, function at a certain level that is not that of the guarantee
given to the mode of production, but rather of its constitution. [. . .] A
system of power like sequestration goes far beyond the guarantee of
the mode of production; it is constitutive of it.[33]

The power of sequestration or disciplinary power not only guarantees
the capitalist mode of production, but 'it is constitutive of it', affirms
Foucault. In other words, disciplinary power not only *reproduces* the
capitalist mode of production, but *fundamentally constitutes and
produces it by forming the subjected labour power.*

32 *Surveiller et punir*, 140; *Discipline and Punish*, 138.
33 *La société punitive*, 234–5; *The Punitive Society*, 231–2.

We should note that this passage is a tacit critique of the Althusserian theory of 'reproduction'.[34] In his article on 'Ideology and Ideological State Apparatuses', Althusser asserts that repressive state apparatuses, such as the police and the army, and the ideological state apparatuses, notably the school apparatus, reproduce relations of capitalist production by subjecting the subjects: 'for the most part, it [the reproduction of the relations of production] is secured by the exercise of state power in the state apparatuses, on the one hand the Repressive State Apparatus, on the other the Ideological State Apparatuses'.[35] However, in Althusser, the question is only the 'reproduction' of the relations of capitalist production by the superstructure or the state apparatuses, since the relative or absolute primacy of the economic base over the superstructure is maintained, whereas Foucault insists that disciplinary power not only reproduces the relations of production in the capitalist mode of production (relations between the bourgeoisie and the proletariat), *but also fundamentally constitutes and produces the capitalist mode of production or capitalism itself by disciplining and normalizing worker-subjects.*

4 Disciplinary dispositives and the state apparatus

To conclude, let us now return to the question we initially asked: what is the relationship between disciplinary power and the state apparatus? We start with the quote from Foucault which clarifies it:

What is interesting is the position and interplay of these instruments of sequestration in relation to what we usually call the state apparatus. I have picked out a kind of tendency to centralization at the end of the eighteenth century, a tendency of the state to take over the means of control that are at work in society at that time. Now, when we see all these flourishing and proliferating instruments of sequestration, we

---

34 See the section 'On the reproduction of the relations of production' in 'Ideology and Ideological State Apparatuses': *Sur la reproduction*, 285–92; *On the Reproduction of Capitalism*, 246–53. On this point, we are inspired by the following article: Julien Pallotta, « L'effet Althusser sur Foucault : de la société punitive à la théorie de la reproduction », in Christian Laval *et al.* dirs., *Marx & Foucault : Lectures, usages, confrontations*, Découverte, 2015.

35 « L'idéologie et les appareils idéologiques d'État », in *Sur la reproduction*, 286; 'Ideology and Ideological State Apparatuses', in *On the Reproduction of Capitalism*, 247.

have the impression that there is, rather, a spreading that in a sense escapes the state. They are often the result of private initiative; and for some of them the state, in the strict sense, only follows initiatives that are not its own. But we should note that most of these establishments take the state structure as their model: they are all little states that are made to function inside the state. They still rely on the state appara- tuses for a whole system of referrals and reciprocities: the workshop could not function in the structure of the convent or barracks if there were not the police or the army alongside. All these establishments, whether or not they come directly under the state, still refer, despite everything, to state apparatuses, even though they are not themselves state apparatuses but, rather, relays-multipliers of power within a society in which the state structure remains the condition for the functioning of these institutions.[36]

The power of sequestration or disciplinary power is not reduced to the state apparatus, but relies on repressive state apparatuses, such as the police and the army, and it models itself on punitive state apparatus like the prison. In other words, using the punitive state apparatus principle of 'supervision and punishment', the disciplinary power disciplines and normalizes individuals to transform them into labour power and thus produces and reproduces capitalism. In this sense, the disciplinary dispositives function as the 'relay-multipliers' of capitalist power and the state power that supports it.

At the same time, concerning the relationship between disciplinary power and the state apparatus, Foucault specifies as follows:

> I do not think that power can adequately be described as something located in state apparatuses. Maybe it is not even sufficient to say that the state apparatuses are the stake of an internal or external struggle. It seems to me rather that the state apparatus is a concentrated form, or even a support structure, of a system of power that goes much further and deeper.[37]

While disciplinary systems are the 'relays-multipliers' of capitalist power and state power, the state apparatus is 'a concentrated form' of a 'deeper'

---

36 *La société punitive*, 214–15; *The Punitive Society*, 209.
37 Ibid., 233; 229.

power system, namely, disciplinary power. In other words, a punitive state apparatus, such as prison, is a concentrated form of disciplinary power that produces and reproduces capitalism.

We are now ready to compare Foucauldian 'disciplinary power' with Althusserian 'ideological state apparatuses'. In Althusser, the main element of the ideological state apparatus is the school apparatus, which inculcates individuals with the dominant ideology, the class relation and the 'know-how' to transform themselves into subjected worker-subjects, and it thus reproduces the relations of capitalist production. In this sense, Althusserian 'ideological state apparatuses' are centred on the school apparatus, even if ideological state apparatuses are always in the plural. On the other hand, in Foucault, the main element of disciplinary power is *the principle of 'supervision and punishment'*, or *the tactics (dispositives) to subject the body according to this principle*, which produces and reproduces subjected worker-subjects and thus the capitalist mode of production. Disciplinary power penetrates the prison (the punitive state apparatus) as well as the school, hospital and factory (in which are disposed disciplinary dispositives irreducible to the punitive state apparatus) to form the set of micropower dispositives which encompass the whole of society in a capillary manner.

At the same time, the state, independent from the economic base, supports the development of capitalism by organizing a punitive state apparatus such as the prison. This perspective allows us to reinterpret the Foucauldian notion of 'diagram' that Deleuze extracted from Foucauldian philosophy:[38] disciplinary power is a set made up of lines of force from above (i.e., the punitive state apparatus) and from below (i.e., the disciplinary dispositives irreducible to the state apparatus); these two lines of force intersect and consolidate each other to produce and reproduce capitalism. In this sense, *disciplinary power is not necessarily non-state power but a set of power relations where the lines of state force (from above) and the lines of non-state or capitalist force (from below) intersect and consolidate each other*. Of course, the power relations appear to be a more complicated whole, since they involve other lines of force (from below) made of the resistance by worker-subjects. In

---

38 Gilles Deleuze, *Foucault*, Minuit, 1986, 44; *Foucault*, University of Minnesota Press, 1988, 36: 'What is a diagram? It is a display of the relations of forces which constitute power'. Translation modified.

this sense, power relations mean both the intersection of state and non-state dispositives as well as that of domination and dominated.

Foucault found a third instance that is deeper and irreducible neither to the economic instance nor to the state instance: it is a 'disciplinary power', the set of tactics of micropower which produce and reproduce capitalism and worker-subjects, and which are disposed in a capillary manner throughout society. In order to differentiate this set of micropower tactics — diagrammatically composed of lines of state force and non-state force — from the Althusserian 'state apparatus', Foucault called them 'power dispositives'.

Conclusion to Part II
Contingency, Materiality

We discussed two problems in Part II: first, the alteration of psychoanalytic theory and the introduction of contingent elements in Derrida and Althusser; second, structural becoming and contingency.

In the fourth chapter, we dealt with these two problems in Derrida through his reflection on the 'death drive'. He approaches — by *speculating* (double entendre intended) on Freud's 'speculation' of the death drive — the question of state cruelty [*Bemächtigungstrieb*] and seeks ways to transform it. The Derridian strategy of resistance (or, rather, resistances: hospitality, gift, forgiveness) involves an auto-hetero-affection which, by introducing an *unheimlichen* other, disrupts and subverts the cruelty of the state system. We then observed the same mechanism as that of the death drive which, as *Unheimliches* of the drive, disrupts the psychic economy and threatens the human organism. At the same time, however, Derridian resistance also relates to another modality of the death drive: that which serves the survival of the subject, the death drive without cruelty which resists the death drive with cruelty. In its relation to political resistance, we have defined this second modality as 'the beyond of all passiveness', 'the resistance of non-resistance' and which opens up a space for the irruption of the other or an eventual rupture, thus preparing the 'democracy to come' situated beyond the cruelty of the state.

In order to present this strategy of resistance, it was essential for Derrida to construct a new theory that alters Lacanian psychoanalytic theory at its base. Derrida opposes his own thesis ('a letter can always not arrive at its destination') to Lacan's ('a letter always arrives at its destination'). This intervention in Lacanian theory, that of subject formation and repetition, opens the theoretical basis for the auto-hetero-affection of the subject and of social formation. If, in Lacan, the subject is barred by the original inscription of the drive which leads it to repeat, to fill its own lack in the vain search for an object of satisfaction, then only non-transformability (rather than transformability) of the subject exists. On the other hand, in Derrida, the modality of the inscription of the drive is plural (there is not a single original inscription; there are only *multiple inscriptions* [Niederschriften]), and these multiple inscriptions allow the transformation of the subjective modality. A very simple fact follows: the subject is susceptible to being transformed by the affectibility of the other. As far as social formation is concerned, Derridian resistance opens up the field for the irruption of the other and prepares for altering the cruelty of the state.

In Althusser, there is a strategy to alter psychoanalytic theory, quite close to that of Derrida. But at the same time, the Althusserian strategy presents itself, in its modalities of intervention and alteration, differently from that of Derrida. In his theory of ideology, Althusser aims to alter and *materialize* the theoretical dispositives of Lacanian psychoanalysis, despite using many terms borrowed from Lacan. In the latter, the subject is sutured by a signifier of lack, namely the 'phallus'. The subject's lack is then sutured by an excentric centre: the Other. We have called this excentric instance the 'transcendent(al) instance', criticizing Žižek's attempt to extrapolate Lacanian psychoanalytic theory onto social theory. Žižek's theorization induces the transcendence of the ideological apparatus (which corresponds to the law, in his work) along with the impossibility of thinking about resistance to power.

In contrast, the Althusserian theory of ideology is not a simple 'extrapolation' of psychoanalytic theory to social theory: it contains a radical alteration of psychoanalytic theory. According to Althusser, the ideological suture is effected by 'ritual' practice, which inculcates dominant ideology. It designates transference to, and the restructuring of the ego on, the dominant ideology. Ideological subjection is thus realized through the mechanism of the unconscious.

Althusser nevertheless thinks that the ideological suture is not perfectly realized: he points it out in the difference between the Primary Ideology and the secondary ideology. The dominant ideology that the ideological state apparatuses aim to inculcate deviates in the process of ideological interpellation/introjection. It is in this deviation between the dominant ideology (Primary Ideology) and the ideology internalized by the subject (secondary ideology) that the effects of resistance (class struggle) appear. Althusser discovers a possibility of resistance in this ideological deviation. Even if the subjected subjects are produced and reproduced by the ideological state apparatuses (which Foucault reformulated as disciplinary dispositives: the set of state and capitalist dispositives to subject the subjects), they are not perfectly sutured by the dominant ideology or by capitalist dispositives: they can de-subject themselves through class struggle or collective struggle against power. And it is this collective struggle of de-subjected subjects that can bring about ideological deviation and structural change. The reality of resistance ('another reality') figures, as effect, in the ideological *deviation* that intervenes as a *material contingency* (deviation from the reproductive law of capitalist society) in the process of ideological interpellation/ introjection. This point constitutes a radical difference with the 'destinal' theory of Lacan. What we provisionally called the 'break' of Althusserian theory in relation to Lacanian theory clearly indicates this introduction of *materiality* to the theory.

In a 1982 text, Althusser cites Epicurus and Lucretius's notion of *clinamen* to illustrate his 'aleatory materialism': the *clinamen* (the infinitesimal deviation of an atom) provokes 'an encounter with the atom next to it, and, from encounter to encounter, a pile-up and the birth of a world'.[1] This 'encounter' caused by the deviation of the law corresponds, in Althusserian theory of the 1960s, to the *Verbindung* as *immanent cause*. On the other hand, the metonymic causality of Lacanian theory was characterized by the *absent cause*.

In his seminar on 'The Four Fundamental Concepts of Psychoanalysis', Lacan also evokes the *clinamen* to clarify the notion of *tuché*: the latter, which designates the real, the non-symbolizable trauma beyond the pleasure principle, is opposed to the *automaton*, which signifies the symbolic, the repetition of signs in the pleasure principle. We should note that the *tuché* is formulated as an unassimilable 'missed encounter' which imposes 'an apparently accidental origin' on the subject.[2] In

---

1 « Le courant souterrain du matérialisme de la rencontre », in *Écrits philosophiques et politiques*, T. I, 541; 'The Underground Current of the Materialism of the Encounter', in *Philosophy of the Encounter*, 169.

2 *Le séminaire*, livre XI, « Les quatre concepts fondamentaux de la psychanalyse », 54–5; *The Seminar*, Book XI, 'The Four Fundamental Concepts of Psychoanalysis', 55.

other words, this missed encounter (the unassimilable as the real) forms
the subject:

> If [the individual's] development is entirely animated by accident, by
> the obstacle of the *tuché*, it is in so far as the *tuché* brings us back to
> the same point at which pre-Socratic philosophy sought to motivate
> the world itself.
>   It required a *clinamen* at some point. When Democritus tried to
> designate it, presenting himself as already the adversary of a pure
> function of negativity in order to introduce thought into it, [. . .] what,
> then, did he say? He said, answering the question I asked today, that
> of idealism, *Nothing, perhaps?* — *not perhaps nothing, but not
> nothing.*[3]

Lacan seeks to show here that in the history of individual development,
it is through the missed encounter (*tuché*) inscribing the lack in the
individual that the subject is formed. This is how accidental (but also
necessary) trauma has the effect of constituting the subject through the
functioning of negativity ('not nothing'). Lacan's position is absolutely
clear: the *tuché* is defined as a 'missed encounter' with the Other, and it
inscribes lack in the subject. It will thus have the effect of forming a
divided subject and suturing it by its non-symbolizability (the suture of
the lack produced by the fantasy). The *tuché* then functions as a negative
factor that ensures the suture in a dialectical manner. In other words,
contingency in Lacan inscribes the lack in the subject and thereby establishes the dialecticity of the suturing process. On the other hand,
Althusser does not grasp the *tuché* in this negativity ('missed encounter'), but in the positivity of the singular encounter.

In order to conceptualize the logic of structural becoming, Althusser
reflects on the contingency of the singular combination of elements.
This question is evident in the Althusserian thought of the 1960s, especially in the conflict between overdetermination and determination in
the last instance. On the one hand, there is determination in the last
instance through economic contradiction, but on the other hand,
contradictions interchange their roles and are condensed in the political
conjuncture (the class struggle). Political contingency thus intervenes in
the economic and reproductive law and disrupts it. This is what Althusser

---

3 Ibid., 61–2; 63–4.

sought to theorize in the discrepancy [*décalage*] between 'the definite and the indefinite', 'the necessary and the unforeseeable'. The Lacanian contingency (*tuché*), as negativity establishing a dialectical movement, paradoxically ensured the suture of the subject *in a destinal manner*. On the other hand, Althusser introduces contingency to subvert this Hegelo-Lacanian dialectic. The Althusserian contingency introduces the *materiality* of the deviation into the dialectical order and disturbs it. In other words, for Althusser, *contingency signifies this material deviation*.

In this sense, the Althusserian theory is clearly distinguishable from the Lacanian 'philosophy of destiny'. Nor was it, at least until the 1970s, the philosophy of the political roll of the dice [*coup de dés*] (Negri).[4] In our view, the singularity of Althusserian philosophy consists in limiting itself to the discrepancy between the definite and the indefinite, between the necessary and the unforeseeable. This is the reason we have interpreted the Althusserian theory of the 1960s and 1970s through that of the 1980s (aleatory materialism). Let us analyse the problem of ideology. The ideological apparatuses seek to suture the subject by ritual practices; however, the ideological suture is not perfectly realized by virtue of the intervention of the deviation in the process of the ideological interpellation/introjection (as an effect of the class struggle). This failure of the ideological suture ensures the possibility of de-subjection for the subjected subject. If the process of ideological suturing synchronically reproduces the social formation, the deviation of ideology intervenes in it in a political and contingent manner.

We could evaluate structural becoming in the same way. Althusser conceptualized social formation as decentralized. There is no privileged instance in social formation; each instance has relative autonomy in

---

4 « Pour Althusser : Notes sur l'évolution de la pensée du dernier Althusser », in *Futur antérieur*, « Sur Althusser. Passages », 94. Dealing with the manuscript entitled '*Machiavel philosophe*' (dated 11 July 1986), Negri compares the Althusserian theme of the aleatory to the Mallarméan '*coup de dés*': 'In addition to the dialectic, the roll of the dice only determines being insofar as it discovers being as negative one, as void. It is not the determination that is in the foreground, in this game, but the simple "roll of the dice": "the roll" is a "hazard" — the determination is aleatory, not dialectical, and if the "roll" determines being, it determines being only as a void of predetermination, of finality, of fixity. Determination is the indeterminate'. Nevertheless, what matters to us is not the Althusserian thought of the 1980s that exclusively affirms the aleatory, but his thought that prevailed until the 1970s and which remained at the discrepancy between the necessary and the unforeseeable, between the law and the contingency.

relation to the others. How, then, is this system of instances without centre compatible with determination in the last instance by economy? According to the dialectical law or the determination in the last instance, there is a primacy of the economic contradictions over the other contradictions; however, in order that the contradictions bring about structural becoming, the law must be disturbed by the displacement and condensation of the contradictions (overdetermination) within the class struggle. In this sense, social formation is not completely 'sutured' by the economic instance, since the primacy of the economy is disturbed by the irruption of materiality (the political 'conjuncture' or the class struggle). We are faced here with the most delicate point. The economic law or determination in the last instance must absolutely exist, but it is insufficient in order to irrupt the new structure: the irruption of contingent materiality is indispensable so that the contradictions cause structural becoming. Contingency in Althusser is an irruption of political materiality that intervenes in economic contradictions, actualizes them and transforms them into an 'explosive' force for structural change. We can, therefore, deduce the following two points: first, in Althusser, the introduction of the notion of contingency never leads to a simple political occasionalism — contingency means material deviation from the law; second, the Althusserian insistence on the determination by the economic instance suggests the decisive importance of *the analysis of capital's movement, which is inseparable from the political conjuncture*. It is exactly in these two respects that we appreciate most positively the Althusserian theory of the 1960s. Althusser thus firmly holds the two ends of the chain: economic law and political contingency.

In 1972, he modified his thesis on determination in the last instance ('the hour of the determination in the last instance never strikes'). From our perspective, the notion of the determination in the last instance is about to be abandoned and the shift to the aleatory materialism, which emphasizes political contingency, has silently started. From that moment on, he constantly meditated, *within the political field*, on structural becoming in the discrepancy between the necessary-to-actualize and the unpredictable contingency; in other words, in the necessity of contingency.

Let us now come back to Derrida: in *Specters of Marx*, does he reflect on the rupture only from the perspective of political contingency? The answer is *no*. We can notice that he introduced the notion of 'messianic promise': promise of rupture, of emancipation. The rupture is neither programmed, as in Hegelian-Marxist teleology, nor impossible to access, as in the Kantian regulatory idea.[5] The idea of democracy to come [*démocratie à venir*] promises, as *future-to-come* [à-venir], the realization of justice. In our view, this Derridian position is very close to that of Althusser, who remains at the discrepancy between the necessary and the unforeseeable. We obviously cannot identify the messianic promise with 'the necessary', because this promise is not programmed. But it is clear that Derrida does not think of the problem of the rupture only in the simple political contingency. He analyses the break in the conflicting relationship between promise and contingency, thus placing himself at the discrepancy between ('disjunction' of) these two poles: the emancipatory promise and the unpredictable irruption of materiality.[6] The problem is not, of course, only the identity, but the difference between the Derridian and Althusserian philosophies. What we mean is that the philosophy of the event in Althusser and Derrida is not the simple theory of the political 'roll of the dice'. It must be inscribed in the disjunction between the necessary and the unforeseeable, which is clearly demonstrated in two apparently different philosophies on the question of event-ness.

To clarify the difference between Derrida and Althusser, we will discuss their position on the temporality of the event. As we have seen, the temporality of Althusserian theory of the event is limited to the present time. Refusing Hegelian teleology, he finds the moment of structural becoming only in pure actuality. In other words, the discrepancy between the necessary and the unforeseeable is, in his theory, exclusively limited to the actual conjuncture. On the other hand, by taking a position on the critique of teleology, Derrida thinks of the event in eschatological time ('a past end'),[7] namely in the intertwining of the

---

5 See *Spectres de Marx*, 110; *Specters of Marx*, 81: 'At stake here is the very concept of democracy as concept of a promise that can only arise in such a *diastema* (failure, inadequation, disjunction, disadjustment, being "out of joint"). That is why we always propose to speak of a democracy *to come*, not of a *future* democracy in the future present, not even of a regulatory idea, in the Kantian sense, or of a utopia — at least to the extent that their inaccessibility would still retain the temporal form of a *future present*, of a future modality of the *living present*'. Translation modified.

6 On the event as materiality in Derrida, see Jacques Derrida, « Le ruban de machine à écrire *(Limited Ink II)* », in *Papier Machine*, Galilée, 2001.

7 *Spectres de Marx*, 68; *Specters of Marx*, 45: 'In the experience of the end, in its insistent, instant, always imminently eschatological coming, at the extremity of the extreme today, there would thus be announced the future of what comes. More than

past and the future, the memory and the future-to-come, which is the
meaning of 'spectrality':

> No justice — let us not say no law and once again we are not speaking
> here of laws — seems possible or thinkable without the principle of
> some *responsibility*, beyond all living present, within that which
> disjoins the living present, before the ghosts of those who are not yet
> born or who are already dead, be they victims of wars, political or
> other kinds of violence, nationalist, racist, colonialist, sexist, or other
> kinds of exterminations, victims of the oppressions of capitalist impe-
> rialism or any of the forms of totalitarianism. Without this *non-*
> *contemporaneity with itself of the living present*, without that which
> secretly unhinges it, without this responsibility and this respect for
> justice concerning those who *are not there*, of those who are no longer
> or who are not yet *present and living*, what sense would there be to ask
> the question 'where?' 'where tomorrow?' 'whither?'[8]

Eschatological time is this 'non-contemporaneity with itself of the living
present' which orders the responsibility of justice towards 'those who
are no longer or who are not yet present and living'. This intertwined
temporality of the past and the future (the *transcendental* temporality,
namely the 'spectrality') demands, as an injunction, the responsibility of
resistance in the present moment. The appeal of the spectres thus opens
up a space to the affectibility of the other in a transcendental manner. In
other words, the temporal 'disjointure' of the emancipatory promise
(unforeseeable irruption *to come*) and of the *actual* practice of resistance
is a *categorical or transcendental imperative*[9] which comes from the

---

ever, for the future-to-come [*à-venir*] can announce itself as such and in its purity only
on the basis of a *past end*: beyond, *if that's possible*, the last extremity if that's possible, if
there is any future, but how can one suspend such a question or deprive oneself of such
a reserve without concluding in advance, without reducing in advance both the future
and its chance? Without totalizing in advance? We must discern here between
eschatology and teleology, even if the stakes of such a difference risk constantly being
effaced in the most fragile and slight insubstantiality — and will be in a certain way
always and necessarily deprived of any insurance against this risk. Is there not a
messianic extremity, an *eskhaton* whose ultimate event (immediate rupture, unheard-of
interruption, untimeliness of the infinite surprise, heterogeneity without
accomplishment) can exceed, at each moment, the final term of a *phusis*, such as work,
the production, and the *telos* of any history?'

8 Ibid., 15–16; xviii

9 On the 'transcendental figure' that commands Derridian resistance, see Étienne

appeal of spectrality and which commands the resistance of non-resistance in the present moment. We could then conclude: what constitutes the difference between the Derridian and Althusserian theories of resistance is the difference between the primacy of *disjointure* (the transcendental) and that of *conjuncture* (the actual) in the temporality of the event.

The problem is not to choose the most 'reasonable' thought between Derrida and Althusser. We limit ourselves here to affirming that one of the common possibilities of their thoughts is that they both resist Lacan's 'destinal' theory and the simple affirmation of contingency. Derrida develops his thought in the 'disjointure' of the *promise* of democracy *to come* and the unforeseeable irruption of the other, and Althusser develops his thought on the discrepancy between *the necessary* of the law (the economic) and *the unforeseeable* of the conjuncture (the political). These attempts to think about structural becoming open up a new possibility in the philosophy of event. 'Aleatory materialism' is only a name given to this endeavour.

Balibar, « Une philosophie politique de la différence anthropologique », *Multitudes* 9, 2002.

Conclusion
What Is Resistance?

We have deduced two strategies of resistance to power: first, in Foucault and Deleuze/Guattari, through the transformation of subjective modality and the constitution of singularity; second, in Althusser and Derrida, through the structural change caused by the irruption of contingency.

In the framework of the first strategy, resistance signifies the transformation of the subject's subjected modality. In Foucault, the issue is, for subjects subjected by the investment of power, 'to transform themselves, to change themselves in their singular being'.[1] In Deleuze and Guattari, the focus is on transforming the oedipalized *topical* subject into an *economic* subject which incessantly becomes through its impersonal power [*puissance impersonnelle*] and its multiple singularities. We called Foucauldian resistance 'becoming-self' and Deleuzo-Guattarian resistance 'becoming-other'.

Nevertheless, despite their relative difference, there is a commonality between the thoughts of Foucault and Deleuze/Guattari: resistance consists, for them, in transfiguring the subjective modality and the 'way of thinking and living'.[2] In other words, for the subjected subject, the

---

1 *L'usage des plaisirs: Histoire de la sexualité 2*, 16; *The Use of Pleasure: The History of Sexuality, Vol. 2*, 10.

2 Michel Foucault, « Préface » in *Dits et écrits*, T. III, 134–5; 'Preface' in *Anti-Oedipus*, xiii. See also, Gilles Deleuze/Félix Guattari, « Mai 68 n'a pas eu lieu », in *Deux régimes de fous*, 215–16; 'May '68 Did Not Take Place', in *Two Regimes of Madness*, 234: 'The possible does not pre-exist, it is created by the event. It is a question of life. The event creates a

issue is to transform his style of thought and life by constructing his singularity (Foucault), or by liberating his impersonal singularities (Deleuze and Guattari). This is what we have called the construction of 'immanence'. The possibility of this transformation exists, in Foucault, in the reflexive gaze as auto-affection caused by the other, which then fulfils a function other than regulatory; in Deleuze and Guattari, it exists in the transformation of the hierarchical subjected group into a trans-versal subject-group of the schizos through a struggle of interests that finally detaches the desiring production from the pursuit of interests. And this de-subjection of the subjected subject is always possible through collective struggle, since, as Althusser demonstrated in his theory of ideology, the subject is not perfectly sutured by power. When the de-subjection is realized collectively, it becomes the 'anti-pastoral revolution' (Foucault), in which the subjects refuse to be governed *in any way* in order to construct a radically autonomous collective subjectivity.

Let us turn to the second strategy of resistance. In the theories of Althusser and Derrida, we tried to find a possibility of changing the social formation. The issue for them is to transform the capitalist structure constantly reproduced by power dispositives. To reflect on this possibility, we insisted on the notion of 'contingency' in Althusser and Derrida. However, if we limit ourselves to saying that structural change is brought about by contingency, we say nothing, since contin-gency does not refer to any causality. On the other hand, what we have called 'contingency' designates the element capable of disturbing static reproduction, an 'other' in the reproduction process. In Althusser, the structural becoming is thought to be in the conflicting relationship between the political instance and the economic instance. According to the thesis of determination in the last instance, there is a hierarchy in the contradictions — the primacy of the economic contradiction over the political contradiction. But in order that the structural becom-ing arises, the principal (economic) contradiction and the secondary (political) contradiction must exchange their roles ('displacement' of contradictions) in the political conjuncture (the class struggle), and these contradictions, whose roles have been 'displaced', must merge ('condensation' of contradictions). In this process of 'displacement'

---

new existence, it produces a new subjectivity (new relations with the body, with time, sexuality, the immediate surroundings, with culture, work . . .)'.

and 'condensation', we found the emergence of contingency or the 'deviation' of the law. In other words, it is this singular encounter [*Verbindung*] of contradictions, this irruption of *eventual materiality*, that causes the law of reproduction to 'deviate' from social formation and that of the primacy of economy over politics, and which finally causes the structural becoming. To think about this eventual rupture, Althusser inscribes his theory in the discrepancy between the necessary law (the economic) and the unforeseeable contingency (the political). He therefore attempted to subvert the Hegelian dialectic by the thought about the actual 'conjuncture', which he calls the 'finite' theory (exclusively limited to the actual phase). Thus, for Althusser, the possibility of becoming exists only in the actual phase of 'capitalist exploitation' (the cause of the class struggle) and the actual political 'tendency' (conjuncture).[3]

Derrida, for his part, proposes another political strategy: the resistance of non-resistance, namely gift, forgiveness and hospitality. For example, hospitality is a strategy to alter social formation and its static reproduction through the indefinite acceptance of others in the existing society. This acceptance will eventually disrupt the cruel system of state sovereignty and alter it (irruption of the 'event'). Derrida *speculates on* this possibility of eventual alteration, even though 'limitless' acceptance of others also implies a threat of social disorder. Unconditional resistance as an 'impossible experience' is required or exists only for this alteration of state cruelty. What we have called the 'death drive without cruelty', which threatens society with its unpredictability but which, at the same time, includes the possibility of altering state cruelty, is this 'impossible' but really 'imminent' political injunction. The promise of 'democracy to come' [*démocratie à venir*] then signifies a future eventual rupture and is also a *categorical imperative* for resistance in existing society. We emphasize this temporality of the event as future [*avenir*] or future-to-come [*à-venir*] and the temporal 'disjointure' of the event (to come) and (actual) resistance. Derridian resistance is thus based on transcendental figures: the promise of the event to come (*disjointure* of the future-to-come and the present) and spectrality (temporal intertwining of the future and the past) which command the actual practice of resistance in a transcendental manner. This transcendental

---

3 « Le marxisme comme théorie 'finie' », in *Solitude de Machiavel*, 285; 'Marxism as Finite Theory', *Viewpoint Magazine*, 14 December 2017, viewpointmag.com.

temporality constitutes, in Derrida, a difference with the Althusserian notion of event ('necessity of contingency'), strictly inscribed in the 'actual moment'.

We could call this resistance to social reproduction 'resistance to destiny'. Then the process of 'auto-hetero-affection' of philosophy through the intermediary of psychoanalysis, this 'other' of philosophy, holds an important place. As Althusser points out, the new structure, once irrupted, reproduces itself 'atemporally, exactly like the unconscious'.[4] This social reproduction is based on the interpellation of the ideological state apparatuses omnipresent in social formation. The ideological *interpellation/introjection* and *atemporal* reproduction of social formation are two fundamental concepts of the theory of power which are both brought by psychoanalytic theory. We can bring these two formulations together in a more literally 'structuralist' theory, that of Lacan. In him, the inscription of the drive in the unconscious — in other words, the inscription of the lack in the subject — is given once and for all (the original repression), and from this moment, this original lack motivates the desire in a repetitive and 'atemporal' manner. If Lacanian theory thus constitutes a dialectic of lack and repetition, it does not constitute a theory of the transformation of the subject and the structure, even if it is indeed a theory of formation and repetitive reproduction of the (barred) subject or the unconscious as a structure. What Althusser called 'a philosophy of destiny'[5] corresponds to this Lacanian theory of the repetitive reproduction of the subject and the structure. To theorize the alteration of the structure determined in a 'destinal' manner and reproduced in an 'atemporal' manner, Althusser proposes the notion of 'deviation' (irruption of *material* contingency), and Derrida proposes that of 'dissemination' (*plural* inscriptions of drive). We see here a kind of response from philosophy to psychoanalysis that affected it — a process of auto-hetero-affection of philosophy in its relation to psychoanalysis.

The thought of resistance to the 'destinal' is shared, in the form of a theory of subject transfiguration, by Foucault and Deleuze/Guattari, since both 'becoming-self' and 'becoming-other' designate a strategy of

---

4 « Lettre à D . . . », in *Écrits sur la psychanalyse*, 93; 'Letter to D . .', in *Writing on Psychoanalysis*, 62.

5 « La découverte du Docteur Freud », in *Écrits sur la psychanalyse*, 204; 'The Discovery of Dr. Freud', in *Writings on Psychoanalysis*, 92.

resistance to the subject's subjected modality reproduced in an 'atemporal' manner by power dispositives. As we have seen, this strategy becomes possible for them with the introduction of the notions of 'singularity' (Foucault) or 'impersonal singularities' (Deleuze), which resist the Lacanian dialectic developing around the lack of the subject and the other.

If there is a 'post-structuralism' in relation to 'structuralism' — the latter of which is a theory of the repetitive reproduction of the structure and formation of the 'excentric' subject — it must be a theory of the alteration of the subject and structure modality determined in a 'destinal' manner. Facing this 'destinal' determination, Foucault and Deleuze/Guattari sought to transfigure the subject's subjected modality by constructing an immanence; Althusser and Derrida aimed to alter the fixed structure of the social formation by the irruption of eventual materiality. It is precisely at this point that the 'structuralist' theories of power arrived at the end of their 'auto-hetero-affection'.

Who, then, are the carriers of resistance? For these philosophers (including Althusser[6]), the carriers of resistance are not limited to the proletariat in the traditional Marxist sense. The lesson of May '68 is the fact that the class struggle includes the struggles of minorities, and it is these minority struggles (struggles of women, colonized people, LGBTQ people, victims of pollution, foreign workers, precarious people, etc.) that affect the majority (proletarian men) to de-subject it. Proletarian struggles and minority struggles must therefore be articulated in a transversal manner. In order to overthrow capitalism, the majority must become minoritarian and de-subject itself in forming the subject-group: this is the tactic that Deleuze and Guattari proposed in *A Thousand Plateaus* following the analysis of the situation post-'68.[7] As we saw in Appendix 1, actual neoliberal politics *individualizes* us through its principle of competition. It is exactly for this reason that *transversal collective struggle* becomes essential. In a contradictory way, the generalized neoliberal precariousness and the environmental destruction by

---

6 See Chapter 5, note 58.

7 *Mille Plateaux*, « 13. Appareil de capture »; *A Thousand Plateaus*, '13. Apparatus of Capture'. We discussed this point in detail in our book: Yoshiyuki Sato/Jun Fujita Hirose, *Mittsu no kakumei: Duruzu-Gatari no seiji tetsugaku* [*Three Revolutions: Political Philosophy of Deleuze and Guattari*], Kôdan-sha, 2017; *Comment imposer une limite absolue au capitalisme ? : Philosophie politique de Deleuze et Guattari*, Hermann, forthcoming.

capitalism (see global warming and the Fukushima nuclear catastrophe[8]) commands, as a categorical imperative, the construction of radically democratic and transversal counter-power. By the transversal struggles which include minorities, we must realize an 'anti-pastoral revolution' in which the subjects refuse to be governed in any way.

To conclude — or not to conclude — we now open up a possible direction for the philosophy of resistance and structural becoming. In *The Logic of Sense*, Deleuze distinguishes two kinds of becoming: on the one hand, the 'static genesis' as the becoming of sense through the effect of the corporeal in the field of virtual and incorporeal multiplicity, 'which would lead from the presupposed event to its actualization in states of affairs and to its expression in propositions'; on the other hand, the 'dynamic genesis' as the becoming from the virtual to the actual, and 'which leads directly from states of affairs to events, from mixtures to pure lines, from depth to the production of surfaces'.[9] If he tried to reflect on the difficult coexistence of these two logics of becoming in *The Logic of Sense*, we might say that he changed his direction in *Anti-Oedipus*, written in collaboration with Félix Guattari, in order to develop the logic of 'dynamic genesis'.[10] But after having followed practically the same direction in *A Thousand Plateaus*, their collaboration ends, in *What Is Philosophy?*, in a thought which aims at the creation of concepts on the 'plane of immanence', the virtual multiplicity of the thought that is 'philosophy'. They deal there with the problem of resistance as follows:

[B]ecoming is the concept itself. It is born in History, and falls back into it, but is not of it. In itself it has neither beginning nor end but only a milieu. It is thus more geographical than historical. Such are

---

8 We discussed the Fukushima nuclear catastrophe in detail in our book: Yoshiyuki Sato/Takumi Taguchi, *Datsu genpatsu no tetsugaku* [*Philosophy of Abandoning Nuclear Power*], Jimbun-shoin, 2016. The French version of the Conclusion of this book is accessible on the following site: « Philosophie de la sortie du nucléaire », Laboratoire d'analyse critique des modernités, 20 July 2021, Laboratoiredanalysecritiquedes modernites.wordpress.com.

9 *Logique du sens*, 217; *The Logic of Sense*, 186.

10 In *Organs Without Bodies*, Slavoj Žižek discusses the Deleuzian passage from *The Logic of Sense* to *Anti-Oedipus* and judges that Deleuze 'escap[es] the full confrontation of a deadlock [incompatibility between dynamic genesis and static genesis] *via* a simplified "flat" solution'. Žižek, who estimates positively the rich field of the virtual in the logic of static genesis, comes to judge *Anti-Oedipus* as 'Deleuze's worst book' (Slavoj Žižek, *Organs Without Bodies*, Routledge, 2004, 20–1). However, we who seek the possibility of a dynamic genesis choose a diametrically opposed perspective to Žižek.

revolutions and societies of friends, societies of resistance, because to create is to resist: pure becomings, pure events on a plane of immanence. What History grasps of the event is its effectuation in states of affairs or in lived experience, but the event in its becoming, in its specific consistency, in its self-positing as concept, escapes History.

'Resistance' here involves the creation of concepts as pure becomings, pure events in the virtual field that escape History. It would be possible to see there, at least as far as the notion of resistance is concerned, a sort of regression from the 'dynamic genesis' (reversal of the power of desire in *Anti-Oedipus*) to the 'static genesis' (the ontology of the virtual). This static genesis corresponds, in *The Logic of Sense*, to 'becoming which divides itself infinitely in past and future and *always eludes the present*'.[11] Through this temporality, Deleuze develops an ontology of the event in the virtual and incorporeal field (transcendental field). And as we saw, Derridean resistance is motivated by certain transcendental figures: the 'messianic without messianism' as the 'event *to come*', and 'spectrality' as the *intertwining of the past and the future*. To these transcendental temporalities of the event, we simply oppose 'the philosophy of actuality'. What Foucault called the 'historical ontology of ourselves' just before his death in 1984 constitutes a thought which finds historical contingency in the actual modality of the subject and tries to transform its subjected modality.[12] And what Althusser called the 'finite' theory in 1978 forms a reflection on actuality which seeks possibilities of becoming for the subject and for social formation.[13] The philosophy of actuality is thus only prefigured. It is from there that we must seek, in the theory of actuality, a possibility of 'dynamic genesis'.

---

11 *Logique du sens*, 14; *The Logic of Sense*, 5.

12 « Qu'est-ce que les Lumières ? », in *Dits et écrits*, T. IV, 574–8; 'What is Enlightenment?' in *Essential Works*, Vol. 1, 315–19.

13 « Le marxisme comme théorie 'finie' », in *Solitude de Machiavel*, 285–6.

Index